Negotiating Discursive Spaces

Juan de la Cuesta Hispanic Monographs

FOUNDING EDITOR
Tom Lathrop†
University of Delaware

EDITOR
Michael J. McGrath
Georgia Southern University

EDITORIAL BOARD
Vincent Barletta
Stanford University

Annette Grant Cash
Georgia State University

David Castillo
State University of New York - Buffalo

Gwen Kirkpatrick
Georgetown University

Mark P. Del Mastro
College of Charleston

Juan F. Egea
University of Wisconsin - Madison

Sara L. Lehman
Fordham University

Mariselle Meléndez
University of Illinois at Urbana - Champaign

Eyda Merediz
University of Maryland

Dayle Seidenspinner-Núñez
University of Notre Dame

Elzbieta Sklodowska
Washington University in St. Louis

Noël Valis
Yale University

Negotiating Discursive Spaces: Censorship and Women's Narrative in Spain (1950s - 1960s)

by

LISA NALBONE
University of Central Florida

Juan de la Cuesta
Newark, Delaware

No portion of this book may be reproduced in any form without permission from the publisher. For permission contact: libros@juandelacuesta.com.

Copyright © 2023 by Linguatext, LLC. All rights reserved.

Juan de la Cuesta Hispanic Monographs
An imprint of Linguatext, LLC.
103 Walker Way
Newark, Delaware 19711 USA
(302) 453-8695

www.JuandelaCuesta.com

MANUFACTURED IN THE UNITED STATES OF AMERICA

ISBN: 978-1-58871-393-3

To Robert and Mary

Table of Contents

Acknowledgments 9
Introduction 11

CHAPTER 1. Censorship: Theories and Practices 25
CHAPTER 2. Authorized Texts: Normative Thematic Threads and Character Portrayals 46
    Carmen Laforet: *La isla y los demonios* (1951) 47
    Ángeles Villarta: *Mi vida en el manicomio* (1953) 54
    Mercedes Rubio: *Las siete muchachas del liceo* (1957) 59
    Carmen Martín Gaite: *Entre visillos* (1958) 64
    Concha Castroviejo: *Víspera del odio* (1959) 69
    Liberata Masoliver: *Barcelona en llamas* (1961) 77
    Observations 87

CHAPTER 3. Tolerated Texts: Boundaries of Transgression 91
    Carmen Conde: *En manos del silencio* (1950) 93
    Elena Quiroga: *Viento del norte* (1951) 100
    Eugenia Serrano y Balañá: *Perdimos la primavera* (1952) 108
    Mercedes Formica: *La ciudad perdida* (1953) 112
    Concha Fernández Luna: *Martín Nadie* (1954) 120
    Observations 127

CHAPTER 4. Texts Authorized with Revisions and Excisions 129

Elisa Brufal: *Siete puertas* (1964) 131
Isabel Calvo de Aguilar: *La danzarina inmóvil* (1954) 139
Carmen Kurtz: *Al lado del hombre* (1961) 146
Concha Alós: *El caballo rojo* (1966) 152
Observations 163

CHAPTER 5. Rejected: Suppressed Texts: From Moral to Ideological Threat 167
Rosa María Cajal: *Un paso más* (1956) 172
María Josefa Canellada: *Penal de Ocaña* (1965) 183
Dolores Medio: *Celda común* (1963/1996) 192
Susana March y Ricardo Fernández de la Reguera: *La boda de Alfonso XIII* (1965) 203
Observations 216

Works Cited 219
Index 237

Acknowledgments

THIS PROJECT HAS RECEIVED the support of many, and for this I am grateful. My ability to research the censorship files was possible due to the dedicated staff at the Archivo General de la Administración in Alcalá de Henares, Spain, in particular Daniel Gonzalbo Gimeno. Support from the Biblioteca Nacional de España's librarians also facilitated my access to invaluable materials. I wish to thank the University of Central Florida for the support in terms of resources, the most valuable of which was that of time during my sabbatical semester to make strides toward the completion of this book. I thank Lucía Montejo Gurruchaga as well as Laureano Bonet for providing me with crucial insights as I formulated and developed this project. Input, encouragement, and support from colleagues who are familiar with my project have been invaluable: Yunsuk Chae, Francisco Javier Fernández Urenda, Patricia Orozco, Francisco Javier Sánchez, Renée Silverman, and Robert Simon, as well as Sarah Sierra. Lastly, these words only begin to express my gratitude to Sean, Fran, Alex, and Kat.

Introduction

THE LITERARY LANDSCAPE OF mid-twentieth century Spain frequently references a set of authors who have distinguished themselves by cultivating the socially engaged novel, defined as one whose political ideology denounces the standard of living in Spain during the years prior to the Spanish Civil War (17 April 1936 to 30 July 1939) or aligns in the postwar decades with the dictatorship under Francisco Franco. Authors most readily recognized for their social realist novels—Camilo José Cela, Luis Romero, Miguel Delibes, José Suárez Carreño, Ignacio Aldecoa, Jesús Fernández Santos, Juan Goytisolo, Ana María Matute, Rafael Sánchez Ferlosio, and Luis Martín Santos—published thematic threads aligned with the tenets espoused by the absolute power of Franco's dictatorial rule, most successfully through paradox and irony as a subversion of the "mythic and heroic ordering of history offered up by historians of the Regime" (Herzberger 12).[1] In order to achieve this balance, their novels often depict scenes of compelling situations of daily life in a style termed Social Realist or Neo-Realist, a contemporary adaptation of the traits of late-nineteenth century Realist literature that describes scenes objectively rather than outwardly critiquing social constructs in depicted scenes. Authors who oppose the conservative dictatorship must live with this conviction in

---

[1] David K. Herzberger proposes viewing history's role in shaping identity and its effect on remembering official events rather than discerning to what degree history reflects the truth: the privileging of affirmation over confirmation (*Narrating* 35-36). He distinguishes between history, the "occurrences of events in time," and historiography, "the inscribing of events into a narrative form" (44).

silence—if not live in exile—and must avoid any suggestion of threat to the regime in their writing.

The postwar period in Spain saw a proliferation of women writers, though the ones most commonly referenced and critically studied represent only a fraction of female authors who cultivated a variety of genres with a robust thematic reach. Literary analyses of novels published during the dictatorship often focus on the writing of four prominent authors: Carmen Laforet, Ana María Matute, and Elena Quiroga, as well as, for her early works, Carmen Martín Gaite. However, a veritable boom of women's writing encroached upon Spain's mid-twentieth century literary scene. Raquel Arias Careaga, Raquel Conde Peñalosa, Carolyn Galerstein, Kathleen McNerney, Janet Pérez, and Katharina M. Wilson have made significant inroads in identifying scores of postwar women writers in their dictionaries and encyclopedias that have been crucial in laying the groundwork for the selection of the majority of authors who comprise this study on women's mid-century narrative.[2] Their biblio-biographical contributions that point to the study of women's narrative in Spain during the twentieth century have had an enormous impact on bringing to light (many of) the names and works featured here. The current status of scholarship that focuses on lesser-known women writers during this period consists of a limited number of critics who have identified dozens of women novelists; many won literary prizes at the time their novels appeared and moved within Madrid's or Barcelona's circles of cultural and literary hegemony. Their studies usually include a discussion of the highlights

---

2   Catherine Davies, in *Spanish Women's Writing 1849-1996*, succinctly summarizes the changes toward women in society between the 1940s and 1975 in a sections dedicated to women's writing in Francoist Spain in which she discusses social, cultural and political shifts that progressively granted women expanded liberties (in education, marriage, family dynamics, workforce, and finances). Davies focuses primarily on Matute, Martín Gaite, Tusquets, and Quiroga. With secondary mention of Dolores Medio, Concha Alós, and Elena Soriano, Davies also dedicates chapters to Mercé Rodoreda, Lidia Falcón, and Ana Diosdado. Davies makes passing reference to Mercedes Ballesteros, Mercedes Salisachs, María Aurèlia Capmany, Carmen Conde, and Josefina Rodríguez Aldecoa (191).

of the author's novels and a brief biographical sketch or limited bibliographical references of secondary studies, often contemporary to the time of the novels' publication; fewer studies undertake a critical analysis of their work. Clearly, a principal value of these studies rests on the premise that these writers' texts will be cast in a future critical light and that subsequent textual analysis will attempt to uncover their intrinsic value as cultural artefacts of mid-twentieth century Spanish literature.

This study examines twenty women novelists who published their works in the middle decades of Spain's dictatorship, including the four canonical ones listed above, but also featuring others whose literary production merits closer attention because of the compelling themes they explore and the way they narrate their stories. Modern critics often disregard the literary, historical, and cultural relevance of many of these novelists for a variety of reasons. To begin, implicit censorship restrictions legally mandated in Francoist Spain, and later a shifted focus on writers whose literary message the regime valued, situated the writing of these authors at considerable remove from the critical eye. Also, writers who went into exile during or following the Spanish Civil War more readily garnered favorable critical attention, particularly in the United States where some writers lived or taught at institutions of higher education, since their life in exile correlated to wider accessibility of their writing among the reading public.[3] I bring to light writing that reflects a feminine consciousness through my reading of the nov-

---

3   Conde Peñalosa signals the need for further study on women's novels in exile, pointing to a gap in scholarship on works published outside of Spain or influenced by the exile experience. Notable authors referenced are Rosa Chacel, María Teresa León, María Zambrano, María Rosa Alonso, Cecilia de Guilarte, Felisa García Rata, María Dolores Boixadós, Luisa Carnés, Aurora Betrana, Concha Castroviejo, and Carmen Mieza (153). The production of Isabel Palencia and Carlota O'Niell also merits closer critical attention. Several foundational sources for this topic are Joaquín de Entrambasaguas y Peña's "Las novelistas actuales," Josebe Martínez's *Exiliadas: escritoras, guerra civil y memoria*, Paul Tabori's *Anatomy of Exile*, and Paul Ilie's *Literatura y exilio interior: escritores y sociedad en la España franquista*. Publications by Grupo de Estudios del Exilio Literario (GEXEL) are useful as well, beginning with the proceedings of their first conference in 1995, pub-

els' censorship files to provide a framework that guides my discussion. I examine the role censorship played in literary output, as part of both the creative and dissemination processes—termed pre- and post-publication by Beate Müller (4)—by analyzing archival documentation that methodically evaluates books that were granted or denied permission for publication and others that required textual modification, deletions, or both prior to publication.

After theorizing on censorship practices in the first chapter, chapters two through five examine the patterns in women's narrative production of the 1950s and 1960s that led to the censors' decisions to a) authorize a work for publication (Chapter 2), b) authorize publication as a *tolerated* work (Chapter 3), c) authorize a work with revisions and/ or excisions (Chapter 4), or d) deny publication (Chapter 5). No such study currently exists, as critics who examine the censorship files usually discuss the nature of textual modifications required and the effect on the product approved for public consumption. Within the second to fifth chapters, I present each novel in chronological order based on the year of its authorship. The analysis and contextualization of the report against the interpretation of the novel, rather than a uniform word count, determines the length of each section. Further, this book is intended to change the way we think about the term *censored*, in that the products readers consumed were *authorized*—rather than *censored* or *banned*—considering also that readers were precluded from reading censored material and texts. I therefore propose adopting the terms the censors employed in my discussion of the censorship outcomes: authorized or authorized with revisions, tolerated, and the parallel terms: not authorized, denied publication, or rejected for publication.

I have chosen the decades of the 1950s and 1960s because of the emergence of a social consciousness as a thematic narrative element that was at best burgeoning in the 1940s and had declined in popularity given the gradually evolving political climate of the 1970s. Writing in the 1940s served as a precursor to the social realist novel for its thematically similar depiction of daily life but in styles that included

---

lished in 1998 under the editorship of Manuel Aznar Soler under the title *El exilio literario español de 1939*.

the *tremendista* esthetic or an existentialist bent. Creative writing in the first postwar decade proffered immediate reactions to the negotiation of the social dynamics that the dictatorship strove to create in a totalitarian society rife with the fissures that separated the victorious and the vanquished, in lines staunchly delineated by social class and ideologies. Authors who successfully published in the 1940s do not comprise a uniform group in their writing style: indeed, novelists in the first postwar decade such as Concha Espina, Gonzalo Torrente Ballester, José Antonio Zunzunegui, and Pedro Álvarez Fernández, for example, are difficult to classify under the rubric of forming part of a particular literary trend. While some continued developing their writing style as conveyed in the 20s and 30s, others were finding their literary voice. Precisely due to the general lack of experimentation in the narrative of the 1940s (Yndurain 328), notwithstanding Carmen Laforet's *Nada* (1945) as relevant to this present study, the selection of novels here begins with those published in the 1950s. Yndurain identifies the 1950s as one of substantive enrichment due to the proliferation of social realist novels, encompassing a noteworthy degree of literary innovation (331). Also pertinent, "The novelists of the 1950s, in their eagerness to expose the 'true reality' concealed by official propaganda, were attracted to realism because of its unproblematic, authoritative mode of narration" (Labanyi 54-55). Then, within the decade of the 1960s, Yndurain identifies three predominant themes in fiction—the novels of the Civil War, existential novels, and social novels (320)— that open the critical space in which to situate writing of this period as socially and culturally engaged. However, Chris Perriam et al. identify two primary challenges to the contextual interpretation of writing between 1962 and 1975: the "role of ideological control and censorship, the privileging of certain ideas and styles, and the pressure on alternative expression to silence or disguise itself" (15) and

> the existence of increasingly dominant, established voices of individuals and groups of writers in exile, mainly in Europe and the Americas, in dialogue with their more silenced partners who are at first in inner exiles of varying kinds, and then, as the 1960s prog-

ress, increasingly exposed to the possibilities of freer expression within Spain. (15)

Further, politically and economically speaking, Cristina Palomares asserts that "The 1960s have been regarded as the most important years of the Francoist era: they saw the end of the hegemony of the Falangist "Blueshirts" and celebrated the revival of the economy" (15) as the country began to move away from autarkic practices following the implementation of the Stabilization Plan in 1959. Economic growth came about both from Spain's shift from a rural to an industrialized nation during this time, which prompted a migration from rural areas to urban centers where workers encountered increased job opportunities, and also from the promotion of the tourism industry. These two decades, indeed, were witness to a socio-economic shift that set them apart from the previous one, but they also differ from the subsequent decades, as the final years of the dictatorship became imminent. The 1950s and 1960s are also remarkable in terms of the content of censorship files and the rather streamlined processes that the censors followed relative to the 1940s, given the establishment of the Ministerio de Información y Turismo (MIT) in 1951.

Mid-century authors who wrote novels thematically and semantically aligned with censorship norms did so by virtue of their ideological support of the regime or of their awareness that their compliance was necessary, if only to convey the essence of support. Fernando Larraz and Cristina Suárez Toledano have constructed a two-pronged framework within which future critical inquiry may build upon their evaluation of social realist texts' adherence to censorship practices. They offer "una interpretación del paradigma del Realismo social hegemónico en los años cincuenta no como una mera elección estética, sino también como una solución a la coacción comunicativa impuesta por el contexto" (67). Further, following recent critical inquiries that have centered on this period, for example, Patricia O'Byrne's *Post-war Spanish Women Novelists* (2014) and the initiatives geared toward the Recuperation of Historical Memory, this study contributes to fostering a dialogue about authors whose work has been overlooked, forgotten, even dismissed, in critical commentary.

My reading of the novels discussed here distances itself from formalistic discussion of what it means to write as a woman rather than a man, or to be a female writer as a distinct experience from being a male writer. I adopt a reductionist stance in this regard that gestures toward the act of writing as a purely individual pursuit inspired by the author's experiences, vision and creativity, and I place on this pursuit Judith Kegan Gardiner's vision of female identity as a process, "typically less fixed, less unitary, and more flexible than male individuality" (353).[4] Within this framework, the reception of literary production is determined by social constructs associated with the reader's contemporaneity coupled with the historical contextualization that aids in interpreting this production.

While the role of gender can certainly not be discounted, I reject the premise that women's writing is different from men's writing based solely on biological differentiation. My approach promotes a holistic interpretation of the writing because it allows us to examine the message and the creative output or evaluate it on its own merits. By contesting the notion that one author's work is superior to another's, we open a space that activates a deeper understanding and fuller appreciation of the mosaic of literary production in Spain in the 1950s and 1960s.

The majority of the texts I have selected for this study rests beyond the canon of authors that appear in Joan Brown and Crista Johnson's *Confronting Our Canons: Spanish and Latin American Studies in the 21st Century* (2010). While I stop at explaining in detail the reasons the many of the texts studied here live outside of the canon, I will continue John Guillory's observations on viewing the noncanonical in terms of its exclusionary positioning and explore his assertion that "the social referents of inclusion and exclusion—the dominant or subordinate groups defined by race, gender, class, or national status—are now represented in the discourse of canon formation by two groups of authors and texts: the canonical and the noncanonical" (9).

---

4   Kegan Gardiner recognizes that her statement "necessitates an immediate theoretical proviso argues against binary polarization. Male identity is not a static product either" (353).

Implicit in this paradigm is examining what configures the exclusion. In discussing the notion of canon, for Brown and Johnson the factors that contribute to entering the canon relate to accessibility, historical significance, and the attractiveness to the critics (quantity and quality of studies, multiple readings). Brown and Johnson, following Judith Fetterly, explain the role of 'resisting reader' in canon formation, when much canonical space is attributed to male authorship: "women [...] must enter male worlds, forced to identify with the opposite sex in order to experience a work of literature" to suggest that when males are not resisting readers of a text written by women, that text is more likely to be well received" (52). That the panorama of writers examined presently represents only a fraction leaves open the possibility that future inquiry will uncover the names and works of other women writers. The aim is not to revise the canon but to follow the approach for which Beatriz Suárez Briones advocates: "la recuperación de autoras olvidadas y el establecimiento de un canon alternativo" (28), to cast a critical eye toward women's narrative produced in the period under study, whose contributions often ignored or forgotten.

Throughout this book, I address—whether implicitly or explicitly—factors that may allude to a less-than-robust reception of women's narrative of mid-twentieth century, guided by John C. Wilcox's observations of two poets from the early twentieth century: Ernestina de Champourcin and Concha Méndez. Wilcox identifies a prevalent practice of excluding their writing from mainstream literary circles based on five reasons that also apply to many female novelists several decades later: the feminine/feminist character of their texts, their departure from the traditional image of women, the employment of gynocentric metaphors, their occasional participation in a deliberately infantile poetic vision, and the subversive and critical analysis to which they submit masculine ideals from an anti-androcentric perspective. Despite reservations or questions expressed by some critics regarding the literary worth of some of the writings examined here, the cultural patrimony of these writers begins to emerge through their involvement in literary endeavors, such as their role as literary critics, anthology editors, journalists, prologue writers for other women's novels, or jury members for literary prizes.

What makes the novels written by these women worthy of study? The initial response is at best a subjective one; considering that many of these novels are out of print and almost exclusively housed in a scant number of university libraries or used book stores,[5] the question is certainly valid. The rich novelistic production of these women often serves as testimony to daily life in Spain as well as to the events of the immediate past dealing with a country torn by the Spanish Civil War. Indeed, the war influenced these writers a number of ways, ranging from the thematic elements based on this event to its repercussions in the post-war period and beyond. Their pages feature a wide array of characters who challenge the normative portrayal of women as mothers and wives. They eschew marriage. They are single, whether young or mature. If they are married, they occasionally provide the point of view of 'the other woman'—which is not necessarily to say *femme fatale*—a circumvention of the typical portrayal of the idealized domestic women of their time. They may not work or be self-reliant. They often lack the ability to discern the meaning of the situations that surround them. They may be self-absorbed. Female characters may be marginalized by gender, age, social class, or place of origin. They at times maneuver in environments dispossessed of power and voice. The protagonists pose no threat to the hegemony; many are perceived as cultural cast-offs, live on the fringe, or observe from the margins. Why does this portrayal of feminine subjectivity proliferate in mid-century Spanish narrative? This study attempts to offer a response by recovering literary voices that offer myriad representations of women in their social, cultural, and historical milieu.

The selection of authors almost necessarily involves a sort of generational grouping: the authors who comprise the bulk of this study were born between 1907 and 1925. They are homogenous in terms the historical events they experienced yet disparate in terms of the age at which these experiences unfolded and in terms of how they narrate these events. References to several authors outside of this range prove

---

5   The first, and oftentimes only, edition consisted of a print run of 500-2000 books, leading perhaps to the thought that this reading material could be viewed as disposable.

helpful in contextualizing or interpreting trends in literary expression and practices. Rather than following a rigid outline of what constitutes a literary generation, I resist attaching specific or traditional generational names (Generation of 36 or Generation of the 1950s for example) because this paradigm does not allow for an accurate portrayal of the literary terrain during the 1950s and 1960s that has often been framed by practices of exclusion rather than inclusion, although the notion of "Lost Generation" captures the level of critical reception received by authors beyond Laforet, Martín Gaite, Matute, and Quiroga. The task of creating a classification system within any literary category, whether generational, stylistic, or thematic, is problematic in its implicit demarcation of what resides inside and outside of the prescribed boundaries. This is precisely what Francisca López comments upon in stating that many examples of women's writing, and women writers for that matter, fall beyond neatly defined categories thus contributing to their exclusion or minimalization (16). For the homogeneity the women writers share by virtue of writing during decades of the 1950s and 1960s, it has been helpful to follow Karl Mannheim's consideration of a generation as a social phenomenon influenced by a specific time and space, with social and historical intersections (290-91).[6] Here, this concept relates to the reality of daily living during the middle decades of the dictatorship as adult women. Mannheim discusses the idea that certain characteristic modes of thought and experience, and a characteristic type of historically relevant action, influence production, and in this way, we will recognize how multiple women writers shaped the literary landscape, not merely populated, but populated with rich and vibrant characters and content. The writers are a product of their environment, often incorporating into their narrative discourse their lived experiences. For David K. Herzberger, "In the novel of memory in postwar Spain, history does not stand outside individual consciousness as an imposed form but, rather, impinges on the consciousness of characters and forces its way into their considerations" (*Narrating*

---

6   See Mannheim's *Essays on the Sociology of Knowledge* and also "The Problem of Generations," Jane Pilcher's "Mannheim's Sociology of Generations: An Undervalued Legacy," and Paloma Aguilar Fernández's *Memoria y olvido de la Guerra Civil Española*.

the Past 38). I follow José Colmeiro's distinction between collective memory and historical memory as two distinct concepts, with the former constituting a part of the latter. According to Colmeiro, the interpretation of historical events from a critical perspective is attached to historical memory. The idea of a historical consciousness or awareness is a necessary part of historical memory insomuch as historical value of things remembered is sidestepped in the formation of collective memory (17-18).

Writers presently examined capture historical memory not as a political construct legally defined in a democratic society but as an organic product of framing their life history. They provide the reader with glimpse, at times colorful, at times bleak, into the life contemporaneous to the period of their writing and often informed by events in the preceding decades. Their testimony inherently precurses the notions of preserving their past by virtue of fictionalizing their present, often harkening to historical events that occurred during their lifetime.

I will demonstrate that many women writers advocate for a society that liberates women from patriarchal tradition, not by refuting it but by acknowledging it and working from a space contextualized by gender. This transformation, however, must first conform to the rigidity of censorial restriction as it attempts to reveal a powerful and passionate testimony on the difficulties and inequalities that the fictionalized women face, in some instances, masked behind autobiographical narration. The forum for analyzing patriarchal traditions from within the family unit belies that very tradition. The death or otherwise absence of the father figure in most of the novels under study here inhibits the healthy nurturing of the unit he is to support. Compounded by the death, absence, or inadequacies of the mother, the daughter must rely on extended family members, members of society, or simply herself to forge an identity, which does not always conform to extant, acceptable gender codes.

The failure of the female protagonist to achieve true independence, to enter the workforce, to exercise political power translates into the question: how do we evaluate women's independence when the parameters are defined by patriarchy's power paradigms, including censorship legislation? What happens when we explore new paradigms, ones in which female agency is defined by the women themselves? The triumph of these women lies in their autonomy driven from within, rather than defined from outside forces. In this way, many of the protagonists that populate the pages of women's novels of the 1950s and 1960s wrangle with issues of self-identity marred by confusion, questioning, and incomprehensibility, while also exhibiting characteristics of fortitude taken in its broadest sense.

Coalescing with the analysis of the censorship outcomes, the analysis of the rich novelistic production serves as testimony to daily life in Spain as well as to the events of the immediate past dealing with a country cleaved by the Spanish Civil War. Indeed, the war seems to have influenced mid-century writers a number of ways, ranging from the thematic elements based on the event itself to its repercussions in the post-war period and beyond. Writers negotiate the discursive space and time in which to locate their female characters, often marginalized by gender, age, social class, or place of origin. Novels under study here take place in urban or rural areas in Spain while some venture abroad in their settings. Temporal markers include the time contemporary to the moment of writing, a specific set of dates during the beginning of the twentieth century, or a span of multiple years or decades. Some authors' writing mirrors their life experiences whereas others enter more decidedly the fictional world. Many of their protagonists maneuver in an environment dispossessed of power and voice and as such present themselves as nonthreatening to the hegemony.

In some instances during the editorial process, the authors interact directly with the censorship board. Whereas previous studies on the actual files discuss the nature of textual modifications required of one author, or in the words of some, 'mutilations', my research situates the censorship reports within their sociocultural context to illustrate how the censors arrived at their decision as to whether or not to authorize publication. Some cases point to the transactional nature of the censorship process not exclusively limited to a vertical or top-down imposition but rather one that exists on a continuum that allowed for the interaction with the authors—either via their publishers or in letters they wrote directly to the censorship board—who at times negotiated the terms of the required textual modifications. In these cases, the outcome both satisfies the powers that fuel the censorial machine and contributes to the permissible consumption of the product. From this perspective, creative writers as intellectuals negotiate their role as agents of power as they craft literary output that they ultimately intend to reach readers' hands with censorial approval, which is not to say free from censorial stricture.

Chapter 1.
Censorship: Theories and Practices

> Let nothing limit us.
> Let nothing define us.
> Let nothing hold us down.
> - *Simone de Beauvoir*

CENSORSHIP, DEFINED IN ITS broadest sense as the practice of restricting the flow of information and ideas, seeks to control the messages that reach the public through legally sanctioned practices, presumably under the premise of preserving political and social order. Pierre Bourdieu, however, moves this definition to the realm of the metaphorical to tease out the interconnectedness between who gains access to cultural products and how the process that determines access is mediated: "The metaphor of censorship should not mislead: it is the structure of the field itself which governs expression by governing both access to expression and the form of expression, and not some legal proceeding which has been specially adapted to designate and repress the transgression of a linguistic code" (138). In this way, censorship is guided by its own internal workings that negotiate the relationship between access and form.

I employ the term censor as Harold C. Gardiner defines it: "A censor is one who not only disagrees with something (or someone) but who is able to enforce that disagreement with some channel of authority" (10).[1] Therein lays the notion of censorship bound to the

---

[1] Censors in Francoist Spain who evaluate literature often adhere to a third-person assessment of a piece's contents (plot, theme, characterization)

principle of power and oppression as explained through the lens of Michel Foucault:

> There exists a system of power which blocks, prohibits, and invalidates this discourse [that of the intellectual who speaks the truth to those forbidden to speak it themselves] and this knowledge, a power not only found in the manifest authority of censorship, but one that profoundly and subtly penetrates an entire societal network. Intellectuals are themselves agents of this system of power—the idea of their responsibility for 'consciousness' and discourse forms part of the system. 207

Following Foucault, positioning the intellectual as the agent of a system of power allows us to enter a space of critical inquiry that examines literary output not just as a product for consumption but as a product of social, political or Bourdieusian cultural capital. The power and oppression dialectic likewise surfaces in Kate Burns's claim that "Whether driven to protect children, ensure national security, prevent moral decay, or suppress rebellion, censorship aims to restrict the distribution of specified information. The degree to which it is successful often depends on the power of the person or group enforcing the regulations" (12-13). Furthermore, censorship promotes and protects political ideology by couching output, for example through literary production, as encircling a homogenous society with little bend to social arches. Analyzing censorship practices and outcomes of these practices in the form of cultural products offers numerous avenues of exploration in their application to literature that move beyond the ways in which an authoritative body controls the words that reach the public eye to include for instance the study of self-censorship, the types of political attacks to thwart, or the analysis of how original manuscripts evolved to their published forms.

What guiding principles deem a literary text suitable or not for public consumption? This study attempts to analyze, by overlaying

---

and conclude with a first-person opinion when rendering their assessment of that piece. Evaluations at times include assessments of the text's literary worth and likelihood of commercial success.

the censorship reports with the author/novel's cultural context, the power continuum in Francoist Spain to draw conclusions on what plots, themes, characterization, and linguistic expressions would meet the threshold for publication. Contextual observations that may also effect the evaluation outcome include, for example, the author's previous record of publication or social standing, the size of the print run as an indicator of the novel's potential reach, or a narrow, sometimes erroneous, interpretation of the text.

The analysis of censorship reports on novels submitted for authorization to publish renders a thematic taxonomy associated with the censors' decisions as to whether or not authorization would be obtained. It provides us with a language to address the censors' textual interpretations against the upholding of censorship laws. In addition to evaluating a range of authors' engagement with the aforementioned plots, themes, characterizations, and linguistic expressions that censors would surely scrutinize before authorizing publication, this study also draws conclusions on what degree of transgression censors deemed suitable for public consumption.

LEGISLATIVE PHASES OF CENSORSHIP IN FRANCOIST SPAIN

The purpose of this section is to highlight in overview fashion the salient characteristics of censorship practices as legislatively mandated, the people involved in executing this legislation, and certain processes the censorship board followed. It is not intended to provide a comprehensive description of censorship legislation or the implementation of that legislation from a legal perspective.[2] Following a brief chronology of where censorship protocols were housed, the discussion continues to the topic of a critical overview of how these protocols affected narrative output.

Much has been said about the history of censorship under the totalitarian rule of Francoist Spain in the context of writing and publishing. These studies address publishing original work intended for

---

2   The introduction of Montejo Gurruchaga's *Discursos de autora: género y censura en la narrativa española de posguerra* provides an overview of censorship practices and laws beginning in 1938 (23-36).

initial publication concurrent with the time it was written, imported texts, translations of literature in languages other than Spanish, and literature published before the implementation of censorship legislation. Hans Jorg Neuschäfer offers a concise delineation of censorship's regulatory structure under which anything published, performed, broadcast, or projected for public consumption was subject to scrutiny: from 1939 to 1941 it was regulated by the Ministerio del Interior; from 1942 to 1945, it fell under the Vicesecretaría de Educación Popular de la Falange; from 1946 to 1951 the Ministerio de Educación was at the helm; and post-1951 Ministerio de Información y Turismo—in two legislative stages—took charge. The evaluation of films (by 10-20 censors) and theatrical works (often more than 10 censors) was more rigorous than that of literary works (usually one to two censors) because they reached a wider audience and were therefore more likely to sway public opinion away from Francoist messaging (Neuschäfer 50). Although the guiding premises to protect the political regime and uphold standards of moral values and religious convictions existed across all products of public consumption (movies, theatre performances, television and radio programs, music, comic books, newspapers, journals, magazines, advertisements) the scope of this study is genre specific as relating to novels and recognizes that the other products of public consumption have received varying degrees of critical attention with the need as well for expanded critical inquiry. Neuschäfer's work is fundamental to understanding the overall structure of censorship practices, explaining that anything publishable was subject to scrutiny.

1939-1941

During the first phase of censorship legislation (1939-1941) under the Ministerio del Interior, censorship was primarily concerned with daily or weekly newspapers and periodicals. In a society reeling from the immediate aftermath of the Spanish Civil War and gaining a sense of what dictatorial society looked like, literary production was minimal during this first phase of censorship legislation. The 1938 Ley de Prensa constituted the initial attempt to demonstrate the scope of totalitarian rule whose reach included regulating publication of literary texts, writing of any sort intended for public consumption, or performances.

A primary reason for enacting this legislation still during wartime was to suppress the Republican press; it also addressed the problem of scarcity of resources by establishing the frequency periodicals could publish and the size and quantity of the pages.

1942-1945

Once the purview of censorship moved from the Ministerio del Interior to the Vicesecretaría de Educación Popular de la Falange in 1942, practices became more streamlined, and they formally outlined what was a previously a less rigorous process to select the censors. It is in this second phase of censorship that the literary scene gradually gained its footing to witness two of the most canonical pieces of their time: Camilo José Cela's *La familia de Pascual Duarte* (1942) and Carmen Laforet's *Nada* (1945). During this period, the process to select the censors was formalized, as was the reporting method of the censors' textual evaluations. As Eduardo Ruiz Bautista explains, on 16 February 1942, Patricio González de Canales, in his role of Secretario Nacional de Propaganda of the Sección de Censura de Libros, discharged all of the censors working under him and began to replace them in a process that accepted applications of candidates who met several of the following requirements. The aspiring candidates needed not be intellectuals or be familiar with creative writing as a profesión or as a form of socio-political/cultural protest. The qualifications were as follows:

Ser licenciado en cualquier de las Facultades.

Haber publicado, o presentar al Tribunal, algún trabajo (aunque no esté terminado) de investigación científica o crítica literaria.

Traducir algún idioma.

Pertenecer a la Vieja Guardia o al requeté antes del 18 de julio de 1936.

Ser Militar (en todas sus situaciones) Provisional y de Complemento.

Ser Sacerdote (del Clero regular o secular).

Los militantes del Partido que se crean con méritos suficientes para ello por los servicios prestados a España y a la Iglesia Católica. (Ruiz Bautista, "La censura," 55-56)

The process continued with their selection based on the finalists' performance in three areas: an interview to measure their qualifications and merits, an evaluation and critique of a text, and a translation. On 15 June 1942, six men were named to the post of censor: Leopoldo Panero, Libori Hierro, Enrique Conde, Carlos Ollero, José María Peña, and Antonio Sánchez del Corral (Ruiz Bautista, "La censura," 56). Their responsibilities remained constant under their tenure, as they were tasked with evaluating a text and identifying infractions—including the identification of page numbers where these infractions appear—to the fundamental, guiding questions listed on the report that leads with the header "Informe del lector":

¿Ataca al Dogma o a la Moral?

¿A las instituciones del Régimen?

¿Tiene valor literario o documental?[3]

Below these questions appears the phrase "Razones circunstanciales que aconsejan una u otra decisión" under which the censor usu-

---

3   By way of comparison of this time in the United States, guidelines, rather than laws existed beginning in 1939. Thomas F. O'Connor summarizes that code of the National Organization for Decent Literature declared publications objectionable that: "(1) Glorify crime or the criminal. (2) Describe in detail ways to commit criminal acts. (3) Hold lawful authority in disrespect. (4) Exploit horror, cruelty or violence. (5) Portray sex facts offensively. (6) Feature indecent, lewd or suggestive photographs or illustrations. (7) Carry advertising which is offensive in content or advertise products which may lead to physical or moral harm. (8) Use blasphemous, profane or obscene speech indiscriminately and repeatedly. (9) Hold up to ridicule any national, religious or racial group" (Qtd. in O'Connor 400).

ally provided a plot summary, character outline, and assessment of the text's literary merits. To conclude, the censor determined suitability for publication and in the case of denying authorization, identified the reasons. When circumstances allowed for textual revision and then resubmission, the censor identified on the report the corresponding manuscript pages and marked the suspect passages directly on the manuscript. Practices included handwritten—in blue or red ink—underlining, bracketing, striking, drawing a vertical line in the margin, and marking an X to indicate where revisions and deletions must occur. At times, censors conveyed emotion by writing a question mark or exclamation mark in the margins near certain passages that caught their attention.

1946-1951
Following the 1945 dissolution of the Vicesecretaría de Educación Popular under the Falange Española Tradicionalista y de las Juntas de Ofensiva Nacional Sindicalista (FET y de las JONS), the purview of the censorship board transferred to the Ministerio de Educación until 1951. In this five-year period, censorship practices remained legislatively unchanged. However, the most significant difference between this phase and the previous consisted of the revised reporting form the censors completed. During this phase, the form under the shortened header of "Informe" was expanded to allow for a more nuanced evaluation of threats, which now separated Dogma from Morality, added the category of the Church, positioned the regime and its institutions as separate, and added a category to account for those who collaborated or have collaborated with the regime:

¿Ataca al Dogma? Páginas

¿A la Iglesia? Páginas

¿A sus Ministros? Páginas

¿A la moral? Páginas

¿Al Régimen y a sus instituciones? Páginas

¿A las personas que colaboran o han colaborado con el Régimen? Páginas

Resultando

This form, used until 1966, included blank spaces for the censor to indicate the day, month, and last two numbers of the year: Madrid, _____ de _____ 19__, followed by another blank area to sign after the word "Lector." In the footer appeared the sentence "El lector deberá indicar de manera concreta si las tachaduras indicadas arriba califican el contenido total de la obra o se refieren a aspectos parciales."

Post-1951, Phase 1 (1951-1962)

The next major changes in censorship enforcement occurred with the creation of the Ministerio de Información y Turismo (MIT) on 18 July 1951 with the official decree pronounced on the following day. Under the leadership of Gabriel Arias-Salgado, the MIT was charged with: "control y censura de la información y estímulo del turismo extranjero" (Gubern 122), a task carried out by the "Sección de Inspección de Libros." The evaluation form remains the same as in the previous phase (1946-1951). In this post-1951 phase, according to Ruiz Bautista, because *lectores* were reading an average of 500 texts per month, he surmises they were glossing over them to identify whether to authorize or suspend publication or to indicate which passages would need to be suppressed ("La larga noche" 85). This also could account for the arbitrariness, subjectivity, and textual misreading. He further recognizes the difficulty in assessing the myriad implications of the attack on morality and asserts that censors focused on requiring revisions to textual references to sexuality in its broadest sense, rather than attempting to eradicate all potentially questionable attacks on morality, such as those relating to sinful actions (envy, wrath, pride, etc.) or to criminal acts (murder, robbery, etc.) (Ruiz Bautista, "La larga noche" 95-96). This phase was the most robust in terms of the number of texts evaluated relative to the thoroughness of the reports. Thirteen of the novels discussed here saw publication during this period.

Post-1951, Phase 2 (1962-1975/1977)
With the MIT's new leadership under Manuel Fraga Iribarne beginning in 1962, the grip of censorship began a gradual repositioning:

> Si es cierto que la censura informativa y cultural se mostró en algunas ocasiones y aspectos como más tolerante, no es menos cierto que su 'apertura' fue arbitraria y zarandeada por los avatares de la coyuntura política de cada momento. Con Fraga Iribarne, por ejemplo, se institucionalizó lo que podría denominarse 'censura selectiva' [...]. Pero también es cierto que su modesta apertura suscitó fuertes resistencias entre algunos miembros del propio Gobierno y en los grupos de presión integristas. (Gubern 184)

During this phase, the "Orientación Bibliográfica" became the new name for the "Sección de Inspección de Libros" as an intended way to suggest greater transparency during the latter part of the dictatorship. As Francisco Rojas Claros explains, however, "la nueva nomenclatura eufemística de este organismo hacía referencia, no a la imposición de censura y prohibición (que en definitiva, seguían siendo sus funciones principales), sino a una simple 'orientación'" (*Dirigismo* 47).

Then, in 1966, censorship's regulatory practices experienced their first legislative shift in 28 years. Ruiz Bautista remarks upon the role of the censors prior to 1966: "lo precario y subalterno de su ocupación no se modificó sustancialmente a lo largo de la dictadura" ("La larga noche" 85). The Ley de Prensa e Imprenta passed on 18 March 1966, under Fraga Iribarne's leadership of the MIT, constituted an attempt to ease censorial restrictions. Also known as "Fraga's Law," it represented a restrained broadening of the 1938 Ley de Prensa. With this law enacted, the onus of primary censorship efforts occurred the editorial level, with the editors working with authors/journalists to ensure that nothing published would be offensive within the framework of the guiding questions. Authors were still required to deliver their published works to the MIT offices, and the office retained the right to sanction or fine individuals, suspend publication, or close newspapers and publishers. Further, the MIT implemented a revised set of guiding questions on an updated reporting form. The guiding questions, still under the heading "Informe" remained largely the same, with the replacement of "Resultando" after the guiding questions with "Informe y otras observaciones":

¿Ataca al Dogma? Páginas

¿A la moral? Páginas

¿A la Iglesia o a sus Ministros? Páginas

¿Al Régimen y a sus instituciones? Páginas

¿A las personas que colaboran o han colaborado con el Régimen? Páginas

Los pasajes censurables ¿califican el contenido total de la obra?

Informe y otras observaciones.

Manuel L. Abellán clarifies that when this law took effect, "La censura, mucho más que antes, se convierte en instrumento represaliador según las simpatías políticas manifiestas o latentes de libreros, escritores o editores. Formalmente hablando, la nueva ley ofrecía, en su falacia, resquicios de libertad. Pero como tantas veces ocurrió durante el régimen de Franco, las disposiciones legales no eran concreción de una voluntad política sino remedio y cortina de humo" ("Fenómeno censorio" 24-25). Despite the proposed changes, this law represented, according to Georgina Cisquella et al., "la regulación, mediante una ley ordinaria, de una censura marcial que había funcionado de forma excepcional y obsesiva desde 1938" (28). The modification of previous restrictions, as stipulated in the various articles of this law, led to the granting of wider freedoms with regard to publishing that Román Gubern outlines: freedom of editorial expression (article 1), and freedom of the press (article 50), "aunque sometidas a ciertas condiciones" (185). This new law maintained a stance of upholding respect toward the truth and morals (Gubern 185), though truth and morals continued to be defined within the parameters of the regime.

However, the work of Rojas Claros, especially in his *Dirigismo cultural y disidencia editorial en España (1962-1973)*, is fundamental to correcting critical misconceptions encircling the censorship process during this phase. He cautions against viewing this period as a relaxing of censorial practices by explaining that publishers could apply to join the "Registro de Empresas Editoriales," which entailed meeting specific criteria in order to qualify to exercise editorial judgement to publish creative work. He delineates the following five points: "el titular se hallaba en pleno ejercicio de sus derechos civiles y políticos, una declaración comprensiva de los fundadores y gestores de la empresa, el reglamento de la editorial, una descripción del patrimonio de la misma y, por último, una exposición del plan editorial y financiero y los medios con que contaba para realizarlo" (60). The confirmation of publishers' budgets is necessary to identify potential irregularities between income and expenditures that would indicate unidentified, suspect sources of external funding. Under this revised legislation, when publishers simply "deposited" the final printed copy after the print run and marketing of the book, they would be motivated to adhere to the censorship guidelines so as not to risk financial loss—due to seizing of the print run, fines, or legal action against them—should the censorship board deny publication or require revisions. Ultimately, with the rise of democracy in post-1975 Spain, censorship disappeared. The legislation that dismantled the system of repression pertaining to print, visual and sound modes of production was the Decreto Libertad de Expresión, adopted on 12 April 1977. Notably, the decree does not contain the word censor or any of its derivations.

Censorship Practices and Literary Production in Spain

The pioneer in identifying the practices, relevance, and implications of censorship in Francoist Spain is literary historian Manuel L. Abellán, whose insights and observations foreground almost every critical study that illuminates the role of pre- and post-publication censorship during the dictatorship. In his 1980 foundational study, *Censura y creación literaria en España (1939-1976)*, Abellán outlines predominant censorship practices and processes in the context of writing and publishing in Francoist Spain. Abellán presents an overview of the submissions by a large number of authors from Spain and the outcome of their evaluations, including in many cases a narrative of the circumstances surrounding the acceptance or rejection of numerous literary pieces. In his study, Abellán explains the processes censors followed and ways specific the censorship board interacted with the authors and their texts. Román Gubern's 1981 foundational work on censorship in Spain, *La Censura. Función política y ordenamiento jurídico bajo el franquismo (1936-1975)* is also noteworthy. He explains that "Las razones que se han invocado tradicionalmente para mantener la justificación de la censura, y la de la censura cinematográfica en particular, han sido la de la protección del 'bien común, la de preservar las 'buenas costumbres' y la de mantener el 'orden público'" (12). Abellán's and Gubern's analyses contribute to an understanding of censorship practices through their examination of what comprises these authoritative bodies and how they are charged with adhering to a particular rhetoric in their evaluations of texts.

More recently, critics have identified what texts censors ban from publication or approve only after proof that required revisions have been implemented, offering further insight to the censorship process to show the impact of excising or revising a text. Cisquella et al., O'Byrne, Lucía Montejo Gurruchaga, and Alejandro Herrero-Olaizola have likewise made substantial inroads in examining the interplay between censorship and literary output of mid-twentieth century writers by comparing novels' original manuscripts with their published versions that have implemented the requisite modifications, in some cases discussing the revisions, excisions—or, in the view of Montejo Gurruchaga, "mutilations"—that texts have suffered in order to gain authorization for publication.[4] Cisquella et al. discuss censorship in terms of the authors' negotiation of *temas malditas*, which will be discussed in more detail below. O'Byrne has also tackled the subject of censorship in women's novels from the perspective of narrative strategies authors employ to evade censure. Montejo Gurruchaga has made

---

4   Pilar Godayol's essay on the censorship process relating to Jean-Paul Sartre's novels and their translation to Catalan references multiple studies on the topic of foreign authors' experiences with censorship during the dictatorship (60).

salient strides in examining censorship practices and explaining how they affected the published version of many authors' works, with special attention to the novels of Concha Alós, Carmen Kurtz, Dolores Medio, and Mercedes Salisachs. Further, in *The Censorship Files: Latin American Writers and Franco's Spain*, Herrero-Olaizola offers compelling scholarship on the topic of censorship practices in the 1960s and 1970s as they relate to Boom writers Guillermo Cabrera Infante, Gabriel García Márquez, Manuel Puig, and Mario Vargas Llosa, elucidating the ways these writers approached writing and publishing in Francoist Spain. Each of these critics discusses the censorship laws and practices to the degree that censors inhibited literary production, its dissemination, or both. These studies often contextualize the author's ideology and reference creative strategies that rather effectively bypass censorial stricture.

In returning to Neuschäfer, he follows Freudian psychology to explain strategies that writers used to circumvent censorial reproach by incorporating allusive or indirect language, moderating their discourse, or disorienting the censor by disfiguring the text through camouflage, mask, code, or the roman à clef mode of expression (56-57).

Indeed, Sue Curry Jansen theorizes on the concept of double-meaning, which:

> treats equivocal forms like allegory, analogy, metaphor, and metonymy as valuable interpretative strategies. A theory of double-meaning [...] acknowledges the critical importance of rhetoric as a way of knowing: a means of creating community and securing truth-claims. [...] it assumes that the equivocal nature of language is essential to communication: These discursive strategies not only contribute to a novel's authorization for publication but also become tools authors implement to communicate nuances outside of their texts that transgress normative portrayals of characters and their life circumstances. That it not only makes communication necessary, it makes it possible. 197-8

Jansen's theory may be expanded to consider the censorship review process over time, when authors have multiple experiences over the span of their careers and therefore may learn from an initial experience how to better navigate the process in subsequent manuscript submissions. Discursive strategies in addition to those Jansen identifies include the difficult-to-measure self-censorship, ellipsis in place of questionable material, irony, or rhetorical questions. Authors themselves at times have discussed these discursive strategies in interviews, letters, and autobiographical or memoir writings. José María Martínez Cachero quotes several authors who recount their experiences with censors (182-84); among them is José María Gironella, who describes the harmful effect of self-censorship in literary production that represents numerous authors' experiences: "La censura realmente importante es la que el escritor se ve obligado a ejercer a priori sobre su obra en la elección de tema y en la manera de desarrollarlo" (Qtd. in Martínez Cachero 285). Regarding the practice of self-censorship, whether implicitly or explicitly imposed, Judith Butler offers insight into the relationship between the power of censorship regulations and the creative process as an "operation of that constraint" (247), elaborating that "agency in speech is conditioned by the workings of implicit censorship, by that which renders unrealizable an unconstrained notion of sovereignty" (248).[5] A less frequent, but no less effective, strategy to gain authorization to publish is that at times authors' convictions lead them to communicate directly with the censorship board through written correspondence either to ask for another reading considering the circumstances put forth in that communication, or to negotiate the terms of authorization. These strategies demonstrate the complexities that come into play when moving beyond the reductionist structure of writing a novel, submitting it for authorization to publish, and implementing any required revisions.

The Terms *Censor* and *Lector*

Catherine O'Leary succinctly describes censors in Francoist Spain as "guardians of morals and political correctness" (73). In Antonio

---

5   Implicit self-censorship refers to the author's attempts to repress or modify her own writing while explicit self-censorship results from repression and modification that occur at the suggestion or demand of another, such as an editor, publisher, or censor.

Beneyto's view, "El censor no era hombre poderoso y, por lo general, tampoco ejercía su labor como profesión principal ni mucho menos prestigiosa" (51), and also "El censor era una simple ruedecita de la gran maquinaria de control. Y aunque la gigantesca máquina no funcionaba a la perfección, de un modo u otro atrapaba a los autores entre sus engranajes y entorpecía su trabajo" (52).[6] Indeed, little has been written about the censors as individuals, as they are often viewed collectively as mediators of the governmental agency that oversees the censorship process. The discussion of who exactly evaluates literary texts; declares their suitability for publication; and completes the initial, substantive evaluation on the censorship report is imperative to clearing up generalizations or misconceptions relating to the terms *censor* and *lector* (reader), which are often used interchangeably. Institutionally speaking, the former constitute a small group of named officials, whereas the latter group benefitted from having their identities shielded from the public. While terms like *Jefe de Lectorado* or *Director General* point to people in the upper echelons of bureaucratic hierarchy that sign off on final decisions based on the commentary the *Lectores* provide in their reports, all of these titles encompass the role of censor. This distinction has rather eluded garnering critical commentary, such that the term *censor* is often limited to referring to the *lector* and/or the *lector* is euphemistically called a *reader*, a point echoed by Rojas Claros (*Dirigismo* 47), who further elaborates that in any given year there were on average 25 *lectores* classified as "especialistas" (in law or religion, for example), "fijos" or "ocasionales" (*Dirigismo* 53-54).[7]

---

6 It is worth noting that of the 43 writers whose experiences Beneyto analyzes in *Censura y política en los escritores españoles* (1977) three are women: Rosa Chacel, Mercé Rodoreda, and Carmen Martín Gaite. His study is representative of others for its focus on men's writing that then opens the space of examining women's writing in the context of censorship.

7 In his subsection titled "Los censores en la época de Fraga," Rojas Claros discusses nuances of the number of censors, their disparate backgrounds, and their work volume, as well as pointing to additional archival resources with information about their names, salaries, and assignments (*Dirigismo* 52-55).

I would like to emphasize and acknowledge that the term *lector* is not devoid of authority, as the *lectores* are the first point of contact with the texts. These are the individuals who write the censorship reports. Their assessments carry much weight, and their decisions are largely upheld when the *Jefe de Lectorado* or *Director General* certifies, or literally rubberstamps, the decision on a blue index card. I recognize the distinction in the prevailing language of Francoist censorship legislation between *censor* and *lector* but reject the premise that the *lector* was simply a reader when his role, in fact and in practice, was to determine whether to authorize, or not, literary texts' publication, for approval at the next bureaucratic level. Interestingly, expanding upon Abellán's research, O'Byrne remarks that the censor "liked to be known" as a *lector* ("Spanish Women Novelists" 201).[8] Rojas Claros offers a study on literary censors who were women, remarking that there were few, and most often they were tasked with evaluating juvenile literature or assisted in reviewing adult literature in special circumstances—for instance in times of increased volume, notably, around the time of the 1964 *Feria del Libro* in Madrid—in the capacity of "censores ocasionales" ("Mujer, censura" 111). Rojas Claros, writing in 2019, suggests a gender anomaly through his article subheading that redundantly marks gender in his discussion of "mujeres censoras" ("Mujer, censura" 107-12). The shrouded identities of the readers at the time they were working perpetuated their anonymity. Strategies of obfuscating their identities when signing the reports included most often their representation as a number, the illegibility of their signature, the use of the first name only, or the use of initials instead of full names. After the mid-1960s, however, the identities of the *lectores* were less guarded, and it became more and more known that they worked as censors as a secondary job, some with little experience in literature, some affiliated, to differing degrees, with the church[9]. In this present study, my use of the term censor when analyzing the censorship archives refers, unless

---

8   O'Byrne offers further insight into the censors' job description, accuracy in textual interpretation, and workload ("Spanish Women Novelists" 202).

9   Censors with the title *lectores* usually worked part time, often dating their reports on Tuesdays.

otherwise noted, to the *lector* as the first point of contact in the texts' evaluations.

When discussing censorship in Spain during the dictatorship, it is useful to move beyond the associations between literary production and consumption, between writer and censor, or even between writer and reader, to contemplate what it means to evaluate literary creation and thereby assess its suitability for public readership. Relevant to this discussion is addressing the relationship between power and censorship as well as the arbitrary nature of censorship as a product of a particular place and time noted in, among others, Michael Holquist (17) and Jean-Paul Valabrega (115). Gubern comments on the legitimizing role of the power dynamic between the creative product and the decision to make it available to the public: "Se entiende por censura aquella restricción administrativa a la libertad de información o de expresión que se fundamenta en el poder ejecutivo y de él recibe su legitimidad" (10). Valabrega takes this idea one step further to claim that censorship as the legalization of the arbitrary (115). The censors' purpose was to enforce censorship laws, but their lack of a cohesive formation and background in literature was the cause of much of the oft-cited arbitrariness the authors themselves at times contested (Abellán 99; Montejo Gurruchaga, *Discurso de autora* 90; Behiels; and Cisquella et al. 47-64) or remarked upon in autobiographical writing and interviews. To provide just one of many examples, O'Byrne references Dolores Medio's response to her evaluation of *Instancia de parte* (1961) that identifies a lack of guidelines writers could follow and an inconsistency in what they allow from one writer to another ("Spanish Women Novelists" 202-03).[10] We shall see in subsequent chapters instances of this unpredictability during the censorial processes of Francoist Spain and state here that both the lack of a cohesive and formative educational background or training in literary analysis as well as an often cursory or quick reading leads to textual misinterpretation. This matter is further problematized by the lack of a formalized rubric beyond the guiding questions that appear on the report.

---

10   The full text of Medios's inquiry and copies pertaining to the novel's censorship file appear in Montejo Gurruchaga's *Discurso de autora* (250).

CENSORSHIP TAXONOMIES

Based on the censorship report's guiding questions, some critics have created thematic taxonomies to categorize what controversial, provocative, or threatening themes censors would disapprove of appearing in published works and remark that writers avoid these themes. I disagree with statements such as "El divorcio, el adulterio, el aborto, las juergas de las 'señoritas de su casa' quedaban borradas de un plumazo de toda narración" (Guillermo and Hernández 11). While this is certainly true in some cases, what I have found in my review of the files is that writers do indeed include these themes within the bounds of what censors would—to use their term—"tolerate," or authors create an underlying justification to include them. Often, this justification deals with some sort of punishment or suffering the character must endure. In the case of political resistance, works are likely to be published if authors depict this theme through subaltern characters, particularly if they live on the fringe or their lives are in some way projected as unstable. Authors destabilize their narratives in order to push the boundaries of acceptability. To note, generally a single theme, plot point, or characterization in isolation is not grounds for denying publication; for instance, a novel whose protagonist is an anarchist and espouses anarchist ideals would not be automatically denied publication rights. What censors would reproach was a favorable or sympathetic portrayal of anarchy. In terms of morality, which subsumes sexuality, authors may broadly portray characters whose being or behavior conflicts with normative expectations. Characters are promiscuous; commit suicide; clash with institutions of law and order; commit adultery, murder or acts of terrorism; and undergo abortion. Authors hint at characters' homosexuality, at times when censorial rigor does not allow explicit identification as such.

In the context of these textual maneuverings, the authors may need to revise or remove passages or words, or they may need to create a different set of textual circumstances to ensure that questionable material is adequately treated in order to comply with censorship norms. Cisquella et al. identify a slew of *temas malditas*, themes that threaten Francoist ideology in historical and political terms; that cast Marxism or anarchism in a favorable light; that contain a non-normative portrayal of sexuality, morality or social customs; or that criticize religious texts (25). Maria DiFrancesco elaborates that "Subjects deemed inappropriate for publication included the Second Republic [...], noted Republican individuals, seizure of resistance members, court tribunals, torture, capital punishment, unionization, devaluation of the *peseta*, overall weakening of the economy, food or housing shortages, and the monarchy" (169). I diverge from DiFrancesco's assessment because even critical treatment of these topics does enter the narrative, for instance, topics ranging from legislation passed in the Second Republic that allows for divorce (*Víspera del odio*), to food and housing shortages (*El caballo rojo, Barcelona en llamas*), to a critical view of the monarchy (*La boda de Alfonso XIII*). One of the goals of this current project is to correct long-standing inaccuracies surrounding what censors would or would not allow to proceed to publication by explaining nuances of plot, theme, and character developments, through a discussion that also takes into account the contents of the censorship files. Further I endeavor to move away from sweeping generalizations regarding publishable and non-publishable material to clear up misconceptions surrounding the censorship process by situating the novels under study in their literary context.

In part, this chapter aims to provide a context for understanding censorship in Spain as a process that contributed to shaping the literary legacy readers experience today, with a focus on women's writing the 1950s and 1960s, when the censorship procedures had matured and become more streamlined compared to the first postwar decade. It allows for a reading that clarifies past inquiries and invites further critical review. For example, future study may unpack statements such as "Female authors, like male authors, were subject to rigorous scrutiny. Nonetheless, their position may have been particularly challenging due to their second-class status under the dictatorship. Censors banned Ana María Matute's (1926-[2014]) *Luciérnagas* (1953; Fireflies) and suppressed publication of 19 pages of *Los hijos muertos* (1958; The Dead Children), even though the latter won Spain's National Literature Prize that same year" (DiFrancesco 170).[11] Of the first statement, future critical inquiry

---

11   As a point of clarification on *Los hijos muertos*, my review of the archival documentation did not show 19 pages that were suppressed, but

may adopt a comparative approach to ascertain to what degree censorial evaluation may have been a gendered construct and to determine the degree to which "rigorous scrutiny" played a role in the evaluation of men's and women's writing. Preliminary archival research points in the direction that the author's relative degree of renown played a role, problematizing the issue of manuscripts submitted under a pseudonym. Additional scholarship may examine specific ways women's writing, in comparison with men's writing, may have been subject to more, or less, difficulty in receiving authorization for publication.[12]

---

rather, 35 pages that contained questionable content. Rather, according to Abellán: "cortes en diecinueve de sus páginas bastaron para concederle el visto bueno" (*Censura y creación* 169). In all, revisions mostly consisted of removing phrases considered offensive, such as "¡Los vencidos son como la peste! ¡Como la peste!..." (Ts. 32), which would have appeared in the novel on page 34 in reference to one of the protagonists, Juan, a supporter of the defeated Republican cause during the Civil War. The name of Republican captain (Rafael) López Tienda was replaced with the surname Arcos. Censors also called for tweaks to vocabulary choice, for instance changing *guerra civil* to *guerra* and removing words or phrases considered objectionable, such as *cabrón, blenorragia*, and *¡Mierda! ¡Puñetera mierda, marica!*

12   For instance, Juan Antonio Zunzunegui was already a well-regarded author, with a career spanning three decades, when he submitted *La vida como es* (1953) for evaluation. The censorship folder includes a letter that calls to overturn the decision to authorize publication, but in the end the decision was upheld. Ultimately, the level of threat was considered acceptable. The evaluation on the censorship report reads, in part: "Novela de tema barriobajero y truhan que sirve a la boga neopicaresca de cierta novelística actual. El estilo es descarnado, violento muchas veces, malsonante otras, y siempre huyendo de florituras o retóricas. No se puede hablar de un argumento. La acción se desarrolla en los barrios bajos del Madrid de los últimos tiempos de la monarquía y los personajes son ladrones, 'espadistas', 'carteristas', invertidos, maridos 'consentidos', esposas infieles, porteros venales, toda la picaresca en sus costumbres, su idioma, sus luchas, sus ambiciones, su moral, poniendo tono en primer plano. Por la novela desfila la vida de estos personajes que ninguno es más importante que otro. En definitiva no ataca a la Iglesia, a sus ministros, a la moral; *solo ataca al buen gusto*" (File *La vida como es*, emphasis added).

The Archives

Censorship files are indexed and housed in the Archivo General de la Administración (AGA) in Alcalá de Henares. Although the task of analyzing the censorship files is daunting and requires dedicated time in the AGA, it is nonetheless a rewarding experience. Those whom I depended upon in the AGA to make materials accessible to me were helpful, informative, and accommodating, and, diligently implemented established security protocols. After submitting my credentials, I received an identification paper that I needed in order to be assigned to a table in the research area. Following a brief orientation session, I learned how to navigate the locked Excel document that contains the information on records of the censorship files. The electronic database, accessed solely in the AGA, is searchable most identifiably by author or title in ascending or descending alphabetical order, without the option to sort for two search terms. It is uneditable and unavailable for download. Files for each entry reference a number sequence that corresponds to a box number and file number. Once the box number is identified, the researcher notes the box numbers (up to ten) in numerical order, submits them electronically to initiate their retrieval, and waits up to 30 minutes for the boxes to arrive. The boxes are held in a separate area adjacent to the research room in order that they may be consulted one at a time. Inside each box are a number of individual envelopes containing reports, one per title—generated on books submitted from around the world—that range in quantity from one or two reports to about thirty, with an average in the boxes I consulted about 15. The envelopes appear to be numbered in the order in which they were received. Retrieved boxes may be stored for a week in the adjacent holding room, giving the researcher ample time to view the contents. Based on my experience, copies may be made of any report and any portion of the envelope's contents, including the typescript and related correspondence. Researchers interested in accessing censorship files should consult the AGA's website ahead of their visit to familiarize themselves with relevant information related to specific procedures, schedules, and rules in the reading room.

Chapter 2.
Authorized Texts: Normative Thematic Threads and Character Portrayals

> I am rooted, but I flow.
> - *Virginia Woolf*

THE FAVORABLE OUTCOME OF a majority of novels without the need for revision takes place due to three primary reasons. First, the text is viewed as innocuous to the notions potentially under threat (dogma, religion, regime, etc.). Second, the text is tolerable despite borderline threats to maintaining the integrity of these notions. Third, it may be published in the edition under review, but any subsequent editions are subject to scrutiny. This last demarcation was reserved for texts whose reception might be considered questionable or whose contents could be perceived as volatile with the passage of time.

Novels that easily gained authorization for publication in many cases featured themes, plots, and characters that aligned with dictatorial discourse, or justifiably contextualized straying from this discourse. According to Raquel Arias Careaga,

> El personaje femenino arquetipo de la novela de estas dos primeras décadas de posguerra es un ama de casa menesterosa, temerosa, pudorosa, católica practicante, simple en sus planteamientos, amante de su marido y sus hijos y sin vida personal, que representa la estabilidad familiar. Su lucha, si se plantea, es una lucha interior, que no traspasa las paredes de su propia casa. (155)

The fact that many authors' works were initially authorized for publication does not mean that they were complicit with Francoist ideology. A case in point is Carmen Conde. She moved from her native Cartagena to Valencia at the beginning of the war and then to Madrid in 1939 to live in hiding during the early postwar period in order to avoid detection and imprisonment or persecution for her connection to Republican forces as her husband was a radio operator in Lorca during the Civil War. She published four of her eight novels during the dictatorship with little or no need for revision; her novels were apolitical in nature and fell within the bounds of acceptable portrayals of morality. On the other hand, censors identified nine questionable passages in the deeply conservative Liberata Masoliver's *Telón* (1967) that they permitted to appear in the published novel—"dado el carácter de la publicación" (File *Telón*)[1]—and required her to revise multiple sections from one of her latter novels, *Un hombre de paz* (1969 completion and evaluation, 1970 publication), for unacceptable material relating to morality, religion, and the representation of political events.

This chapter discusses the thematic threads and character portrayals that the censorship board viewed as favorable in light of the guiding questions that appear on the censorship report. Novels under study are the product of the writing by Carmen Laforet, Ángeles Villarta, Mercedes Rubio, Carmen Martín Gaite, Concha Castroviejo, and Liberata Masoliver.

Carmen Laforet: *La isla y los demonios* (1951)

The enduring literary legacy of Carmen Laforet (1921-2004) is testimony to the groundbreaking inroads she made to shaping postwar narrative, beginning with the publication of *Nada* in 1945. This section aims to shed light on the uneven interpretations censors gave the novels they read by discussing censorship in the context of Laforet's

---

1 After summarizing the plot, the censor concludes: "Narración limpia, sin extremismos descriptivos de ningún tipo. A título informativo, se señalan algunos párrafos que hacen referencia pasada y sin profundidad, a algunos momentos de la política española. Pags. 15, 24, 25, 29, 44, 145, 183, 337 y 338. Creemos que *no tiene importancia lo señalado dado el carácter de la publicación, público al que va destinada y precio*" (File *Telón*, emphasis added).

first two—*Nada* and *La isla y los demonios* (1951)—as novels that easily passed censorship review to gain authorization to publish.[2] Analysis of Laforet's censorship experience with her second novel through comparison with her first sheds light on the censors' interpretation of novels deemed non-threatening to the tenets listed on the censorship report. The subjective evaluation Laforet experienced with her critically acclaimed breakout novel reveals that censors did not recognize the potential for popularity or cultural significance that would come to be associated with this master work. Misreadings such as this one occur due to a variety of factors beyond the volume of texts censors had to evaluate, which came into play especially in the early iterations of censorship practices: cursory readings and lack of academic training in identifying literary nuance among the top two. Indeed, the censors' task is to determine suitability for public consumption, yet the complete dismissal the literary merit of Laforet's novel opens the space to examine why this may have occurred.

The first censor evaluated the novel in the following terms on 27 March 1945: "Novela morbosa de tipos bajos sin fin moral alguno," supplying an exclamation mark in response to the question "¿Ataca al Dogma o a la Moral?" and responding "no" to the questions "¿A las instituciones del Régimen?" and "¿Tiene valor literario o documental?" (File *Nada*). The reaction to the question regarding the threat to dogma or morality indicates that the novel's contents merely caught the censor's attention, and the negative responses to the remaining questions safeguarded the novel from the censors' literal red pen. Three weeks later (17 April 1945), the second censor responded "no" to the three guiding questions and based his decision to authorize publication on the following assessment of *Nada*: "Novela insulsa, sin estilo ni valor literario alguno. Se reduce a describir cómo pasó un año en Barcelona en casa de sus tíos una chica universitaria, sin peripecias de relieve. Creo que no hay inconveniente en su autorización" (File *Nada*). The novel, considered inferior in literary value despite having won the

---

2   Other published novels include *Una mujer nueva* and the unfinished trilogy *Tres pasos fuera del tiempo*: *Al volver la esquina*, *La insolación* and *Jaque mate*, the last of which has not been published. Laforet published as well short stories and essays, including the travelogue *Paralelo 35*.

inaugural 1944 Nadal Prize, gains authorization on 20 April 1945 to run a print of 3000 copies without the need for revision.

Regarding the exclamation mark on the first censor's report, probable questionable content relates a variety of sources: for example, the paucity surrounding Andrea's daily vicissitudes in her relatives' Aribau home, complicated by scarce food, unemployment, and limited energy sources, which appear not as a socio-cultural critique but rather underscore commonplace struggles of postwar Spain. Ideological threats are assuaged by Laforet's narrative balancing in which she positions her uncles Juan and Román as falling on opposing ideological sides in the Spanish Civil War. Laforet's anecdotal representation of the war mostly reaching the reader second- and even third-hand (through Gloria's conversation with her mother-in-law that Andrea hears in Chapter 4) is a narrative strategy that locates the war at considerable temporal-spatial remove from events in the novel. The romantic relationship between Andrea's aunt Angustias and her boss ends with her entering the convent to remind readers of the notions of redemption, repentance, and salvation. This outcome is particularly fitting considering that Angustias represents the narrative embodiment of the moral censor to uphold and safeguard Andrea's normative behavior (García Blay et al. 6). Román's death teeters both ambiguously and textually between suicide and accident. References to the war appear, but are not central to the novel's plot: a cathedral burned during the war, a group of houses now in ruins in the aftermath of war, rusted boats sunk during the war that now look like skeletons, and a minor character orphaned as a result of the war. Laforet had intended to publish a lengthier novel, one in which she narrated the precarious situation of Polish refugees seeking safe shelter from the atrocities of World War II, but following the advice of her editor and future husband Manuel Cerezales, she removed the two chapters with this content from the final manuscript presented to the censorship board (Johnson and Rolón-Barada 573, n. 7).[3] The exclusion of questionable content, while potentially border-

---

3   The content of these two excised, self-censored chapters "dealt with finding safe houses for Polish refugees" in the context of World War II (Rolón-Barada 122). It can only be surmised that this content may have been authorized had it portrayed the refugees as marginalized and accentuated

ing on the transgressive, keeps the novel within the realm of fiction that meets the criteria for publication.

While it is true that Laforet elided censorial stricture for what she did not narrate, as expressed in the following manner by Gabriela de Lima Grecco and Sara Martín Gutiérrez: "escenas eróticas, léxico tenido por vulgar o inmoral, alusiones directamente políticas o irreverencias religiosas" (88) combined with a direct and testimonial writing style, my work on interpreting and contextualizing censorship reports aims to demystify the notion that Lima Grecco and others claim in statements such as "Para una censura que se atendía más al detalle que al fondo, que utilizaba un criterio muy puntilloso en lo religioso y que ejercía un puritanismo excesivo, *Nada* no parecía ser una amenaza para el régimen" (88). Statements such as these do hold some truth, but the swath is larger, especially when considering that censors often do allude to *el fondo* in their reports, as various files include adjectives that specifically describe it, such as *inmoral, moralizador, político, psicológico, religioso, reprobable*, or *surrealista*.

Nada exemplifies the type of novel that on first read appears to be an innocent representation of everyday life, in this case, of a university student in a new city, a young woman who demonstrates no political engagement and does not pose any real or potential threat to the political regime; nor do Andrea's daily activities outwardly challenge moral codes of conduct. By focusing this interpretation on the main character's meanderings through Barcelona as a veritable lost soul against an environment of family dysfunction, if anything, critics' existentialist and *tremendista* readings surfaced; the novel did not at first register as a compelling postwar narrative. Critical inroads now lead to the prevailing thought that *Nada* set the stage for the emergence of the postwar novel. Thus, the reading of the novel deemed the apolitical, timeless story of a lost soul during the early years of the dictatorship has evolved in recent scholarship to challenge its purported apoliticism or anormativity and to offer modern interpretations we read today through multiple critical lenses.

---

the hardships of their plight rather than glorifying or sympathizing with an ideological representation.

The novel's famed protagonist, Andrea, embodies the *chica rara*, who, as Ellen Mayock summarizes, seeks to escape confinement and therefore celebrates life on the street. Her actions demythify typical feminine stories of the past, her physical appearance takes on a secondary or non-existent role, and she eschews flirting and very self-consciously examines her own 'interior' spaces. She thereby takes on a role of spectator and witness (21). Andrea as *chica rara* tests gender expectations and in many way subverts the courtship customs Carmen Martín Gaite famously outlined in her *Usos amorosos de la postguerra española* (1987) not only by eschewing behavior assigned to her gender but also by adopting behavior assigned to men. In the first case, she falls outside the circle of young girls, who "en espera pasiva de que algún día la manipulación de la especie llegara a estar en sus manos, ensayaban sus vagos anhelos de maternidad entregándose al paraíso ficticio de coserle vestidos a una muñeca de trapo o de cartón" (*Usos amorosos* 120). In the second case, she often wanders through the streets of la Ciudad Condal, opening a space in which to interpret the vertiginous atmosphere of her surroundings as a gendered female who had yet to "find herself," in contrast to the opposite sex encouraged to learn the wiles of sexuality by cofraternizing in public spaces; as Martín Gaite states: "los chicos…buscaban soporte en la calle para el aprendizaje de su masculinidad" (*Usos amorosos* 109). Life outside the confines of the house for Andrea and her sister heroines, according to Roberta Johnson, takes on new meaning in their positioning in public spaces: "la tentación de la calle no surge identificada con la búsqueda de una aventura apasionante, sino bajo la noción de cobijo, de recinto liberador" ("Chica rara" 389). Andrea's display of independence within both the harsh home atmosphere and the boundaries of her tight-knit circle of friends gestures toward the potential for an unconventional evolution to a new concept of feminine subjectivity in which this strange girl will journey on an unforged path.

To understand how the feminine subject evolves in Laforet's writing, the intersection of biography and fiction reveals what the author herself attempted for many years to occlude: the blurring of fact and fiction, one of the principal threads in Ana Caballé and Rolón-Barada's biography on Laforet titled *Una mujer en fuga* (2010). This leads to linking Laforet's *Nada* and her subsequent three novels with the development of the writer/protagonist as moving from *chica rara* to her version of the *femme seule*, whom Janet Pérez perceives as "the liberated single woman, financially independent and content with [her] life" (54), a rather infrequent character type to populate the pages of Spanish fiction of mid-century.

Laforet's second novel, *La isla y los demonios* (1952), is set in 1938-1939 in Gran Canaria during the second half of the Spanish Civil War and deemed by Caballé and Rolón-Barada as an indisputable combination of fact and fiction biographically speaking (270). It narrates the ways the protagonist, Marta Camino, negotiates stifling family dynamics against her indefatigable desire to resist the sense of confinement that this relationship imposes upon her (Del Mastro, 50). As a 16-year-old young woman, the developmentally driven yearning for independence accentuates Marta's much sought-after escape from her birthplace and propels her to move to Barcelona by novel's end.

As a prequel of sorts to *Nada*, *La isla y los demonios* easily passes the censorship process. The report on the novel, dated 31 December 1951, is extremely sparse and only indicates the outcome: "Puede autorizarse" (File *La isla*). If *Nada* gained authorization without the need for revision, a novel by the same, generally speaking, young author set further back in time, featuring a younger protagonist, and removed spatially from big city environs on the peninsula, gave the censorship board no pause.

Also contributing to the novel's authorization to publish is Marta's safe portrayal in terms of the potential threats on the listed censorship form. Like Andrea, Marta exhibits traits of the *chica rara*: "Una característica común a estas heroínas [...] es la de que enumerated no aguantan el encierro ni las ataduras al bloque familiar que las impide lanzarse a la calle. [...] Quieren largarse a la calle, simplemente, para respirar, para tomar distancia con lo de dentro mirándolo" (Martín Gaite, *Desde la ventana* 113). The characterization of a young girl with an invalid mother, left to her own devices, reads more like a variation of a modern day, gender-shifted picaresque, minus the bouncing from one shifty authority figure to another.

Another theme that figures prominently is that of maternal loss, which would contribute to a sympathetic reading of the protagonist. Marta, whose mother is ill, has few to no friends and relates poorly to those around her, and in this regard she resembles many of her literary sisters. Women's writing in the 1950s and 1960s features a preponderance of female characters beleaguered by a sense of isolation as a compelling thematic undergirding. With the prevalent narrative construct of fragmented families in the literature published during the Franco regime, a theme that emerges is that of maternal loss due to the mother's death or illness, or due to mother-daughter estrangement. Another way the authors portray this situation is through the childless woman. Female protagonists under study here are almost exclusively motherless or childless, as examined in subsequent sections.

Marta resists confinement within the walls of her suffocating home and navigates a world shaped through her adolescent vantage point as restricted by the adults around her: "son casi siempre las personas de otra generación—padres, tías o abuelos—quienes tratan de persuadirla para no busque fuera de los muros de la casa patrones de conducta subversivos" (Martín Gaite, *La chica rara* 391). The mediation of the adults as enforcers of social order is also a contributing factor relating to the novel's favorable review.

The novel's setting in Las Palmas is important to the discussion of censorship on two levels. First, the representations of the Spanish Civil War are at geographic remove and at best are benign, with the circumstances under which Marta's extended family members arrive from the Peninsula to the Canary Islands shrouded in secrecy. This representation of Las Palmas as a location of escape from the Civil War shields the reader from direct contact with wartime hostilities and their implications on daily survival. The physical distance away from the battles of war that are imperceptible to the young protagonist contribute to the favorable censorship review. Also, taking place amidst "un paisaje fantasmagórico" (García Viñó 84), the atmosphere Laforet creates borders on "pura fantasmagoría" populated with "un círculo de seres estrafalarios" in a world constituted by "lo irreal, lo telúrico-fantástico" (Iglesias Laguna 179). The environment accentuates a fictional space that exists outside the realities of the atrocities of war. Johnson moreover remarks that Laforet's second novel "incorporates a personal, oblique and distanced view of political events through which the protagonist matures and decides the future direction of her life" ("Personal and Public" 47).

While documents pertaining to the *historia oficial* reveal an unproblematic relationship between Carmen Laforet and the censorship process in her first two novels, we now know that Laforet, like many authors in her time, crafted her literary products to fall within the parameters of text authorization, often with input from others and following the difficult-to-track process of self-censorship.

Ángeles Villarta: *Mi vida en el manicomio* (1953)

The writing of Ángeles Villarta (1919-2018) spans prose, poetry and journalism. She also worked as an editor of both literary works and literary periodicals. She was the daughter of a well-regarded doctor in Lastres (Asturias) who saw to her education in Switzerland from age 11 to about age 17, when she returned to Spain at outset of the Spanish Civil War. After the war she became aligned with the *Sección Femenina*, which informs the ideological framework of her creative writing and her career as a journalist. Because of her knowledge of English, French, German, and Italian, she began her professional life as an international reporter as a way to break down the complexities of accessing and disseminating news from abroad. Although Villarta appears in a number of bibliographical dictionaries and encyclopedia entries, her writing has only minimally registered on the critical radar. Julia María Labrador Ben traces Villarta's journalistic endeavors in her study on the 1953 Fémina prizewinning *Una mujer fea* (1954), which focuses on the vicissitudes of the titular character and those who inhabit the novel's rural setting. Further, Patricia O'Byrne, who offers a thorough listing of critics who have addressed—albeit cursorily—Villarta's writing, examines the theme of working women and of women and religion in representative narrative pieces that adhere to the tenets of the Sección Femenina. Mar Soria likewise examines the theme of working women and adds to O'Byrne's overview of *Yo he sido estraperlista* that extrapolates the vein of social class disparities from a seemingly uncritical optic aligned with Villarta's ideological conservatism. Soria concludes that the many women working in the black market defied Francoist messaging of the domesticated ángel del hogar, further supported by the female narrator working as journalist (189).

O'Byrne reminds readers that efforts aimed at the recovery of women's voices should be an ideologically "inclusive process" (88), which is particularly relevant to this present study because, often, studies on censorship examine writing that contests, or to any degree resists complicity with, the dominant discourse. The analysis of Villarta's work allows for contextualizing the censorship process on the ideological continuum as a literary corpus that easily gained authorization for publication for the author's ideological alignment with the dictatorship. Villarta's institutional adherence to the *Sección Femenina* would certainly have afforded her a favorable position before the censorship board, as evidenced by her multiple publications in the postwar literary landscape written largely in a journalistic vein that privileged objectivity over critique in her thematic development. This censorship experience would continue with *Mi vida en el manocomio* (1953), her exposé on a marginalized social group: women institutionalized in a mental health hospital. The novel was authorized for publication on 15 January 1953, absent censor remarks on the report (File *Mi vida*). Notwithstanding Villarta's ideological conservatisim, she presents institutional practices in the psychiatric hospital with a journalistic subtlety that leads readers to gaining access to the typically unobservable spaces of the facility's open and closed wards: common rooms, bedrooms, exterior gardens, and rooms where medical procedures take place. Villarta's act of narrating her experience subverts the notion of inaccessibility of this marginal space.

Villarta decenters the narrative in multiple ways. She translocates the action from Madrid to Oviedo since she could not gain entry to any of the psychiatric hospitals in the capital city. By moving away from the culturally hegemonic geography into the now bulldozed walls of La Cadellada Psychiatric Hospital, she insinuates a space of multi-faceted alterity. Known as "el manicomio de La Cadellada," the space takes on historical significance in both the medical and political realms. Designed in 1924 and built beginning in 1927, it was a state-of-the-art micro-city intended to allow for maximum success in the recuperation of its patients' mental health (Crespo Vázquez et al. 26, Secades Fernández 132-33). However, the facility suffered considerable damage during the Spanish Civil War when the Republican-held city suffered a devastating defeat by the Nationalist forces in 1937, with the help of the Legión Condor that blanketed the city with bombs.[4] The hospital was then repurposed as a concentration camp from October 1937 to at least April 1938 ("Los campos de concentración"). After the war it was rebuilt and returned to its use as a psychiatric hospital[5] but has since been demolished. The setting of this novel published in 1953 would have jogged historical memory to evoke the dialectic of victors and vanquished and would have been a powerful institutional marker in pro of the dominant ideology.

Villarta, however, destabilizes the narration by explaining that, rather than conversing with the medical staff about the patients' clinical diagnoses, she relies on the patients themselves to communicate their conditions and constructs her novel as one based on numerous unreliable narrators. She openly reminds readers that she is not trained to diagnose the women around her, although she clarifies that she informed herself of psychiatric conditions by immersing herself in medical literature. She bolsters authenticity by incorporating the clinical terminology of dozens of illnesses, ranging from bulimia, hypochondria, exhibitionism, manic depression, schizophrenia, obsessive compulsions, paranoia, suicidal ideation, catatonia, and numerous types of other phobias and manias. The female patients who interact with Villarta experience psychosis, disorientation, or hallucinations and undergo treatments that range from medicine to brain stimulation treatment, from injections to brain surgery. Indeed, *Mi vida en el manicomio* is a documentary novel, a hybrid text that combines the reporting of facts woven with narrative techniques of dialogue, plot

---

4   The strategy known as carpet bombing, or saturation bombing, for the ways that the repeatedly fired bombs blanket the target to maximize destruction is now considered a war crime by the Geneva Convention. This warfare tactic also appears in Liberata Masoliver's *Barcelona en llamas*.

5   The complex was demolished in 2004 to allow for the new construction of the Hospital Universitario Central de Asturias.

development.⁶ Villarta's undercover, investigative writing captures with a detached objectivity her recounting of myriad mental illnesses in the lives of the women she observed during the week she lived as if she were a patient, where the medical director knew who she was, and the staff only knew she was not a typical patient. Furthermore, Villarta pushes readers to question the labels of sanity and insanity, a subtle paradox considering the gender-based power of those who define these terms.

Villarta challenges from the outset the misconception that someone may be nefariously institutionalized at the whim of another in collusion with a sinister doctor by stating that it was surprisingly difficult for her to gain entry because in order to do so, it is necessary for the patient to have a mental illness and for that illness to be medically, officially certified (11). She also states that, to her knowledge, no one of sane mind has ever lived in a mental health institution undercover with permission from the director and reported on the experience, although she does acknowledge the existence of accounts by people with clinical conditions upon leaving the institution and the reporting by a woman who feigned mental illness to gain entry and then wrote about her experience. Villarta begins narrating the details of her arrival at the hospital by engaging directly with her reader, her *lectora amiga* (16), as the interlocutor of the first-person narrator, a signpost that this literature is destined for a female audience. The identification of her readership as women suggests the innocuity of content vis-à-vis the guiding questions on the censorship report. This posture is accen-

---

6   There is a discrepancy in the timing of her investigative reporting. In the book, she claims that she was a little older than 20 years old but in an interview she said she was about 30 years old. The dates are also problematized by the inconsistencies in her birth year, which in her own words was 1919, and which is supported by her accounts of returning to Spain after studying in Switzerland at age 17 in 1936, although other sources identify her birth year as 1913 or 1921. The temporal reference to the Civil War as distant (47) aligns with the author's references to her previous experiences living among black marketeers, garbage collectors, and miners suggests that her age was closer to 30 in the late 1940s, which would gesture toward the 1919 birth year.

tuated by Villarta's claim that "no fui al manicomio con intenciones moralizadoras, ni tengo el orgullo ni la aspiración de creer que voy a mejorar el mundo" (48), which may account for the absence of any untoward details about the women's treatment or living conditions.

If, as Soria concludes, the locus of the home is asphyxiating (189), the woman confined to the insane asylum breathes with even more difficulty. Villarta finds herself in a constant state of vigilance as she reconciles the potential dangers in the patients' volatility she faces while interacting with those patients who roam freely about the facility. By pushing through the gradations of confinement among the women, readers begin to resist the patients' social marginalization as a collective phenomenon. While it is true that some of the patients present with clinical conditions that would seem to require their institutionalization, others exhibit symptoms that fall outside of clinical diagnoses. For instance, one of the patients named Charín lives with "obsesiones [...] de tipo político" (185), and within her ramblings about political leadership and governance, she offers a critique of masculinity in the context of marriage: "Un hombre inexperto es un hombre torpe, y no puede hacer la felicidad de una mujer" (188). She further states that men are "presuntousos y cobardes" (189). Such attitudes echo what Soria interprets in Villarta's *Yo he sido estraperlista* (1950), that her narration "parodies and subverts the romance novel's idealized portrayal of men as intelligent" (188). Charín's critique is permissible in terms of censorship parameters because it comes from a woman sidelined from full participation in society, even though Villarta had believed her to be sane.

Villarta also references gender in the context of medical doctors. For this, she describes the case of Elisa and Pruden whose illness she identifies as *masculinofobia* for the present term of androphobia. The two women believe that female rather than male doctors should attend to female patients. However, instead of serving as an indictment on the lack of gender equity in medical professionals, Villarta offers a corrective to justify the idea by saying that female patients often fall in love with their male doctors, which subsequently has the potential to worsen their conditions, a situation that would be circumvented with female doctors. This method of granting the patients a voice points to a larger narrative of living in the dictatorship without transgressing the political regime, religion, or morality.

Villarta's narrative challenges the degree to which some women's confinement is necessary. Even though the purpose of the narrative is to serve as an exposé of what life is like within the walls of the hospital, some of the women's attitudes and experiences refer to sociocultural disparities in the sum of society. Nonetheless, for her alignment with the dominant ideology, her non-threatening portrayal of marginalized women, and her non-critical stance toward the living conditions in the hospital, Villarta gains easy authorization to publish her text.

Mercedes Rubio: Las siete muchachas del liceo (1957)

Scant bio-bibliographical background on Mercedes Rubio and the limited critical reception of her only published novel offer an entry point to literary recovery of writing on the margins.[7] On the one hand, that Rubio won the Barcelona publisher Garbo's Elisenda de Montcada literary prize in 1956 for her novel *Las siete muchachas del liceo* suggests at least the potential for success in the literary world, yet on the other she fell victim to circumstances that precluded her from furthering her career at the expense of financial and familial exigencies: she worked as a translator while fulfilling her role as wife and mother of two children. Although Rubio referenced in her press interview upon receiving the Montcada accolade the authorship of other novels and short stories and her anticipated continued writing, nothing beyond her first novel was published (Montaner 79).[8] This inconsistency opens the possibility that she wrote under a yet-to-be-discovered pseudonym.

The novel gained authorization for publication without the need for revision in a report issued on 6 April 1957:

---

7   The dates of Rubio's lifespan do not appear in the materials consulted.

8   Rubio states in this interview that she began translating novels 14 years earlier. During the 1950s and 1960s, she translated multiple novels from English to Spanish by authors such as Rosamond Marshall, W. Somerset Maugham, Edwin Radford, Frank G. Slaughter, and Frank Yerby for various publishers in Barcelona. Presumably, the financial gain through her translation work would have that of her creative production.

> Novela en que se narran la vida, ilusiones y desventuras de siete muchachas estudiantes de música en el liceo, que tomaron parte en el estreno de *Parsifal*, en el coro de Ángeles y de las que sólo una triunfa como concertista, a cambio de sacrificar su hogar. Se enlaza la acción con una historia retrospectiva de la Barcelona de principios de siglo. No contiene nada censurable y PUEDE AUTORIZARSE SU PUBLICACION. (File *Las siete muchachas*)

Raquel Conde Peñalosa summarizes the content and style of Rubio's novel in similar fashion to Eva Martínez Carmona's *Cuerpo sin sombra* (1956), which "recoge todos los tópicos de la literatura más convencional del momento sin separarse, ni por su prosa, no por sus críticas sociales, de una literatura costumbrista fácil" (211). *Costumbrista* elements include depictions, for example, of holiday celebrations, street scenes as the girls and their families move through the city space of Barcelona, clothing, and some of the girls' ordinary daily lives. The girls' conversations before and after their rehearsals touch upon the music they perform and the books they read.[9] Indeed, the novel's characters ranging from the top tier individuals in the power hierarchy in Barcelona's Gran Teatre del Liceu to the seven girls seem to ascribe to normative gender molds. Protagonist Blanca Galindo's story as rewriting of the Holy Grail narrative, however, positions her in a space of power that seldom constitutes female characterization. Rubio's creative departure from Richard Wagner's opera *Parsifal* (1882) rewrites gender in the legendary narrative to illustrate Blanca's quest for success as a musician. Through a feminized appropriation of the grail narrative, Rubio regenders the male protagonist in Wagner's celebrated opera to create her protagonist who aspires to win a coveted distinction in the conservatory despite numerous obstacles, most notably the opposition of the lead instructor, Sr. Ramírez, a dynamic that evokes the

---

9   For this last characteristic, Nicola Humble points out a feature of middlebrow novels: they "repeatedly portray scenes in which women discuss books, list their favourite authors, or imagine themselves into the plots of their favourite novels" (9).

Fisher King narrative.[10] The implications of these obstacles correlate to the positioning of the feminine subject preceding the Franco dictatorship and make veiled claims, in adhering to strict censorship practices, regarding the broad-based limitations many women experienced during this period of totalitarian reign.

Blanca's portrayal as a career woman, a highly trained, gifted pianist poised to gain international fame, distances the musician from the model of domesticity that would render a simple *costumbrista* narrative. Overt narrative reference to obstacles women face in the working world support Rubio's claim that her purpose in writing the novel was to cast light on "El problema de las personas que avanzan en su carrera artística y chocan con los intereses creados por otras personas que quieren conservar" (Del Arco 27). This statement is implicitly gender coded when considering hierarchical power dynamics relative to the stakeholders in a patriarchal society. At the same time, her remarks are subtly cautionary considering her female readership.

Despite the traditionalist overtones of the coming-of-age trope applied to a successful musician, the protagonist eschews married life and motherhood to travel the world as one of Spain's most distinguished concert pianists. In this way, the story traces the life of the pianist through her formative years, interweaving throughout the novel the life stories of her six classmates from the conservatory. Whereas the other girls could not overcome obstacles to their budding music careers due to various reasons—lack of financial resources to pursue studies or to rent concert halls for self-promotion, poor health that led to an early death, marriage, loss of interest in a career in music—Blanca persevered to study both in Barcelona and throughout Europe, gaining stature as a prominent musician. Her initial fame and success,

---

   10   Tasked with guarding the Holy Grail, the figure of Fisher King is rooted in the 12th Century Chrétien de Troyes's *Perceval*, on which Wagner's *Parsifal* is based. The Fisher King's wound to the thigh, symbolically referencing his impotence both literal and figurative, figures prominently in Arthurian legend; in *Las siete muchachas*, the conservatory director suffers a wound to the arm, as a parallel reference to diminished authority. See "Moving through Time and Space in Mercedes Rubio's *Las siete muchachas del liceo* (1957) via Wagner's *Parsifal* in Barcelona, Spain (1914)."

which implies financial independence, supports the showcasing of her talents as product of Spain's cultural patrimony as she was contracted to travel through Europe and the Americas by novel's end.

Of the seven young ladies, Blanca is the only one who rose to fame as a musician. About two thirds of the novel is narrated in flashback beginning with events some thirty years in her past, while Blanca is jailed for assaulting her musical director in 1934, until her release from the holding cell when the novel resumes the story in the narrative present to recount the details of her defense and trial, her exoneration, and her yet-unchartered path in life. The flashback opens with the time that Blanca's six conservatory girlfriends were rehearsing to sing in the Choir of Angels in the premiere of *Parsifal* in the Gran Teatre del Liceu.[11] This was the first performance Wagner authorized outside of Bayreuth, which began on 31 December 1913 at 11:00 pm and ended at 6:00 am on 1 January 1914.

Rubio's responses in the interview upon winning the prize attest to the opposing views of femininity in Spain's dictatorial society. Though Rubio elides any autobiographical connections with the protagonist or her classmates with a definitive "No" in response to the question "¿Es usted una de ellas?" (Del Arco 27), contrarily a large part of the remaining interview contains numerous intersections between Rubio's life as a musician and the evolution of Blanca's portrayal in the novel: both won numerous awards for their performances, traveled abroad thanks to the generosity of benefactors, returned to Spain upon the illness of their fathers, married and had children, and gave up promising careers in music. Rubio reveals that she was a prodigious musician who played the complete version of Isaac Albéniz's *Iberia*, a notable accomplishment due to the complexity of piece.[12] Rubio, like Galindo,

---

11   The Choir of Angels sings suspended from the rafters, unseen by the audience such that the ethereal effect of their voices accentuates the angelic quality of their performance.

12   An article in the 24 May 1932 edition of *La Vanguardia* reads: "Mercedes Rubio se lanzó a ejecutar íntegramente la *Iberia*, de Albéniz, obra ante la cual se han estrellado no pocas reputaciones pianísticas. Artista bien preparada y conocedora de los recursos del teclado, Mercedes Rubio, si no llegó siempre a traducir con absoluta fidelidad la evocadora poesía que im-

performed and studied in Paris and married before the war. Although she said she had written short stories and other novels (Montaner 79), efforts to locate them have proven unfruitful. Rubio attempts to dialogue with the keepers of cultural patrimony by creating a protagonist inspired by her own experiences, despite denying the correlation with the fictional musician who is a source of pride in national identity formation.

The subtext of Rubio's story proffers a rich understanding of feminine subjectivity in opposition to Francoist discourse that locates the mother and wife within the confines of domesticity. By framing her story through the lens of Spain's Second Republic and likely reframing her own life story, Rubio avoids constituting a female subject who would clash with models outlined through restrictive dictatorial practices because she touches upon elements of wifehood and motherhood in her normative portrayal of Blanca's adult life later in the novel. The censor's comment that Blanca attains fame at the expense her home underscores the prevailing attitudes surrounding femininity and domesticity at the time the novel was published.

The characters evoked in the novel's title immediately move censors away from interpreting them as threatening subjects for their gender and young age. The reader, including the censor, is led to believe that the young women live in the world of the arts, far from the male-shaped political climate of the author's time of writing. The censor's view of the girls as *ángeles* neatly conforms to gender norms. They are heard and not seen; their visible erasure from the opera connotes women's exclusion from the sphere of political, economic, and even familial influence as Blanca experienced in her life, and more revealing, as did her fictional sisters and many women of her time. For her upholding of patriarchal norms, Rubio's portrayal of femininity aligns with official discourse.

---

pregna las páginas de la obra maestra de Albéniz, demostró haber hecho de ella un escrupuloso estudio, y puso de relieve la perfección de su técnica y atinadas intervenciones expresivas" ("Música y teatro" 27).

CARMEN MARTÍN GAITE: *ENTRE VISILLOS* (1958)
Carmen Martín Gaite (1925-2000) has published an impressive body of work over a four-decade period that has secured her place as a literary giant of her time. Martín Gaite's canonical *El cuarto de atrás* (1978) cemented her historiographic legacy as a retrospective portrait of society from the 1930s through the end of the dictatorship and beyond. Numerous studies on this novel and her writing in general—her remaining novels, short stories, essays, poetry, children's literature, and, to a lesser degree, dramatic works—capture nuanced thematic representations and character portrayals that inextricably link history with humanity. Martín Gaite gained easy authorization to publish her writing, beginning with her short story collection, the Café Gijón prize-winning *El balneario* in 1955. Her first full-length novel, *Entre visillos*, winner of the 1957 Nadal Prize, is set against the backdrop of an unnamed *ciudad en provincias* presumed to represent Salamanca and constitutes a snapshot in time through its depiction of female protagonists bound by the ennui surrounding their small-town life. The novel offers commentary on the prospects of the women's future largely determined by gender. Chris Perriam et al. consider *Entre visillos* among "a number of post-war novels in which female characters break with the restrictive models of the patriarchal family binding them to a confined domestic space" in which young women—unlike their *novela rosa* heroines—"are characterized by their desire to escape into the public space of the street and broaden their perspective" (89).

The quotidian humdrum that permeates Martín Gaite's fictional world consolidates the image of peaceful living aligned with Francoist messaging:

> Ultimately, the social project of the New State was simply to impose victory and then to consolidate control. The political system was intended, above all, to depoliticize. The exclusion and punishment of those outside the regime was vital to its strategy of pacification, but life had to become bearable for those who stayed within it, so that it could become at least a 'lesser evil', in conditions which were, for all their shortcomings, better than the social and political conflict which preceded it. (Vincent 169)

The author creatively draws from her own life experiences as a young woman growing up in a totalitarian society to narrate the stories of the young women who live a safeguarded existence, with their lives neatly mapped as a metonymic microcosm of femininity. The autobiographical content, summarized by Joan L. Brown, that nurtures the narrative of *Entre visillos* is presented in such a way that conforms to the regime's ideals: "1) the oppressive conformity of provincial life; 2) the severely circumscribed role ascribed to women in a traditional social order; 3) the nature of education under Franco; and 4) the political circumstances of the era" (38-39).

The classification of *Entre visillos* as a neorealist novel in Spanish literature of the 1950s has contributed to the analysis of the female protagonists as part of a collective unit that abides by gender-ascribed moral codes of conduct, in an atmosphere that by design perpetuates this portrayal. To support this viewpoint, I follow Pablo Gil Casado's interpretation of the social novel: "Trata del estado de la sociedad o de ciertas desigualdades e injusticias que existen en ella."[13] Social realist novelists, identified by Gil Casado as being born between 1922 and 1936, are different from their predecessors because they experienced the war as infants or young children and have little or no recollection of its events. As a result, they take a critical view of their contemporary Spain, and if they revert to references to the war, it is with the intention of gaining a better understanding of the here and now (Gil Casado XX-XXI).

Martín Gaite explained in her interview with Celia Fernández: "*Entre visillos* lo escribí como una especie de rechazo de ese mundo provinciano del que huía. Yo tenía veintitantos años y acababa de llegar a Madrid. Hay una crítica, aunque sin crueldad, de ese mundo pequeño y demasiado cerrado de mi infancia y juventud" (171). For the tone that Martín Gaite adopted, in some instances the novel's reception was less than complementary. It received a scathing review in

---

13 Regarding the social novels, Gil Casado elaborates that "Éstas se refieren a todo un sector o grupo, a varios, o a la totalidad de la sociedad, pero en cualquier caso carecen de sentido individual" (XVI). The testimonial basis of a collective tone of denunciation discerned through the "héroe múltiple" figures prominently in these novels (XVI).

Archivum upon its publication in 1957 in which the critic identified by the initials J. P. V. summarily dismisses the novel on the grounds that: "carece totalmente de interés," "no pasa de ser un relato ñoño, anodino, escrito con torpeza y sin el menor asomo de humanidad," and "No hay quién lo resista" (369). The reviewer faults the author's empty characterization and uneven pacing: "Ni uno sólo de sus personajes, en su contextura psicológica, supera la categoría de máscara de guiñol. Tampoco tiene acción" (369). It is due to these nontransgressive elements that Martín Gaite obfuscated her critique of society, which María Luisa Guardiola explains through the lens of the author's use of space to evade censorial stricture. Guardiola examines the novel from the standpoint of the highly emblematic buildings of the Catedral and the Instituto Femenino de Enseñanza to connote the reach of religious and educational indoctrination and protagonist Pablo Klein's positioning as the "intermediario o *in-between*, que logra inculcar su método de enseñanza innovador en la joven [Natalia]" (27). These textual elements contest the limits of dictatorial powers through the author's strategy of veiling her female protagonist between the curtains, a space Guardiolia identifies as "un lugar transformador donde subvierten y se apropian, parcialmente, de los lugares censurados pertenecientes al patriarcado más acérrimo" (26).

The novel's censorship file summarizes: "Una historia provinciana de un grupo de chicas, sus estudios y sus amoríos. El argumento se centra en torno a la figura del nuevo profesor de alemán del instituto, desde que llega al pueblo a las vacaciones de Navidad" (File *Entre visillos*). The gleaning of patriarchy embedded in this summary aligns with Francoist discourse with focused attention on the male/female divide: Martín Gaite positions the male as the sole authority against the female collective who will benefit from his expertise, to be gained from the outside perspective of the foreign character. The non-transgressive portrayal of characters who align with their gender roles offers the censors every reason to grant authorization for publication.

However, the file exemplifies inconsistencies I have found in the process of making a determination regarding the content in the final printing of the novel. Although the censor continues: "Convendría suprimir dos expresiones groseras, en las galeradas n° 41 y 64. PUEDE

PUBLICARSE," and then a separate note indicates: "Consultado Jefe decía no se toman en consideración las tachaduras propuestas 22-1-58" (File *Entre visillos*), the printed novel includes the suggested—rather than required—revisions even though they were not essential. The changes, few in number, soften indecorous wording by substituting less offensive language. In the published version, the phrase "niñas de las narices" (Ms. 100) replaces "niñas de las puñetas" (Ts. 41), while "que está peor irse de mujeres" (Ms. 153) replaces "que está peor irse de putas" (Ts. 64).[14] Considering that these changes are minimal, and were not made at the behest of the censorship process, it is impossible to ascertain if they were made by the editor or by the author herself. The show of cooperation coupled with the compliance in all other aspects of the censorship guidelines could have contributed to subsequently favorable outcomes with future submissions.[15] These voluntary, albeit slight revisions, avoided any suggestion of impropriety in Martín Gaite's writing. Further, the author's level of relative fame would have made her a known member of influential literary circles of her time also for her marriage to Rafael Sánchez Ferlosio, whose *El jarama* (1955) garnered both the Premio Nadal that same year and the Premio de la Crítica in the category of narrative writing the following year.

Disparities emerge within the subtext of a hegemonic-subaltern dialectic: the tedium the girls experience is countered with the presence of the German school teacher Pablo Klein in the tripartite role of Other in terms of gender and nation, and as the bearer of social capital. The question of gender also plays a predominant role in the

---

14   Throughout this present study, "Ts." (typescript) refers to the typed novel, and "Ms." (manuscript) refers to the published novel.

15   See Montejo Gurruchaga's study *Discurso de autora* on the censorship files on Martín Gaite's work and the outcome of *Entre visillos* in addition to *El balneario* (1955) and *Ritmo lento* (1963). Montejo Gurruchaga notes as well the censor's lack of acumen in evaluating *Ritmo lento*, finalist for the Premio Biblioteca Breve in 1962 (57-59), which underscores a significant shortcoming pointed out in critical studies on censorship in Francoist Spain, that is, the censors' misreading or misunderstanding of the texts under evaluation.

father-daughter paradigm through which readers perceive an existential angst best reflected at the end of chapter 16 in the exchange between Natalia and her father that takes place in his bedroom at day's end. In representation of the patriarchy, he embodies its public discourse. This portion of the novel accentuates what Lauren Berlant calls the female complaint, which "serves in particular to mediate and manage the social contradictions that arise from women's sexual and affective allegiance to a phallocentric ideology that has, in practice, denied women power, privilege, and presence in the public and private spheres" ("Female Complaint" 243). Berlant locates the manifestation of this complaint in the space she calls the intimate public, a space where consumers—for example, a particular cross-section of women—"share a worldview and emotional knowledge that they have derived from a broadly common historical experience" (*The Unfinished Business* viii). For Natalia, beginning the conversation "era dificilismo," and she states, "he arrancado a hablar no sé cómo" (232) before incorporating indirect discourse to enumerate her concerns that include "que la tía Concha nos quiere convertir en unas estúpidas, que solo nos educa para tener un novio rico, y que seamos lo más retrasadas posible en todo" (232-33). Her father's inability to discern her greater aspirations to break from patriarchy combined with her difficulty in articulating her needs is reflected in Natalia's interior thoughts: "no sabía lo que tenía que pedirle" and "he sido incoherente" (233), and is punctuated by her complete omission of talking about her own future: "Lo de mi carrera no le he dicho nada" (234). Natalia's ideas and speech exist as part of women's culture that leads to this poignant moment as an articulation of a symbolic voicelessness mediated by the patriarchy (the prevailing ideology) through both tone and semantics, without yielding change.

Martín Gaite avoided censorial stricture with this novel for two primary reasons. First, by circumventing language that directly engages with oppression, she explicitly and critically positions women on the social continuum aligned with cultural normativity—including the role of education. She also presents political circumstances in a non-threatening manner. Like other social realist authors, Martín Gaite is a product of her environment and incorporates into her narrative her experience of the times, giving the reader a vivid glimpse into the life contemporary to the period of their writing in alignment with the dominant discourse.

CONCHA CASTROVIEJO: *VÍSPERA DEL ODIO* (1959)

Concha Castroviejo (1912-1995) is known primarily as a novelist, journalist, and literary critic who also wrote short stories and children's literature. Critic Antonio Iglesias Laguna identifies Castroviejo as one of the *novelistas combatientes*—a grouping that includes José Luis Castillo Puche, Ricardo Fernández de la Reguera, José María Gironella, Susana March, and Elena Soriano (72)—young adults at the time of the war, for whom historical perspectives mark the cornerstone of much of their writing.[16] In Raquel Conde Peñalosa's view, Castroviejo ranks with Mercedes Formica, Carmen Kurtz, Dolores Medio, and Elena Soriano as "autoras nacidas entre 1910 y 1920, con una marcada conciencia de las circunstancias sociales que rodean y afectan a la mujer en la posguerra y actitudes de talante feminista" (200). For Montejo Gurruchaga, authors born during this decade experienced the war directly or indirectly: "van a reflexionar sobre la guerra civil y sus consecuencias, la cárcel, la degradación del hombre, el odio" (*Mujeres escritoras* 155). Castroviejo left Spain after the Civil War to live briefly in France before settling in Mexico until returning to her homeland in 1949.[17]

Castroviejo's first novel, *Los que se fueron* (1957), recounts the experience of exile in both France and Mexico and gained easy authorization for publication primarily for the disadvantageous positioning of defeated *rojos* forced to abandon their country for ideological reasons.

---

16   Iglesias Laguna classifies postwar novelists into three categories: those who were born between 1875 and 1900 and who were already known writers at the outbreak of the Spanish Civil War (for example, Mercedes Formica, Rosa Chacel, Francisco Ayala, Max Aub, and Ramón Sender); the *novelistas combatientes* identified above; and those like Néstor Luján, Torcuato Luca de Tena, Ana María Matute, and Juan Goytisolo who experienced the war as part of their childhood and whose literature reflects "mayor perspectiva histórica para juzgar desapasionadamente los hechos" (72-73).

17   Detailed bio-bibliographical information on Castroviejo appears in articles by Gregorio Torres Nebrera and by Nanina Santos.

She was the first non-Falangist novelist to gain authorization to publish a novel on the experience of exile (Larraz, "La 'operación retorno'" 182-83). For her second novel, *Víspera del odio* (1959), she received the Premio Elisenda de Montcada, submitted under the pseudonym Pedro López. The novel's structure follows the confession trope, in the form of an extended letter the protagonist Teresa Nava wrote to her friend, aptly named Consuelo. Castroviejo sets the action before, during, and after the Spanish Civil War as a temporal marker to illustrate the protagonist's evolution from a single young woman to a mature married woman in a context shaped by its historical setting. The novel features a woman who avenges her first husband's abusive treatment through the emotional and physical cruelty she inflicts upon him after he falls ill and enters a paralytic state. For Gregorio Torres Nebrera, "Teresa Nava es una de las primeras voluntades feministas de nuestra literatura contemporánea, que lucha contra la presión ejercida por la hipócrita moral oficialista y la familia, y corre tras el espacio de relativa libertad que la revolución le concede" (226). In L. Teresa Valdivieso's summation of *Víspera del odio*, "La guerra civil y la violencia que ésta despertó en los individuos es una presencia constante en la obra" (28).[18] Further, Raquel Osborne contextualizes:

> It is well known that Francoism intended to use as its foundation the denial and the reversal of the ideals of the Republic. The new regime established itself during the Civil War. When the war was over and the dictatorship settled in, it claimed that the degradation responsible for bringing about the clash between Spaniards was a consequence of the abyss to which the country had sunk during the Republican period.
>
> Central to such a negative vision of the 'New Spain' upheld by the Franco dictatorship was the change of status of women fos-

---

18   Carlos Luis Álvarez, in his review of *Víspera del odio*, points to the evolution of Teresa's behavior: "Castroviejo sabe que los dolores inmensos no encenagan, sino que purifican. Un ser humano no transita automáticamente desde el sufrimiento inmerecido a la abyección. Tendrá que haber antes una lucha, cuya intensidad le dará, en último término, la estatura moral del luchador" (134).

tered during the Second Republic through the implementation of gender equality measures, such as the right to vote, divorce and abortion, among others. (512)

Literary critic Melchor Fernández Almagro notes in his review of the novel that "hay que reconocer que el medio geográfico-social no gravita demasiado, por reducirse a telón de fondo sobre el que se perfila la figura de la protagonista" (6), an interpretation that would align with the censors' perspective that the narrative distances itself from an indictment against the war or its aftermath. However, contrary to Fernández Almagro's interpretation, compelling social implications motivate protagonist Teresa's hatred toward her first husband, Braulio Lozano. As Valdivieso explains: "la autora juega con la memoria histórica del lector y así puede crear expectativas de lectura, de algo que no se dice, mediante la simple sugerencia de fechas, lugares y sucesos" (28). By virtue of these suggestions, rather than direct references to events that transpired two decades before she endeavored to publish her novel, Castroviejo circumvented censorial stricture. Yet, references to certain textual elements move beyond the realm of what Valdivieso identifies as suggestion. The novel explicitly describes mass incarceration of Republican soldiers held captive in deplorable conditions for their ideological dissonance. They endure living in cramped quarters in a frenzied atmosphere, marked by the uncertainties of their fate. To name but one example, the novel tells of one of those soldiers who is executed by firing squad because an influential figure on the winning side insisted on his instant death for his alleged egregious wartime activities.

The novel's favorable pass through censorship came notwithstanding the first censor's disparaging summary and the second's reference to the protagonist's moral shortcomings. These two interpreations aside, the political undertones that positioned the Republican forces in a negative light combined with the novel's perception as female focused, outweighed the censors' misgivings about authorizing publication without requiring revisions.

The first report, from 20 January 1959 reads:

Novela en estremo [sic] desagradable, de penosa lectura. Una joven casada por su madre con un ser repugnante de avaricia y lujuria, vive martirizada por él y sus hermanas en un ambiente sórdido insoportable, hasta el año 1936 que por fin huye, encontrando casualmente al hombre de su vida (desechado de perfecciones metido en uniforme de capitan [sic] rojo). Divorciada y casada con su amor, vive feliz con él y su hijo. Terminada la guerra el marido se venga cruelmente, haciendo ejecutar al calumniado capitán; el niño muere y ella dedica el resto de sus días a cultivar el odio a su marido. Paralítico y en sus manos es sometido a todo género de torturas físicas, morales y hasta espirituales ya en su agonía. Más tarde ella muere sin que un compasivo religioso logre traerla al camino del arrepentimiento y la penitencia. No obstante, ateniéndonos al cuestionario adjunto, PUEDE PUBLICARSE. (File *Víspera*)

By adhering to the guiding questions that outline potential threats espoused in the novel under review (¿Ataca al dogma?, etc.), the censor authorizes its publication. The novel's esteemed poor literary quality referenced by the "penosa lectura" did not influence the decision, as the censors at times would—unjustly—remark on the inferior writing or underestimate the quality of the writing when evaluating submissions. The first censor's mention of divorce alludes to the sociocultural and legal contexts central to the novel's plot. Teresa entered the arranged marriage with Braulio but later divorced him when divorce was legal during the Second Republic. The subtlety in the censor's remark that "el marido se venga cruelmente" tellingly reflects his own bias in still considering Braulio her husband, when in fact, Teresa legally dissolved the marriage. During the war, she falls in love with José Yuste, marries him, and has a child with him. José is falsely accused of war crimes and imprisoned due to his affiliation with the Republicans, and Braulio later arranges for his execution as a war criminal. Braulio refuses to recognize the legitimacy of divorce in alignment with the law's abolition in Francoist Spain, and in doing so he delegitimizes her second marriage. Because Teresa asserts her legal right to divorce Braulio, she defies, according to Raquel Conde Peñalosa, "los modelos femeninos que se difunden desde la ideología franquista" (239). Women such as Teresa were marginalized and labeled as adulterous in the discourse of the dictatorship, recalling literary critic and feminist Carolyn Heilbrun's observation of the eponymous protagonist of *Anna Karenina*, who was ostracized for living with a man outside of marriage (88). The women who transgress established social norms suffer grave consequences for their actions, fictionalized in *Víspera del odio* with Teresa's loss of José and of their son together, and the ensuing, lifelong unhappiness. Jo Labanyi has remarked upon "The equation of the Republic with sexual freedom" (51), a notion that may be applied within the framework of *Víspera del odio* in that Teresa felt free to explore love after her divorce, an exploration that led, rather than to following a path of promiscuity, directly to finding her one true love in life, suggesting a redeeming quality in the protagonist.

For all of the domestic violence Teresa experienced at the hands of Braulio, when she learns that he suffered a stroke that has left him paralyzed, she outwardly—publicly—assumes the role of the benevolent wife and caretaker, in a dutiful return to her place in matrimony. Teresa, however, subverts this role in a turn that positions her to exact revenge on him in the cruelest ways she can imagine, a symbolic attack against the patriarchy. Unable to speak or move, the formerly tyrannical Braulio is rendered indefensible and must tolerate daily mistreatment until the day he dies. Although Teresa does not confess her sins—despite the opportunity to do so—and therefore is not absolved of them, her religiosity is not required for the novel to gain authorization.[19] Rather, the presence of the priest at novel's end mediates what Torres Nebrera calls "la narrativa de 'existencialismo cristiano'" (229),

---

19 The topic of religious conversion or repentance appears in several novels authorized as submitted, for example, in Rosa María Cajal's *Un paso más* (1956), Carmen Laforet's *Una mujer nueva* (1955), Concha Suárez del Otero's *Me llamo Clara* (1968), and Anunciación Rivera Tovar's *La otra guerra de la posguerra* (1969). The shift in the protagonist's psychological profile that leads to the change in religious convictions or awareness of actions considered transgressive was driven by the censorship process in the case of the first two novels and was written as part of the character's profile in the last two.

which consolidates Teresa's sacramental contrition in both censors' and readers' minds.

A second reading before the censorship board two weeks later yielded the same assessment to authorize publication:

> Con un argumento muy complejo se sitúa la acción de la novela en los años de la campaña de Liberación Nacional.
>
> Teresa antes de morir escribe a una amiga la historia de su amor con el hombre que eligió su corazón, y la vida que llevó con el hombre que la casó su madre.
>
> Este, por una denuncia, es culpable de la muerte del primero. Y el odio de Teresa no se apagará ni con la venganza, unicamente [sic] parece aplacarse con las palabras del Sacerdote a la hora de su transito [sic]. (File *Víspera*)

The reductive plot summary glosses over Teresa's attack on patriarchy, and this report, like the first, makes mention of the priest. As observed by Montejo Gurruchaga, the narrative positioning of the priest at novel's end as society's moral compass is the device that "salva la novela de la censura" ("Las mujeres escritoras" 103); the mere inclusion of the priest who is willing to hear Teresa's confession reminds readers that salvation is always an option for those who choose it. Further, the discourse on the ramifications of falling on the losing side of the war aligns with the messaging of the Spanish State's totalitarian rule. Also to note from this report is that it teases out one of the various names associated with the Spanish Civil War, named in the report as "la campaña de Liberación Nacional." In a handful of novels, censors rejected the phrase Guerra Civil or Guerra Civil Española and instead imposed its renaming as *Guerra de Liberación, la guerra española, nuestra cruzada, nuestra cruzada de liberación, la cruzada,* or *nuestra guerra de cruzada,* with the ideological implications of the winning side of *nuestra* in opposition to the vanquished. The reframing of war as a "campaign" serves two purposes. It accurately reflects how dictatorial discourse viewed these events, including the motivations behind them, and it describes the sum of events as a necessary vehicle to restore social order. In war theory, however, a campaign is a phase of a war and employing this term would thereby minimize the scope of the conflict. In *Víspera del odio*, the victors' portrayal as victorious, two decades removed from the end of the war, is not only a reminder of the outcome but also asserts the power continuum over the vanquished by recalling their incarceration and execution during both the war and postwar years.

The second report provides a confusing summary of the novel on two fronts. First, the action is not limited to wartime but rather spans multiple decades. Further, the report inverts the order of Teresa's relationships to insinuate that her husband is actually Braulio rather than José, her true love and legally recognized second husband—in the language of the Second Republic—reflective of the postwar discourse that nullifies the legitimacy of divorce. The report's allusion to the possibility of absolution evinces Castroviejo's literary corrective that censors duly noted.

Because Castroviejo tells of one fictional character's response to injustices that occurred on the level of her personal circumstances, she minimizes the potentially deleterious effect of the regime's ability to uphold social order. As Teresa ultimately lives in self-imposed isolation in the home, Castroviejo follows a discursive strategy of constructing what Arias Careaga identifies as: "la creación de un espacio restringido frecuentemente a la esfera de lo privado, que es el espacio reservado a la mujer en la estructura social de la posguerra" (155). Teresa's inward turn to violence as a way to come to terms with the tragedy that befell her reads as a unique circumstance with an inner logic that justifies her actions. In this way, Teresa's transgressive actions unfold within to the domestic sphere wherein she creates her *exilio interior* (Arias Careaga 139). The lack of public display of her aggression is another factor that figures into the novel's authorization for publication. By limiting the violence to the home, Castroviejo avoids the suggestion that Teresa would exhibit cruel and vengeful behavior in the public arena, which contrasts with the normative public display of violence among men when contextualized in terms of war and wartime crimes. Mention of the construct of delineated space also surfaces in the author's personal correspondence with literary critic and essayist Guillermo de Torre who praises the novel's narrative mastery in his letter to Castroviejo:

"En ella se confirma una vez más paradójicamente que a mayor limitación de espacio, de tema, de personajes, mayores posibilidades de ahondamiento y perfección" (Letter 22821/28 [27 January 1964]).[20] In addition, the acknowledgement in the novel's opening that it is a letter intended solely for one recipient, her friend Consuelo, leaves the reader as an unintended observer not incited to emulate Teresa's behavior.

Teresa's refusal in the end to recognize her abhorrent behavior casts her not as transgressive but as irrational or as an exaggerated response to Braulio's earlier treatment toward her in line also with the *tremendista* esthetic of the postwar novel of the 1940s.[21] She lives in a double bind, married in the language of patriarchy, divorced and legitimately remarried in the language of the Republic. Her death without absolution for her transgressions is just retribution for her behavior.

The novel toys with the readers' initial sympathies toward Teresa for her portrayal as a victim of the patriarchy. She survives Braulio's abuse, suffers the loss of true love, and endures fractured motherhood upon the death of her son. By adopting the role of abuser, she subverts the power continuum that privileges patriarchy. The transgressive behavior of a woman as aggressor, coupled with the backdrop of the Civil War and Braulio's responsibility for the execution of José contest the idea that the novel is simply a love story gone wrong as implied by the first report. Castroviejo creates a narrative that negotiates the confines

---

20 Torre continues: "Los caracteres poseen una intensidad inolvidable: se graban en la memoria y no desaparecen como solamente sucede con los de algunos grandes novelistas del pasado: desde Dostoievski a Galdós. [...] Es curioso, mi querida y admirada Concha, que usted—mejor dicho su yo novelesco—se mantiene tan objetivo, tan exenta de odio y rencor. La tragedia de la guerra, ya ha insuflado tan intensamente a las pasiones en un drama personal. Con ello se demuestra que usted, en cuanto novelista, siente y expresa mejor lo individual que lo colectivo. [...] No abandone la novela. [...] Espero, pues, su próxima" (Letter 22821/28).

21 Óscar Barrero Pérez has pointed out the existential qualities of this novel in that the first-person narrator and her solitude open the space of interior reflection and that the protagonist's pessimism leads to a hatred complicated by outside factors (war, first husband's revenge), faith or lack thereof, and evasion of reality (taking refuge in dreams or forgetting) (212).

of feminine subjectivity through the protagonist's privately displayed abusive behavior in order to secure authorization to publish *Víspera del odio*.

Liberata Masoliver: *Barcelona en llamas* (1961)

Catalán writer Liberata Masoliver (1911-1996) authored eighteen novels throughout a career that spanned from 1955 to 1972, publishing at least one novel a year between 1959 and 1969. Although some of her novels, in particular the first three set in Africa, have received critical attention, studies on her work obviate biographical details. Minimal biographic information may be gleaned from literary dictionaries and encyclopedias, which consistently remark on her ideological conservativism. All of her works except for two received authorization to print either as submitted in their original form or with minimal revisions required. It was Masoliver's first novel that was required to undergo minor edits and it appears that, after her initial experience with the censorship board, she adjusted her writing to avoid censure until she reached the latter years of her publishing career.

For Judith Butler, "Censorship precedes the text" (248), a position that views production as an activity construed to the liking of censorial approval, rather than production created then modified to fit within the constraints of regulatory practices. When an author's political ideology coincides with the regime, as it did with Ángeles Villarta, the likelihood of an outcome of "authorized for publication" increases. Such is the case of Masoliver, whose ideologically conservative posture filtered into her writing during the first decade and a half of her literary career before challenging patriarchal norms in *Telón* (1969), the fifteenth of her eighteen novels. Censorship files of her novels, save *Telón*, *La retirada* (1967), and *Un hombre de paz* (1969, censorship file; 1970, publication date),[22] reveal mostly tempered observations, with

---

22 *Un hombre de paz* is the most censored of Masoliver's works for its political content. Similar to *Barcelona en llamas*, she recounts the experiences of Republicans in Barcelona during the war, with revisions required on over 20 pages. Because she portrays events that deride the Republican-occupied city—such as this phrase on the novel's report: "caída en el lado republicano y las atrocidades cometidas contra víctimas inocentes"—she dis-

modifiers of *limpia, ejemplar, moral, delicada,* and *deliciosa,* notwithstanding the comment that one of them "carece de potencia narrativa" (File *La retirada*), and another is labeled "Sucia, mala, pero no tiene importancia" (File *La mujer del colonial*). Thematically, Masoliver's work falls into two primary areas: "una más testimonial sobre la España de la guerra y de la posguerra, y otra más creativa en un conjunto de novelas de ambiente africano que nos alejan de las tensiones psíquicas y sociales posbélicas" (Conde Peñalosa 212). Conde Peñalosa rightly observes that Masoliver "elabora novelas cuidadas y bien escritas mostrando mundos y conflictos nuevos en un panorama literario bastante monótono en cuanto a los asuntos y temas literarios. En general estas novelas no alcanzan mucha difusión y apenas se reeditan, aunque hayan recibido alabanzas en la prensa y galardones literarios" (212). Indeed, Masoliver enjoyed favorable reception in the press with numerous positive reviews of her work at the time of publication. Before discussing the censorial review of Masoliver's fifth novel *Barcelona en llamas,* a novel that passed the requirements outright, remarks on the author's experience with her previous novels provides the context to

---

tances the realities of wartime atrocities from the side of the victors (File *Un hombre de paz*). This is especially true when censors require the removal of phrases such as: "Un millón de muertos...miles de presos de uno y otro lado, que estaban en campos de concentración" (Ts. 146, underline added by censor). One of the most volatile, and therefore excised, critiques appears in this lengthy interior monologue that the censor bracketed and sub-bracketed: ["Llevada hasta el último extremo de miseria, por las ruinas de la guerra, [por la orgía rapaz de la revolución], Franco heredará una España mísera, carente del poco oro que le quedaba al país entregado por Negrín a los rusos a cambio de material de guerra; una nación en deuda con los alemanes e italianos que le ayudaron a alcanzar la victoria... Heredará el rencor acendrado de los de izquierdas y habrá de poner en cintura a los exaltados de derechas que también la odiarán, como habrá de luchar con el odio de las grandes potencias europeas y americanas que no le perdonarán jamás esta victoria... Los obreros tampoco le agradecerán que les hayan arrebatado la alegría y el orgullo del mundo"] (Ts. 195). The censor also notes that the narration presents an autobiographical perspective. See the "Observations" at the end of Chapter 4 for excerpts from the censorship report.

understand how writers—even those adhering to conservative ideology—adapted their writing, shedding light on self-censorship practices.

An overview of Masoliver's initial experiences with the censorship board elucidates the evolution in her writing that led to avoiding concepts originally signaled as problematic to the censorship process. Masoliver's first novel *Efún* (1955) was the recipient of the Elisenda de Montcada Prize. Beyond the love story trope of a young Spanish woman who travels to Equatorial Guinea to be with her fiancé, the novel offers testimony to the image—both conceptions and misconceptions—of the region's people and way of life. Set on a timber plantation whose name inspired the title, and the surrounding areas, the novel's vivid descriptions of the people and places in this foreign land mark a stark contrast the colonizing power over the imperial subject. According to Antonio Carrasco González, Masoliver "Conoció las circunstancias con que adorna su relato gracias a los amigos de su padre que contaban en su casa los pormenores de sus viajes y estancias en la colonia española, donde residían muchos catalanes" ("Novelas de plantación"). Representations of various social strata that comprise the timber plantation's successful operation paint a vivid portrait of class, racial, and gender dichotomies of a cultural imaginary far removed from the author's experience, yet they suggest a keen awareness of nuanced cultural differences between Spain and Equatorial Guinea in terms of local language, cultural practices, and flora and fauna. Although Masoliver never traveled to this country, her narrative contains realistic though stylized descriptions of what she perceives daily life would be like. She typifies her Spanish-born characters as conflicted outcasts from the Peninsula rather than presenting them as most of them were—entrepreneurs attempting to seek a fortune abroad (Carrasco González)—and places them on a racialized dialectic with the local population. Critical readings have led Montserrat Alás-Brun, Kathleen Connolly, Benita Sampedro Vizcaya, and Cécile Stephanie Stehrenberger to push readers to contextualize *Efún* as contestatory and counterdiscoursive to official messaging of colonial rule.

The novel's 16 March 1955 censorship file summarizes the main plot points and indicates three problematic areas:

Pintura de la vida en la Guinea española, eficaz, cruda y muy bien documentada, que parece realizada por un conocedor profundo de aquellas tierra. Ana llega hasta allí en busca de su novio [Juan Esteve] y se desilusiona de él—vivía y tenía tres hijos con una mestiza—iniciando un idilio con Carlos, protagonista de la novela. Ana vuelve a la península, esperándolo, pero Carlos, absorbido por los problemas coloniales carece del arranque necesario para abandonar a los nativos.

Pág. 51: palabra políticamente inadecuada. Pág. 52: error histórico acerca del Movimiento. Las tropas desgraciadamente no se echaron a la calle. Pág. 92 concepto misionalmente poco ortodoxo que podría molestar en los organismos de este género. Corregidos estos detalles y a juicio del lector, puede autorizarse. (File *Efún*)

The casting of the plot as a love story immediately eschews a deeper reading from the censor's point of view, despite ample opportunity to include representations of race and gender in the report, and hints at a tendency to undervalue women's writing.

The censor indicates three instances of inopportune phrasing. In the first, Ana's explanation of her adoptive mother's past reveals an alliance to conservative ideology. She converses with Carlos about the circumstances surrounding the death of doña Elvira's husband: "Fue durante nuestra revolución, ¿sabes? Los rojos querían matar a su marido y ..." (Ms. 80). In the original typescript, Carlos asks "¿Era fascista o de derechas?" (Ts. 51); the censor crossed off the "políticamente inadecuada" term "fascista," and in the published version, the question is reduced to "¿Era de derechas?" (Ms. 80) to assuage the censor's concerns. Masoliver's use of the terms "nuestra" and "revolución" to refer to the Spanish Civil War indicates her alignment with the dictatorial regime's portrayal of the event not simply an ideologically based conflict between two organized groups but as a necessary fight to oust the Second Republic and establish a new political system.

The second problematic area deals with an historical inaccuracy and appears in this same section of the novel, in which Ana explains the circumstances of her parents' death during the war when she was three years old. The original text regarding her father, however, was left intact: "Mi padre era militar y estaba destinado en Madrid cuando las tropas se echaron en la calle" (Ms. 81), remaining in the published novel, which may be due to the fact that it does not glorify the Republican side nor does it portray the Nationalist forces in a negative light. In this section, Ana also reveals that her mother fell victim to one of the worst air raid bombings of the war: "aquel camión lleno de trilita… Fue abandonado en la calle por los milicianos, cuando oyeron las sirenas advirtiendo el peligro de los aviones nacionalistas… Cayeron las bombas y el camión estalló, derribando varios edificios" (Ms. 82). What the narrative omits from the cursory reference to the historically significant 17 March 1938 bombing—the second most deadly air raid in the Spanish Civil War after Guernica—is that the number of casualties ranged from 800 to 1300 (Thomas 866). The glossing over of history misleadingly attributes the casualties to the explosives in the abandoned Republican force's truck such that the air raid siren would have alerted the residents to take cover from the Nationalist-supported bombardment. Although this section as well as several others that reference life on the peninsula are minimal, they nonetheless demonstrate the author's enduring memory of events some two decades earlier.[23]

The third section subject to removal is identified in the censorship report as the "concepto misionalmente poco ortodoxo que podrá molestar en los organismos de este género" (File *Efún*). At this stage in the narration, Ana has just learned about the relationship between Juan and a local woman, Obama, believing that they have two sons together. When Carlos confirms that Isabelita is their third child, he explains the ominous future that awaits her, because she is a female and also because she has inherited biological, i.e. physical, traits more

---

23   The scene Masoliver describes took place in the middle of a Nationalist-driven carpet bombing in Barcelona by Italian and German aircraft 16-18 March 1938. One of the men slated to be in the truck that exploded was Cristóbal Font Casadó, whose 2003 testimonial appears in the article "Era el 21 y me salvé." Font Casadó was counted as the 21st soldier in line and therefore excused from being involved in the transporting of the truck, since only 20 were needed (Vivanco 6).

closely associated with her African, rather than European, heritage. The stricken passage was removed from the final manuscript (appearing here between brackets):

> Para Juan no cuenta esta hija. Isabelita habrá de vivir en Efún, en una miserable *nda*, con gentes sin Dios y sin instrucción. Un día será comprada por un marido. Dormirá como ellas, en el suelo, sobre una estera. [Teniendo eso en cuenta, es más humano dejarla en la creencia de que la poligamia no es un pecado. Entre los blancos, a causa de su color, sería aún más desgraciada.] (Ts. 92, Ms. 153)

Why does this idea catch the censor's attention? Juan's racialized classification of Isabelita problematizes the notion of her potential translocation to the peninsula, unlike her light-skinned brothers who could pass as white, because her mestizo bloodline is physically marked by her skin color. The miserable existence that Isabelita's future holds, then, is acceptable text that may remain in published form because it references the life of the local population in their own homeland. The acceptability of dozens of remarks that portray the local Guinean population as racially inferior would then seem not to be contradictory from the perspective of censorship but would indicate that the geography accentuates the otherness of the colonized subject. One of the numerous examples of how the local population is portrayed in terms of local customs positions the colonial subject as part of a milieu distinct from the imperial subject: "El marido, en la Guinea, trata a la mujer peor que a sus cabras o a sus perros. La hace trabajar en el hogar, en el cultivo de la tierra, y la llena de hijos. [...] África hace florecer demasiado pronto a la mujer y consume pronto su belleza" (121-22). These examples elide censorial stricture for their adherence to the portrayal of an exotic other. With these three areas addressed, Masoliver successfully publishes her first novel. Her subsequent three novels gain authorization for publication without the need for revision.[24]

---

24 Masoliver's second novel, *Los Galiano* (1959), takes place in Barcelona and features a normative representation of female characters defined through the patriarchy. This work has been completely overlooked by critics and merits future study to tease out representations war, gender, or educa-

Barcelona en llamas (1961), Masoliver's fifth novel, paints a picture of the titular city's social fabric during a 12-month period of the Spanish Civil War. It delineates with chronological accuracy, historically speaking, the progression of Republican defeat that culminates with the arrival of Nationalist troops in Barcelona, the takeover which occurred on 26 January 1939. The concluding lines take place during an open-air mass, a reference to the first public mass since the outbreak of the war, celebrated on 29 January 1939 in the iconic Plaça de Catalunya. As a story that from an ideologically conservative perspective glorifies Nationalist victory, the book foregrounds the imminent fall of Madrid at war's end. Masoliver's approach of presenting a timeline of a year during the war reads as a personalized—though fictional— account of the atrocities the protagonist experienced. The observable reality that Masoliver conveys through this novel points to the pro-

tion, for example, that serve as testimony of the many ways women writers made contributions to the literary corpus of their time. In her third novel, a return to a setting in Africa, Masoliver seems to apply what she has learned from her previous experience with the censorship board. In *Selva negra, selva verde* (1959) set in Ethiopia, the exonymic Abisinia, she continues to develop themes of European hegemony, this time dealing with the transition in Ethiopia between Italian rule and independence, through the fascist protagonists Etore and Vittoriano. This novel passes the censorship process with the evaluation of: "Novela en la que, al narrar las vicisitudes que hubo de afrontar Etori Ascari, el italiano prisionero de los aliados en Abisinia, se describen los paisajes, costumbres y modos de vida de los habitantes de la selva. PUEDE AUTORIZARSE (File *Selva negra*). Masoliver adopts a similar stance toward the colonized subject compared with her first novel, featuring the civilizing forces of the benevolent European (Stehrenberger, "Manifestaciones" 640), which align with the Francoist racialized discourse of white superiority over the African subject. In her fourth novel, *El rebelde* (1960)— one that has likewise escaped critical analysis—Masoliver begins a focused portrayal of the Spanish Civil War from the point of view of a Republican soldier. Antonio Campo, in his review of *El rebelde* at the time of its publication, remarks on Masoliver's skilled character profiling as a key feature of the text, as opposed to the fundamental importance of setting and creative storytelling in her novels set in Africa (8).

tagonism of the city of Barcelona, which Laureano Bonet describes in broader terms in the following manner:

> Esa literaturización de la Barcelona, o Barcelonas, en forma de sucesivas sinécdoques está, por consiguiente, oscilando siempre entre lo lírico y lo conceptual, entre lo físico y lo abstracto: biografía, paisaje, estado anímico, reflejos matéricos, imágenes que brotan unas de otras... Sin la menor duda dicha literaturización irá tomando cuerpo a partir de los últimos 1950, estimulada sobre todo por el neorrealismo en su doble filo literario y fílmico. ("Hacia la construcción" 55)

Barcelona en llamas narrates the protagonist Julia Alonso's survival story in one bleak year of the war, beginning with the two months she spends in a Republican jail cell as an accused fascist sympathizer—though she is ideologically apolitical—and ending with the return of her mother and sisters from France upon the occupation of Barcelona by the *Nacionales* in January 1939. After her release from the basement-level cell, where she experienced and witnessed countless atrocities (torture, hunger, squalor) and with the help of her cousin, she assumes the identity of Isabel Morales, a Republican supporter, to live in hiding in the back room of a cabaret as the owner's daughter. From afar, she sees and develops romantic feelings for a cabaret patron, who unbeknownst to her is a priest posing as a Republican soldier. Their brief contact consists of an exchange on one of the nights Isabel at first thinks she is alone in the main dance hall and plays the piano, unaware that Jaime is behind one of the room's curtained sections. As she continues to live in secrecy her thoughts turn to the idealized possibility of a romantic relationship between the two. The daily instabilities of wartime living and, more significantly, Jaime's identity as a priest preclude the viability of this narrative arc. The portrayal of wartime life illustrates the daily challenges that Raquel Conde Peñalosa identifies as marred by: "escasez, emigración, carencias, salarios bajos, estraperlo, cartillas de racionamiento, colas, represión miseria, etc." (158).

The novel proceeded to publication after censor review without the need for revision. Published when the author would have been 50 years old, *Barcelona en llamas* offers a retrospective vantage point of the events she narrates, especially telling considering that the protagonist's age would mirror that of the author, who was 25 years old in the final year of the war. Because minimal information is known about Masoliver's life, conjectures abound regarding autobiographical elements in this novel, as well as in *Un hombre de paz*, as the censor infers in his report of that novel, this considering the narrative distancing achieved through the third-person point of view.

Masoliver presents her version of history, a history in broader terms that for David K. Herzberger, "impinges upon the consciousness of characters and forces its way into their considerations. History supervenes against the discourse of myth in these novels because it both shapes and is shaped by the private affairs of the self" (*Narrating* 68). Does Masoliver write from first-person knowledge? Does she recount experiences she witnessed, read about, or heard? To what degree does she fictionalize the accounts she narrates? Further inquiry is necessary to establish these possible connections and shed more light on the corpus of her works. In sum, with *Barcelona en llamas*, Masoliver devises a compelling narrative as a testament to the recovery of historical events. Woven into the fictional world are proven truths of harsh wartime reality, as the censor observes in this 1961 censorship report:

> "Barcelona en llamas" de Liberata Masoliver, constituye una narración más sobre el tema de la guerra civil española. Barcelona es el escenario de los acontecimientos que aquí se novelan. La guerra civil representa el *telón de fondo*. Los verdaderos ejes de la trama son seres humanos, como Isabel, Joaquín, primo de ésta, Benito, Jaime Vargás-sacerdote, etc.: ejemplares humanos encargados de dar vida a la suma de problemas y experiencias angustiosas que hubieron de vivir quienes, como ellos, habitaron en Barcelona durante la *dominación roja*. Dificultades para conseguir el menguado alimento diario, el inhumano asalto a las viviendas, el desvalijamiento de éstas, el lucrativo negocio de algún capitoste rojo en la venta de provisiones, etc., etc. PUEDE AUTORIZARSE. (File *Barcelona*, emphasis added)

Because Masoliver's primary focus is narrating the challenges, difficulties, and horrors of wartime life in vivid detail as central to the novel's development, I resist the *novela rosa* label that Julio Rodríguez Puértolas applies to this novel in particular—and more broadly to Masoliver's body of work (632)—as a reductionist standpoint that only contributes to moving her work away from critical view. Critics have begun to deconstruct the racial tensions in her first novels, and much more work is needed to dispel the myth that the presence of a romantic interest in a novel written by a woman means it is facile literature to be considered a *novela rosa* unworthy of serious literary study. Raquel Conde Peñaolsa elevates women's writing on the experiences of war in a way that invites expanded critical inquiry: "Las escritoras de posguerra, como sus compañeros varones, levantan un testimonio cronístico de la época que viven, pero desde la realidad que conocen y de la que observan a su alrededor como mujeres" (159). Critical readers may move beyond the budding romantic feelings Isabel develops for Jaime and examine the novel as testimony of a snapshot in time that shifts the notion of the civil war as a mere *telón de fondo* that the censorship file demarcates, to position the sum of Barcelona's wartime society as the novel's protagonist, beginning with the title Masoliver selected for this novel.

The first three lines of the report redundantly state the theme of the Civil War as the novel's backdrop, which I argue is the novel's focal point, as myriad hardships are representative of the perils that constantly threaten the characters' well-being. The atmosphere evokes vulnerable affective states marred by fear, isolation, survival instincts, stupefaction, and chaos. With the continuous reminders of wartime living referenced by disease due to unhygienic conditions; frequent bombarding; intermittent electricity; confiscation of personal items; counterfeit currency; the cacophonous sound of foot soldiers' fast-paced march through the streets; night time aerial bombings; sounds of weaponry discharges; ideologically motivated home searches, forcible removal from home, home invasions, kidnappings, incarceration, and assassination; clandestine meetings; and the adoption of secret identities as a shield of protection during the Civil War or as a way to spy undercover, rather than a mere *telón de fondo*, the war occupies center stage as a force that motivates the characters' every actions.

The experience of Masoliver's novel with the censorship process grants insight to a set of criteria used to measure a given text's suitability for publication. Masoliver galvanizes historical memory through normative representations that elide censorial reproach through the novel's trope of the young, conservative woman living in Barcelona under an assumed identity as a Republican during the phase of *dominación roja*, with romantic interest in a mysterious man. Because Isabel's father had died prior to the events narrated in the novel, and because the beginning of the war caught Isabel's mother and sisters in Paris, preventing their return to Barcelona until January 1939, Isabel negotiated the treacherous living conditions as a familyless young woman. Her portrayal calls to mind the defenseless, motherless daughter who lacks protection and guidance, one whose innocence or lack of political engagement prevents her from posing any moral or ideological threat to the reading public. The novel's representation of the nefarious actions of the Republican army that in essence hold the conservative contingent captive produces an environment of suspicion and uncertainty that not only contributes to the novel's intrigue fueled by rampant *terror rojo* but captures the reality of survival strategies in a politically volatile climate. The author subverts readers' expectations that the text will focalize on the plight of the Republicans because it does much more than that: it provides critical commentary on the disasters of war that ravaged the city not just from the perspective of those who would suffer defeat, but, in retrospect, of a nation as a whole, for its depictions of the deleterious effects of war on Spanish society. The formidable obstacles in daily life of the conservative woman in hiding in Barcelona under Republican siege connotes an expanded perception of the widespread nature of these obstacles in especially war-torn parts of the country.

OBSERVATIONS

Censors authorized publication of the six novels in this section for reasons that correlate to thematic and narrative content. The texts are indicative of the nuances surrounding the favorable pass through the censorship board that go beyond the characterization of a young woman or the absence of a political agenda. The mere existence of characters who are young or marginalized women is not the only determining factor that demarcates the threshold for authorization to publish. Protagonists may experience the Spanish Civil War or its aftermath, but do so tangentially, from the standpoint of the victors, or from the standpoint that underscores the alterity of the vanquished (*Nada, La isla y los demonios, Barcelona en llamas*). The women must eschew any political activity that could be interpreted as threatening, and they must conduct themselves in accordance with the social mores of their time (*Entre visillos*). If they transgress the ideal model of behavior associated with femininity, they must do so in the privacy of their own home (*Víspera del odio*) or in an institutional setting (*Mi vida en el manicomio*). The women may choose a career, but this career must be portrayed as secondary to the role of benevolent wife and mother (*Las siete muchachas del liceo*). Ideological alignment with Francoist discourse had an effect on the decision to authorize a text for publication. Narrative strategies women incorporated in their writing included the coming of age story featuring a normatively portrayed young woman, journalistic exposé to imply objectivity, the trope of the letter to suggest a narrow readership, and the adoption of a secret identity to allow the ideologically conservative protagonist to live undercover as a Republican during the war.

A synthesis of censorship reports on numerous files reveals that some novels were approved because the censors found them simplistic, boring, or of minimal literary value. In other cases, the summary offers an evaluation that is laudatory or neutral in tone. Examples of ways censors described texts authorized for publication without the need for revision appear in the following selected list. The descriptors include selected excerpts from the corresponding censorship reports:

- Concha Alós, *Las hogueras* (1964): "Se trata de una historia más de adulterio, narrada literariamente. [...] De ninguna manera puede considerarse que en la presente novela su tesis sea la defensa o apología del adulterio."

- Mercedes Ballesteros, *Mi hermano y yo por esos mundos* (1962): "Es un libro de humor de codorniz."

- Rosa Cajal, *Primero, derecha* (1955): "La narración es buena y los momentos más crudos y difíciles están expuestos con eufemismos y narrados con dignidad."

- Carmen Conde, *Las oscuras raíces* (1954): "Tiene características de suma originalidad."

- Paulina Crusat, *El mundo pequeño y fingido* (1953): "Carece la obra, en realidad, de un hilo argumental único, [...] interminables soliloquios carentes en absoluto de interés y medida."

- Paulina Crusat, *Historia de un viaje* (1955): "Es estudio sutilísimo y delicado; resulta rollo."

- Carmen García Bellver, *La sangre inútil* (1966): "novela urdida"

- Antonia Guinduláin, *A punta de lanza* (1962): "lectura sana"

- Carmen de Icaza, *Talia* (1951): "graciosa narración"

- Carmen Kurtz, *El último camino* (1961): "Utiliza una temática variada, sacada de la vida cotidiana, de los problemas familiares y personales, para tejer la trama del asunto."

- Concha Lagos, *El pantano* (1954): "literariamente presentado, de escaso valor"

- Liberata Masoliver, *Los Galiano* (1957): "novela deliciosa"

- Liberata Masoliver, *Un camino llega a la cumbre* (1965): "La novela, pues, limpia y puede ponerse en todas las manos."

- Carmela Molina, *Segundos planos* (1953): "novela de escasa acción"

- Elizabeth Mulder, *Eran cuatro* (1954): "novela muy bien constituida y escrita"

- Marta Portal, *A tientas y a ciegas* (1966, Planeta Prize): "Aunque inmoral en el fondo, por cómo justifica el adulterio (por ejemplo, con los razonamientos falaces de las páginas 205-6) y por la ausencia de preocupaciones superiores a las de orden estrictamente social en el ámbito de conducta de la protagonista, la novela, bien escrita y sin crudezas formales, no puede considerarse escandalosa al nivel de la literatura corriente en nuestros días."

- Anunciación Rivera Tovar, *Agua estancada* (1963): "Aunque la acción de este relato discurre lenta, hay un simpático dramatismo que le hace interesante."

- Eugenia Serrano, *Pista de baile* (filed 1955, published 1963): "No faltan en el aderezo novelístico referencias, ni a las drogas, ni a los invertidos... al tercer sexo, y creemos hasta en algunas de estas páginas dedicadas a temas tan apetitosos se exteriorizan alusiones a medios artísticos e intelectuales, muy conocidos en Madrid."

- Concha Suárez del Otero, *Me llamo Clara* (1968): "Clara actuaba como mujer católica."

The novels listed above as well as other novels written by these women provide robust opportunity for future inquiry to the censorship process, as does expanding literary genre, as many of them cultivated short stories, poetry, and, to a lesser degree, dramatic works. Rereading these texts through the lens of current trends in scholarship may continue to shed light on the censorship process by using the censors' evaluations as a starting point. Casting the work of these writers in the critical eye will also make inroads into the recovery of mid-century Spanish literature written by women who are often excluded from such inquiry.

Chapter 3.
Tolerated Texts:
Boundaries of Transgression

> I could not live in any of the worlds offered to me—
> the world of my parents, the world of war, the world of politics.
> - *Anaïs Nin*

THE UNOFFICIAL LABEL OF "tolerated" or "tolerable" to categorize a novel's content, unlike the official censorship outcome of "authorized" or "denied," is revealing for the way it demonstrates stratification within the evaluation process. Reasons the censors provide for their decision to classify the text as tolerated also point to the boundaries of suitability for public consumption. The classification of "tolerada" was granted only sparingly in women's writing and only during a brief period of time, 1950-1954.[1] Of the five texts that received this classification amid the over 200 I evaluated written

---

1   Future inquiry on novels classified as tolerated and written by male authors would allow for further contextualization of this label. I have searched titles from 1950-1962 that appear with this designation in "Fichas de novelas presentadas a la censura." Although this is not an exhaustive list, the following body of novels serves as a starting point, listed by the year they went before the censorship board: *La quiebra* (Juan Antonio Zunzunegui, 1946); *Los hijos de Máximo Judas* (Luis Landínez, 1950); *Sin camino* (José Luis Castillo Puche, 1950); *Lola, espejo oscuro* (Darío Fernández Flórez, 1950); *La noria* (Luis Romero, 1952 [Premio Nadal 1951]); *Los canes andan sueltos* (Ángel Oliver, 1952); *Cuerpos, almas y todo eso* (Santiago Lorén, 1952); and *Tormenta de verano* (Juan García Hortelano, 1961).

by women in the 1950s and 1960s, two were published as presented while the others underwent minor revisions. Texts authorized with minimal or no need for revision serve as baseline levels of propriety and suitability for public dissemination. The authors of the novels that appear in this chapter do not transgress normativity, whether intuitively or intentionally adhering to its boundaries. Indeed, challenges to the schema of the guiding questions on the censorship report exercise the limits of censorial power such that the hegemonic body is satisfied that its strength remains intact. The infrequent application of this outcome as jargon internal to the review process merits mention for the way references, themes, and wording deemed mildly offensive reveal the boundaries of acceptability within the censorship parameters.[2]

One of the earliest examples of a censor labeling a text as tolerated is Camilo José Cela's *La familia de Pascual Duarte* (1944), whose file reads: "Novela de ambiente crudo, enfermizo en que todos los personajes son amorales, infrahumanos y se complacen en acciones repugnantes. El autor ha sabido apropiarse el estilo de nuestra picaresca y esto, creo, es lo único de positivo valor en esta obra. Sin ver recomendable su lectura, creo que pudiera *tolerarse*" (File *La familia*, emphasis added). The evocation of the classic Lazarillo prototype sufficiently overshadows the *tremendista* aesthetic of the grotesque to allow for a small print run not of thousands of copies but of 700. If the reasons

---

2   A text that barely circumvents political threat is Carmen Kurtz's prison narrative *Detrás de la piedra* (1958): "Una novela basada en una sospecha falsa de atraco que determina el ingreso en cárceles de un ingeniero. En la novela se relata con las ideas y pensamientos particulares del encarcelado sobre motivos familiares, morales, etc., etc. la vida carcelaria más o menos bronca y realista. Teniendo en cuenta lo acotado que unas veces roza la grosería y otras la inmoralidad. Puede publicarse" (File *Detrás*). The phrase that describes the content ("unas veces roza la grosería y otras la inmoralidad") signals the novel has stayed within the bounds of acceptability, and in fact, Kurtz did not need to revise the text. Indeed, a woman writing about a man wrongfully jailed bends gender expectations just enough to gain authorization for publication. However, the notion of tolerance is only implied, compared with other novels that include the word *tolerada* in any of its derivations as part of the final evaluation.

for considering Cela's novel tolerable related to the grotesque deformations of death and dying in an atmosphere marked by material paucity and moral bankruptcy, the novels studied here exemplify works that skirt overt morality or politically rooted threats. The reasons connected to the designation of tolerated reflect censors' concerns with the direction of each novel's moral compass, the politically charged reckoning of the protagonists, or both.

By looking at novels classified as tolerable, a framework emerges to delineate in practice rather than in theory the parameters of acceptable literary output vis à vis the tenets the censorial machine is tasked with upholding. The topics under scrutiny above, contextualized with the novels below that either required revisions or generated an exchange between authors and the censorship board, point to the messages authors were permitted to convey to the general reading public that would preserve both moral and political order as well as the balance of power between the government and the people.

This chapter examines novels authorized as tolerated texts by Carmen Conde, Elena Quiroga, Eugenia Serrano y Balañá, Mercedes Formica, and Concha Fernández Luna. The thematic content, character development, and plot points lived at the edge of a negative response to the guiding questions on the censorship form.

CARMEN CONDE: *EN MANOS DEL SILENCIO* (1950)
Carmen Conde (1907-1996), the first woman writer elected to the Real Academia Española (1978), authored eight novels, in addition to her prolific and award-winning poetry in 37 collections published between 1929 and 1988. During her career over half a century, Conde navigated the Spanish literary panorama spanning the dictatorship of Miguel de Primo de Rivera to the transition to democracy, with the publication of her first collection of poetry, *Brocal* (1929),[3] to her posthumously published *Virginia, o La calle de los balcones azules* (2002), written and revised between 1976 and 1984.

---

3   Conde's first collection of poetry was in the form of prose poetry that she began writing in 1914. It was not published until 1955 under the title *Empezando la vida: Memorias de una infancia en Marruecos (1914-1920)*.

En manos del silencio (1950) was the first novel Conde published under her own name, following the release of *Vidas contra su espejo* (1944) under the pseudonym Florentina del Mar. *En manos del silencio* received reluctant censorial approval despite classification as an indirect threat to morality. The novel meets the threshold of the scope of this present study for its publication date, though Conde completed the manuscript in 1947.[4] I include the novel here precisely for its classification as tolerable and also because it breaks thematic ground for its transgressive portrayal of femininity that censors explicitly identified yet allowed to proceed to publication.

En manos del silencio is set primarily in Madrid with textual clues identifying the temporal frame as coinciding tangentially with early events of World War II. The novel describes family dysfunction surrounding the pregnancies by the same man, Manuel, of both the wife (Cristina) and daughter (Myra) of the absent husband/father (Enrique). The resolution of the knotted relationships opens a pathway for Myra's journey through life as an unwed mother. While Cristina miscarries, Myra gives birth to a daughter and decides to remain unwed rather than enter a loveless marriage. By novel's end, Cristina and Manuel die, she in a car accident and he following his move to London and becoming a victim the London Blitz (between September 1940 and May 1941). Enrique leaves his home to begin a life with a new family in the United States; his son, Luis, enters the monastery, derailing

---

4   The primary reason for its delayed publication appears in a letter from her publisher José Janés in which he explained that he already had multiple novels in press and was also experiencing: "las dificultades que se presenten en las actuales circunstancias, con la falta de fluido eléctrico y los impresores trabajando únicamente doce horas por semana. En fin, que me mandaría usted el libro y no podría publicárselo hasta dentro de cinco años" (Letter 32-008). Janés communicates with Conde three years later in reference to the delayed publication: "[e]n circunstancias más propicias que las actuales, su novela hubiera encontrado fácilmente sitio en alguna de mis colecciones, pero desgraciadamente la crisis editorial persiste y he de seguir restringiendo mi plan de publicaciones de modo extraordinario" (Letter 049-098).

the possibility that Myra will enjoy the support and protection of her immediate family.

As one of only a handful of novels that received the designation of *tolerable* following its censorship evaluation, the first observation of note on the report is the response to first guiding question relating to the threat to Dogma or Morality: "Sí, a la Moral, indirectamente," which sets the stage for content scrutiny. The censor's 8 February 1947 remarks read:

> Entendemos que el asunto en sí es inmoral y en parte repugnante. Cierto personaje fundamental en la novela, resulta ser el amante de una mujer casada y de la hija de esta. De ambas tiene hijos, el de la 1ª muere y el de la 2ª no; contrayendo el referido personaje matrimonio con esta última mujer más tarde. Frente a tanta concupiscencia, se destaca la figura del hijo de aquella mujer casada adornado de todas las virtudes familiares. Acotamos por crudeza las páginas 30, 33, 91 y 97. Por la manera de como se trata el asunto, entendemos que la obra es *tolerable* (File *En manos del silencio*, emphasis added).

The novel was published as written, despite the mention of the four passages marked on the typescript with a red X in the margins. In the censor's report, the descriptors "repugnante" and "Escaso valor literario" speak to the evaluator's opinion, rather than factors that influenced the decision to reject or authorize the text. Furthermore, the report reflects a cursory reading of the novel as it misconstrues or incorrectly reflects its content. Cristina's unborn child dies as a result of miscarriage, although she was in the process of seeking an abortion. Further, Myra rejects the prospect of matrimony with Manuel, which prompts him to leave the country. It is difficult to ascertain if the misreading of the text influences the decision to authorize its publication. In the censor's evaluation, there is no explicit value judgement placed on Cristina's infidelity, nor on Myra's sexual relations outside of marriage. Indeed, he seems to focalize the culpability on Manuel, thereby exculpating to a certain degree the two women. Perhaps this renders a sympathetic reading of the female protagonists, mitigated by the trope of Enrique as absent husband and father. And, although, as the report accurately states that Luis, Cristina's son, displays virtuous behavior, he is at best a secondary character. Luis's religious vocation did indeed garner the censor's attention as contributing to the novel's message of salvation, but is comes at the end of the novel and is only briefly developed. Luis enters religious life after his love interest, Amelia, leaves him to pursue wartime work abroad as a Red Cross nurse, citing her answering a call to serve the greater good. The novel classified as "tolerated" reflects Conde's discursive strategies aimed at marginalizing or punishing transgressors combined with highlighting the redeeming qualities of others who adhere to gender-prescribed roles molded by resolutely moral conduct. In this way, Manuel and Cristina die, and the inadequate Enrique abandons both nation and family. On the contrary, Myra, her infant daughter, and Luis enjoy the freedom to follow their own pursuits in life.

Manuel is first displaced in a sort of self-banishment and while abroad in England becomes a tragedy of war. Cristina's death correlates to her marital infidelity and may have been more violent or shocking had she carried through with her planned abortion, averted only by miscarriage just before the procedure was to take place. Her death is representative of Pam Morris's view of the transgressive female's destiny: "One persistent plot pattern is that suffering and death are the inevitable fate of sexually transgressive heroines" (31). As a narrative maneuvering, Cristina's treatment in the text serves as an admonishment against amoral conduct in the discourse of the dictatorship. Myra's salvation, and that of her child born out of wedlock, may be understood in the context of a daughter who fails to grow up in a nurturing family, hinting toward the fractured home environment that would lead to the full—that is, moral—integration of children in totalitarian society. Within Morris's paradigm, if Myra's characterization as the benevolent mother is read in positive terms, "for women, heroism consists of accepting restrictions and disappointment with stoicism" (32).

An analysis of the novel's questionable material, in the censor's view, demonstrates the boundaries of suitability for publication. The first censor-marked passage is preceded by Myra's reflections in the form of a first-person narration in which she describes as "feo, censurable" (45) her transgressive behavior with her father's close friend (Manuel), who could potentially become his son-in-law. She recalls her first encounter with Manuel in his office, predicated by an insinuated lovemaking scene between Manuel and another woman readers will later identify as Cristina, which was interrupted by Myra's knock on the door. Cristina leaves sight unseen through a back door to make way for a visibly flustered Manuel to receive Myra and admonish her for her unannounced visit. To assuage the awkwardness, Myra approaches him: "Y en un afán de quitarle el enfado, de reconciliarnos, me acerqué a su butaca y le acaricié la cabeza" (47). A mutual attraction leads to their first intimate encounter, which the censor marked with a red X in the typescript's margin: "Nos sentimos envueltos en una embriaguez de la que no éramos responsables. Hombre y Mujer, cara a cara, cuerpo a cuerpo boca contra boca, en una arrebatada y transida hora que para nosotros se había desprendido del más secreto de los universos" (Ts. 30, Ms. 47). The cultural mores tilt away from sanctioning the mother-daughter-lover triangle despite the close succession of the women's individual encounters with him, even when compounded by marital infidelity and the age difference between Manuel and Myra.

The second textual reference the censor marked describes the intensity of Myra's relationship with Manuel, who had told her family he would be on a month-long business trip but instead secretly rented an apartment to spend alternating mornings and afternoons with Myra. She explains their physical encounters as: "Es feo comparar mi cariño al hambre, a la sed, al sueño, pero es así como le quise. Con él no había descanso. Se dejaba comer y comía" (Ts. 33, Ms. 49), with *comer* and *comía* underlined by the censor's hand in red ink. The reference to a mutual consumption of the body as a satiating sexual act on par with a basic physical survival needs of food, water and sleep relies on metaphor and is thereby void of the explicitness that would have pushed the contents to revision or excision.[5]

---

    5   Following Abraham H. Maslow's hierarchy of basic survival needs, physical needs occupy the most basic level, and when these needs are not met, fulfilling them becomes an object of intense interest and concern (56-61). Textual references support this outlook in Myra, who is content with Manuel and obsessive in anticipation of their next encounter.

The remaining two cases, also marked with a red X in the margins, deal with Manuel's blurred view of the two women as one being, compounded by the sense of excitement he experiences with each woman. While the first is focalized from Cristina's point of view, the second reflects Manuel's, fragmented through the intervening allegorical narrator identified as "Destino." The degree to which the descriptions of Manuel's perspective attack morality seems more to do with the fact that the women are mother and daughter and know nothing of the other's relationship, and that Manuel intentionally exploits Myra's youth, rather than the infidelity of his relationship with the married Cristina.

In the first example, Cristina has just learned from her son Luis the identity of her daughter's lover and is flooded with emotions. She holds a critical view of Manuel's overlapping actions toward, and words for, the two women:

> Las imágenes deslumbraban batallando con la sangre. Celos furiosos de los dos. ¡Es el castigo! Un cuerpo joven, fresco, en contraste con el suyo propio, hermoso y seguro cuerpo de amor. ¡El hombre en los dos seres amados, mirando, poseyendo la doble imagen, la sangre misma enloquecida! "Solo a ti te quiero" Sí. "A ti solamente amo yo."
>
> Hijos para las dos. Pero el suyo era mayor pecado. (Ts. 91, Ms. 118)

While Cristina clearly sees the differences between herself and Myra, the overlaying images of mother and daughter before Manuel's eyes conveys his blending of the two women as one in the same, as objects of his failure to distinguish between the two. She judges him to be more sinful, which is a plausible reaction since initially neither woman was aware of the other's relationship with him.

The last highlighted section appears in a subsection titled "Confluencia" in the third chapter, "Habla el destino:"

> Para Manuel el amor por Cristina seguía revivificado, con Myra. Con lealtad absoluta para las dos. Y solamente un ángel hubiera

podido tener la gracia para separar de uno al otro amor, sin matar el amante. Aunque, ¿era necesario Manuel? Las dos amadas, doliendo por él, querían retenerle. Un ser así debe constituir el tremendo principio vital, ciego y sordo, desesperadamente puesto al servicio de la continuidad. (Ts. 97, Ms. 127)

These words narrated by "Destiny" focus on Manuel's fusion of the two female characters into one and paradoxically negate and elevate his importance in their lives. Manuel's ability to separate his love for the two would depend the sacrilegious prospect of relying on divine intervention.

The fact that Manuel leaves Spain and is subsequently killed in a World War II air raid in London, coupled with Cristina's miscarriage and, later, her death in a car accident, restores the disrupted social order.[6] Myra, destined for a life as a single mother, embraces what her future holds, although the less optimistic social reality points to her likely ostracization for her misalignment within Francoist discourse pertaining to maternity and matrimony.

Despite the novel's multiple points of censorial rebuke, Conde is not required to address them, and the text is cleared for publication

---

6   Conde also relies on the death trope as an outcome to avoid describing how a character might come to terms with living outside the social boundaries of totalitarian society. The protagonist in her short novel *Solamente un viaje* (1954), Ana, seeks to regain the financial independence she lost upon marrying by taking on a job as a private tutor of Sylvia. The women travel to Italy on an educational trip, but on their overnight stop in Nice before returning to Madrid, when she had decided not to return to her husband, Ana strolls along water's edge where a man offers her a scenic boat ride. The next morning her battered cadaver found shoreside. Ana's symbolic death as retribution for her transgressions problematizes the question of what identity would have awaited her had she attempted to live outside of marriage; her acceptance of the boat ride also suggests that this prospect would have been so insurmountable that she preferred death over domesticity. The censorship report reads: "la narración de un viaje que hace la protagonista—Ana—mujer casada acompañando a Silvia—muchacha joven—en ruta de estudios por Italia, y en su pequeña excursión marítima es víctima de un robo muere asesinada" (File *Cobre: Destino hallado* y *Solamente un viaje*).

in its original form. Conde's novel bookends the limits of the censors' decision and is crucial to the understanding of the thresholds at the borders of what was considered acceptable and what was not. As an author considered primarily as a poet, it was known that her husband Antonio Oliver Belmás (1903-1968), a well-regarded poet in his own right, was decades earlier a known Republican sympathizer, operating radios during the Spanish Civil War. For her ideological stance Conde imposed self-exile, first in Murcia and then in Madrid, to avoid prosecution during the aftermath of the war. Less than a decade into the postwar period, Conde, living as a married woman pursuing a writing career at the time her novel moved through the censorship process, no longer faced the threat of political persecution that would have made her the target of unwanted attention at the time of the novel's evaluation.

ELENA QUIROGA: *VIENTO DEL NORTE* (1951)
Elena Quiroga (1921-1995) was the second woman elected to the Real Academia Española. Similar to the first woman to hold this distinction, Carmen Conde, although Quiroga has received a noticeable degree of critical attention, there is a great deal lacking in the analysis of her individual works and her works collectively as contributions to Spanish literature of her time. She undoubtedly finds a place in studies on literary histories or bio-bibliographies, but a comprehensive study on her writing would contribute to the agenda of literary recovery of mid-century women writers. Though critics have commented on Quiroga's narrative style in certain works, a wider reach of critical analysis, for example, from cultural or gender studies approaches is much lacking. One of the obstacles in assessing Quiroga's writing is that many critics reductively compare her with Emilia Pardo Bazán for her settings in rural Galicia and themes related to the Galician countryside. This approach diminishes the significance and breadth of each author's literary corpus, and it establishes an unparalleled paradigm within which to contextualize their writing. Novels such as *Algo pasa en la calle* (1954) and parts of *La careta* (1955), as well as her contributions to the Novela del Sábado installments—*Trayecto uno* (1953) and *La otra ciudad* (1953)—are but several examples of works with settings

in Madrid, contemporary to the time of writing. Phyllis Zatlin has best articulated the need for original and critical study of Quiroga's writing that cannot be attained with the overlapping of Quiroga with Pardo Bazán because that approach stems from "a male-centered focus that tended to put all women writers, and certainly all Galician women writers, in the same category, and a Madrid-centered focus that failed to appreciate the realities of twentieth-century Galicia" (*Writing Against* 44). To this end, Inés Corujo Martín has made significant inroads to critical recovery of Quiroga's work that may serve as a starting point in synthesizing the reception of this work and in analyzing *La sangre* (1952) and *La careta* from the standpoint of narratology and gender studies, respectively.

In the context of this present study, Quiroga's second novel, *Viento del norte*, the 1950 Nadal prizewinner, contributes to a better understanding of the censorship process.[7] This section first presents an overview of Quiroga's experience with the censorship board, building on Sarah Leggott's conclusions in her essay on censorship in Quiroga's fourth and most critically studied novel, *Algo pasa en la calle*. Leggott explains that the author evaded censorial stricture despite broaching taboo subjects such as divorce and veiling social criticism relating to, for example, female sexuality and political retaliation. Leggot also references Quiroga's own words regarding her experience with the censorship board: "Tuve muchísima suerte, porque la censura la pasé, y no la pasé, porque tenía un amigo en censura lo bastante noble para decirme 'ven mañana; tráeme el libro'. Y me daba la tarjeta de censura y ponía los sellos, y se acabó" (Hermida 1995). Of note to support this claim is that *La careta*, with the publication year of 1955, received authorization to publish on Friday, 30 December of that same year. The exact release is difficult to discern; however, Melchor Fernández Almagro's review on 15 January 1956 gives a sense that the book was already printed and about to be distributed ahead of its authorization date to allow time for display, purchase, review, and publication of the

---

7   Antonio Iglesias Laguna states in his discussion of *Viento del norte* that "Quiroga posee un alma lírica" conveyed with "los temas sensuales y bruscos, tan consustanciales con nuestra época," and classifies it as a naturalist novel (269).

review, all during a two-week period over a holiday period. Further, Quiroga's experience with the censorship process undergoes a shift between the first three novels and her subsequent works. Excisions on the grounds of morality on seven pages were required to gain authorization to publish her first novel *La soledad sonora* (1949), described in the censor's report as: "una novela de indudable mérito literario. Sin embargo, convendrá exigir las tachaduras de las páginas arriba indicadas, cuyas descripciones resultan excesivamente crudas, aun reconociendo la calidad del lenguaje literario" (File *La soledad*). The tone of the reports of her next two works changes from critical or harsh to practically laudatory in the remaining. Whereas the censor called out "episodios que rezuman malicia sensual y valoraciones blandas" (File *Viento*) in *Viento del norte*, whose report will be discussed below, the report for *La sangre* includes the statements: "Novela realmente cruda y hosca, con frecuentes escenas inmorales y de un realismo hiriente y toda ella con un fondo morboso de un naturalismo sensual. Casi todos los personajes o son perversos o son locos" and "Sin que me atreva a calificarla como francamente inmoral, creo que su lectura ha de ser perniciosa para una gran mayoría de los lectores" (File *La sangre*).[8] The

8   The censor who signed this report, A[ndrés] de Lucas in July 1952 used similar phrasing when evaluating Darío Fernández Flórez's *Lola, espejo oscuro* (1950) to assess the novel as "Autorizada con carácter de tolerada." To the question regarding the threat to morality he responds in the affirmative, and rather than listing pages he writes "todo el argumento de la novela" (File *Lola*). His report reads:

"Es la historia de una vulgar prostituta, cínica y egoísta, con ribetes de un histérico sentimentalismo. En la 1ª parte se imita, con bastante acierto, el estilo de la novela picaresca; en las restantes partes el estilo es corriente con profusión de aburridos y estúpidos diálogos entre la protagonista y un tal Juan. Por su fondo la novela es *franca y abiertamente inmoral*. No se desprende tampoco de ella ni la más leve lección moral o ejemplar.

En la forma, aunque no llegue a la pornografía, abunda en palabras y frases groseras y de mal gusto.

Creo que su lectura ha de resultar perniciosa para la inmensa mayoría de lectores.

Si concurrieran circunstancias especiales, creo que a lo sumo podría ser tolerada." (File *Lola*, emphasis added)

censor's estimation of the novel as "perniciosa para una gran mayoría de los lectores" refers to the general reading population rather than discerning readers who may glean sexual innuendo between the lines and extract textual nuances.[9]

The tone of reproach is absent in the report of *Algo pasa en la calle*; despite the inclusion of the aforementioned taboo subjects and themes, no revisions are necessary:

> Novela de tipo realista, [...] dilata y reitera, y se hace confusa al mezclar el presente con el pasado. Está mejor conseguido el "clima" que el relato. (File *Algo pasa*)

In returning to *La careta*, the censor calls attention to Quiroga's deft portrayal of characters and plot development:

> hay de todo: perfiles vigorosos de caracteres, muy difuminados en la intención de la autora, conjugados y contrastados unos y otros en el seno de una familia, cuyos miembros subrayan con parquedad expresiva sus peculiaridades y características encuadrándoles en el marco de la guerra española, y resolviendo aquellas miserias con final doloroso y trágico. (File *La careta*).

Furthermore, references to the Civil War and its deleterious effects on a child whose parents died because of events surrounding the war do not require excision or softening.[10]

Montejo Gurruchaga traces the novel's precarious standing with the censorship board from the time of its first evaluation through the halted publication of future editions until it regained permission to publish in 1964 ("Algunas novelas" 171-77).

9   The term *pernicioso* or its derivations was used, for example, to describe the heavily marked *Nosotros, los Rivero* by Dolores Medio.

10 Reports on her remaining works mostly offer a brief plot summary, for example a) *La enferma* (1955): "Plantea como figura central la vida de una enferma mental recluida en la cama a consecuencia de un fracaso sentimental amoroso. Nada que impida su publicación" (File *La enferma*); b) *Plácida la joven* (1956): "la huérfana que muere al dar a luz a su primera hija, estando ausente el marido—se pintan escenas del medio rural gallego [...]. Nada fun-

The censorship board likewise does not require revisions to *Viento del norte*, which is classified as a "tolerable" novel. Set in and around the Galician *pazo* of *La Sagreira*, the plot traces the evolution of the relationship between Marcela and Álvaro, owner of *La Sagreira*, against the backdrop of social class and gender disparities. The orphaned Marcela grows up under the care of Álvaro's housekeeper Ermitas and marries him at age 16, or perhaps 18 (143)—when he is 50 years old—not for love but out of sense of obligation and as a way to preserve an honorable reputation. An orphan himself, Álvaro was raised by and has a close relationship with Lucía and Enrique, his aunt and uncle who live with their seven children in the nearby *pazo* known as *Cora*.

The censorship report points to questionable material, though it avoids posing a threat to the categories encompassed by the guiding questions. The censor attributes this to the author's dexterous narrative skills:

> Una visión del carácter y ambiente gallego con su credulidad supersticiosa y francas costumbres. En el aspecto moral, algunos episodios que rezuman malicia sensual y valoraciones blandas, si bien poco recomendable por su influencia paradigmática, *tolerable* por la discreción narrativa, su valor expresivo del ambiente reflejado y la indiscutible calidad literaria del conjunto sin par de ejemplos del tono indicado en págs: 2-20-22. (File *Viento*, emphasis added)

The classification of tolerable reveals the boundaries of what does or does not constitute material in need of revision or excision. The pages the censor indicates appear in the opening three chapters, with the others presumably scattered unmarked throughout the text.

The first example the censor notes begins with the eighth paragraph and extends about 40 lines.[11] This section describes the flirta-

---

damental que censurar" (File *Plácida*); c) *Carta a Cadaqués* (1961): "poesía, nada que oponer" (File *Carta*).

11   As a point of reference, the lines begin and end with "Sonrió, socarrón; a ver ahora de qué les había servido el unicornio" (Ts. 2-3, Ms. 9-10), and "Manoteaba, olvidando su respeto al señor, pero es que a veces le parecía que seguía siendo niño, el niño que ella quiso y acunara" (Ts. 3, Ms. 10).

tious dynamic between the men and women who work at *La Sagreira* as they complete their daily chores:

> les bastaba a las mujeres cualquier cosa para poner el grito en el cielo y alborotar [...]. Y los hombres, claro, siempre a la que salta, aprovechaban cualquier revuelo para fingir que las empujaban, tanteándolas. No engañaban a nadie, que buenas andaban ellas para que las burlasen. Pero se hacían las sorprendidas, y protestaban con palabrotas que dejaban chicos a los hombres, cuando soltaban la lengua. (Ts. 2, Ms. 10)

The male-female interaction pushes the boundaries of behavioral propriety and is peppered with indecorous language. This dynamic continues with a coquettish exchange between one of the men and one of the women:

> — Quietas las manos, puerco — clamaba una moza, rubia y ancha como una vaca normanda.
> — Pos déjame que asome la cabeciña.
> — No tienes que hacer aquí.
> — Tengo... Tengo — contestaba el mozo, riendo.
> Y para rubricar sus palabras, atizó un soberano y ávido azote en las robustas ancas de la hembra. Tal no hiciera; volvióse ella encrespada, y le largó un sonoro bofetón. Al volverse divisó al amo apoyado en la barandilla de la solana.
> — El amo — avisó, atragantada, componiéndose las faldas. (Ts. 2, Ms. 10)

The characters' animalization in both description and action privileges their portrayal as savage beings, yet the censor allows this characterization to remain in the printed novel. This borderline level of tolerability may be explained by the socio-spatial distancing of the characters in the rural setting who belong to the lower class that also allows for a certain degree of separation from the perceived civility of the urban landscape.

The second example also refers to a lengthy excerpt, this one dealing with descriptions of activities surrounding the hunting excursions. The focal point is the *leonera*, the room in the home kept locked except for the days before and after the hunting trips, to allow for preparing weapons and provisions as well as cleaning the carcasses when the men return. Among the eight paragraphs the censors mark appears the following text, which, though lengthy, paints the picture of what was considered tolerable:

> Las mujeres andaban esos días más erguidas, más provocantes, excitadas por el fuerte olor a bravío de la caza. Aspiraban hondo, al pasar ante la leonera, se hacían las remolonas, y ellos fingían ignorarlas, aunque, retirado el amo, comenzara la dispersión. A veces faltaban parejas a la cena, y los demás rezongaban. Por tácito acuerdo no se atrancaba la puerta del granero, y se oían, al pasar ante los establos, o si alguien se aventuraba por la fraga, sofocadas voces y risas. Como Ermitas cerraba la puerta a las doce, no queriéndose dar por enterada, la última criada que salía de la lareira, dejaba descuidadamente abierta la ventana. Era la temporada de las rivalidades, la sorda envidia, el despecho entre ellas; las viejas insultaban a las mozas.
>
> — Porque non podes — contestaban las mozas ufanándose.
>
> Madrugaban los hombres. Las altas botas claveteadas resonaban en la casa dormida. Cogían los morrales, preparados desde la víspera. Mientras montaban, frente al portón, se asomaban algunas de las mujeres, desgreñadas, y el verlos a caballo, escuchando su piafar, y el ladrido de los perros, como locos, olfateando la partida, las voces bruscas de los mozos, y sus roncas risas, les hacían sentirse más mujeres, más rendidas.
>
> A la vuelta, sobre el macizo tablero de la mesa, toscamente tallado, amontonábanse las perdices y las piezas muertas. Las rudas manos femeninas las palpaban, buscando con ávida mirada el orificio, negro y ensangrentado, por donde la muerte se coló. Todo el rebullir del pazo se concentraba en la leonera, al abrirse la caza. Es-

copetas, cajas de cartuchos, cananas y morrales, invadían las sillas y las mesas. (Ts. 20, Ms. 24-25)

The lines above may be divided into three conceptual sections. In the first, the women provoke and taunt the men who then become complicit in illicit behavior, and they also enable this behavior from one couple to the next by leaving a window open to allow access to the *leonera* when locked. Young women mock the older women who are envious of the attention those younger women attract. In the second section, correlating to the hunters' morning departure, the women's interactions with the men underscore heightened female sexuality amidst the flurried commotion. Lastly, the cleaning of the carcasses takes place in a frenetic atmosphere in which the women handle the dead animals with the omnipresent reminders of weaponry and ammunition. The coalescence of a primitive sexuality woven into the hunting narrative accentuates a savage existence. Readers may associate Quiroga's representation of hunting in Galician countryside with Pardo Bazán's *Los pazos de Ulloa* (1886), but careful comparison reveals nuanced differences in that the nineteenth century work portrays hunting not from a communal perspective but one focalized on specific individuals and excludes the overtly sexualized encounters between the men and women. Quiroga's narration attests to the creation of a more populous swath of the men and women and illustrates how they interact with one another in a broadened context of social class.

The third example of tolerable text refers to Alvaro's uncle, don Enrique. The first section of the 33 lines the censor indicated deals with the septuagenarian's outlook on life: "El hombre que no gusta de la caza y las mujeres por la madrugada, y del vino a todas horas, es hombre a medias" (Ts. 22, Ms. 26). A self-proclaimed liberal, and "poco amigo de los curas," he challenges religious dogma by making the sign of the cross only out of habit and takes communion only to appease his wife (Ts. 23, Ms. 27). His attitudes toward women also test the bounds of propriety not because he grimaced when congratulated on the birth of his firstborn five daughters but because he "quiso enseñar a las chicas como a los muchachos, ponerlas pantalones y que salieran de caza, y a ver talar la fraga" (Ts. 23, Ms. 27). His progressive mindset promotes his daughters' self-sufficiency, even if for his own financial means in the short term, and clashes with the *ángel del hogar* positioning his wife doña Lucía wishes to secure, "A mis hijas las educo yo. Como unas señoritas" (Ts. 23, Ms. 27). Quiroga maintains social order through Lucía's voice in upholding the tenets of female domesticity by imposing her will over the transgressive ideas don Enrique espouses.

These examples test the bounds of tolerability but do not overstep because they are positioned within the rural masses for their portrayal of actions by anonymous, secondary characters, as in the first two cases, or suggest non-normative behavior with an asserted corrective that upholds normativity as in the third case.

Eugenia Serrano y Balañá: *Perdimos la primavera* (1952)
Eugenia Serrano y Balañá (1921-1991) published four novels and was a frequent contributor to, and section editor of, numerous newspapers and magazines. She belongs to the list of women writers in mid-century Spain who have barely registered on the critical radar. Her plenteous publications in state-sanctioned venues such as *El Alcázar*, *El Español*, and *Medina* or in journals aimed at women, such as *Ventanal*, support Pilar Sáenz's identification of Serrano as a conservative, although Sáenz adds the qualifier "of liberal leanings" ("Serrano" 555). As Sáenz notes, the centerpiece of Serrano's novels is a female protagonist who experiences a coming of age, but the ways Serrano narrates her stories challenge a normative portrayal of these protagonists. Much more critical work, however, is necessary to examine Serrano's literary treatment of feminine subjectivity, particularly since her novels present characters realistically immersed in the temporal-spatial bounds of pre- and postwar Spain. Further, study of her contributions to journalism will situate her in the context of the burgeoning Francoist press, within which articles such "En contra y en pro de las novelistas" (1944) or "Hacia un renacimiento de la novela española" (1951) may further elucidate her literary aesthetic.

Serrano's second novel, *Perdimos la primavera*, is an early example of what Perriam et al. describe as a mid-century shift in the portrayal of Spain's recent past: "By the 1950s, although Falangist fundamentalism had given way to a more pragmatic but still authoritarian political climate, the heroic version of history remained essentially intact in official versions. In the meantime, however, it was beginning to be questioned in a variety of ways by essayists, historians, and creative writers" (44). Serrano's novel is divided into a prologue and three sections. In the prologue "Al lector y más especialmente al crítico," she describes the genesis of the novel, completed in 1948, as a symbolic child that came into being five years earlier (8), and as such offers two historical touchstones of contextualization, one that harkens back to her memories and the other that offers the interpretive lens through the passage of time. The "Primera parte" is focused on the protagonist Carola's early education and continues with the "Segunda parte" as she moves through adolescence. The third, subtitled "1936-1937," recounts her time working with the Misiones Pedagógicas coinciding with the outbreak of the Spanish Civil War and narrates her experiences that run counter to conservative ideology. In this novel covering just over a decade in Carola's life, from about the age of nine to about the age of 20, Serrano presents her characters as products of their environment, the first two thirds in Madrid and the last third in an unspecified town near Soria. It is a choral novel in the first and second parts, with a focus on the young girl who is nonthreatening in terms of the guiding questions on the censorship report. The third part is the most substantive as it pertains to the censorship evaluation for its direct reference to the pivotal moments between the Second Republic and the political challenges to its rule that highlight the significance of the novel's title. As Serrano explains in the prologue, "Perdimos mi generación, adolescencia y juventud. Fuimos un puñado de niños zarandeados de pronto por la vida. Perdimos nuestra infancia, sus inocencias, sus ilusiones. Perdimos el mundo fácil de los mayores" (10). Serrano develops in the third part Carola's social and cultural engagement with her community that comes under attack during the onset of the war. For her pregnancy outside of marriage, she suffers death in the days after childbirth as retribution for her social practices, wayward in the eyes of patriarchy, and her transgressive ideology during the dictatorship. The characters' participation in the Misiones Pedagógicas is the vehicle through which Serrano questions ideological interplay for the ways the Nationalist presence menaces the Second Republican-led initiative and for the ways Serrano imbues her female protagonist with an independent spirit; the prevailing ideology cannot reconcile her independence and therefore erases it.

Though published in 1952, Serrano presented *Perdimos la primavera* for censorial approval in 1948. It was initially denied publication without explanation when it first went before the censor on 27 January 1948 with the final decision stamped of *denegada* on 30 January. The report lists the affirmative answer to the question relating to the threat to morality, elaborating "En general, por el fondo" instead of listing the pages where questionable material appears. The report reads: "No es recomendable su publicación por la perversión moral que describe en un sector de la juventud estudiantil del año 36 (F.U.E.)" (File *Perdimos*).[12]

It is typical that a rejected text or one with questionable content will continue to a second reading either for confirmation of the rejection or for the second censor to arrive at a final decision regarding viability for publication, which occurred with this novel (originally titled *Primavera*) in a report dated 4 March 1948:

> En general el fondo de la obra es reprobable por el ambiente amoral en que se desenvuelve y hasta por el tono de indiferencia con que se enfoca nuestra Cruzada de liberación. Aunque no es claramente inmoral creo que no se debe autorizar sin una reforma "a fondo" de la obra. (File *Perdimos*)

This novel represents one of the rare cases in which the higher-ranking censor—the *jefe de sección*—directly intervenes and overturns the two censors' (*lectores*) assessments. On one of the forms with the Ministerio de Educación Nacional letterhead in the censorship file appears in large handwritten red letters "suspendido 28 enero 48," to which was subsequently added "autorizada con carácter de tolerada

---

12   The Federación Universitaria Escolar (F.U.E.) was formed in protest of educational practices under Primo de Rivera and lost traction after the Second Republic rose to power when its members dispersed into left-leaning educational activist groups.

por acuerdo con jefe de la sección 6-3-48" (File *Perdimos*), and the novel saw publication four years later.

The moral perversion the first censor cites relates to Carola's work with the Misiones Pedagógicas that was part of the Second Republic's initiative to promote education in rural areas, beginning in 1931, before being dismantled by the end of the Civil War. Carola is inspired to undertake this work under the premise that she is contributing to the progress of her country. However, due to hardships associated with wartime life, she lives in squalor, subsists on meager rations, and at times faces scrutiny of the townspeople, one of whom denounces her and her two coworkers, prompting a stressful search of the home where she is living with the coworkers and a host family. As she scrambles to hide two texts subversive to Nationalist ideology, she and one of the soldiers recognize each other from their school days, and he saves Carola and her friends from further scrutiny by ignoring the presence the incriminating texts. Although this textual maneuvering safeguards Carola from political danger, her affronts to the traditional role of women as conservativism was gaining hold place her in jeopardy. Carola's ideas on motherhood complicate the censorial authorization that she ultimately attained in spite of thoughts that include "¿Por qué las mujeres no podrán tener los hijos sin colaboración? Un amante, un marido, puede decepcionar" (273) and "Para una futura madre es más importante tener algunas nociones de embriología y puericultura que traducir con facilidad a Plinio, dibujar con gracia, conocer con relativa profundidad las literaturas románticas" (275).

Contributing to the outcome of "authorized as tolerable" was the textual treatment Carola received at novel's end. The evolution of events that culminated with the protagonist's demise in essence align with Francoist messaging from the onset of the novel, by portraying Carola and her friends beginning two decades earlier when they were young students. Although a dramatic ending, the disillusioned Carola's death in the end reads as a common outcome in novels that depict a woman who rejects the confines of prescribed feminine subjectivity.

MERCEDES FORMICA: *LA CIUDAD PERDIDA* (1953)
Writer and lawyer Mercedes Formica (1913-2002)[13] is widely known as a Falangist supporter during the Spanish Civil War who gradually distanced herself from the ideologically conservative tenets espoused by the regime over the subsequent decades. She was an influential member of the Sección Femenina but her progressive views on women's rights contributed to her leaving the organization in 1962 (Lavail 370). Concha Alborg explains that "after receiving her law degree in 1948 (Alborg, "Formica" 242), Formica used her legal background to expand laws to grant women greater legislative protection in cases of divorce and domestic violence. The shift away from an ideologically conservative standpoint in the first postwar decade to promote the feminist cause prompted her support of legislative changes in pro of women's rights.[14] The watershed moment that brought to light the uneven treatment women received in the court system appeared prominently in the newsfeeds in 1953: the case of a wife who endured years of abuse at the hands of her husband who eventually stabbed her to death highlighted the minimal legal resources women could access to escape domestic abuse. In her scathing commentary published in *ABC* 7 November 1953, titled "El domicilio conyugal," Formica argues that "Nuestro Código Civil, tan injusto con la mujer en la mayoría de sus instituciones" (5) failed to protect basic human rights, setting off a series of debates in the press and in the legal community on ways and reasons to amend the laws. Formica's article drew attention to the unjust law that "llevó a la inútil sacrificio" of the victim (5), in which she clamored for a reversal in existing legislation that favored the husband in cases of domestic disputes. She advocated for and inspired legal reform so that an abused wife could retain property rights and gain custody of her children as well as stay in her home, rather than being legally bound to leave and seek shelter elsewhere when financial limitations would in essence force her into homelessness. Formica's dedica-

---

13 Formica confirms in her interview with Concha Alborg that her surname is written without the accent, even though in numerous sources, including on book covers, it often appears as Fórmica (*Cinco figuras* 104).

14 For an expanded account of the intersection of Formica's biography and her writing see Miguel Soler Gallo.

tion to women's causes had been evident in the years preceding these events; as an example, she was commissioned to write a speech in support of women's employment for the 1951 I Congreso Femenino Hispanoamericano Filipino in Madrid, although it was ultimately pulled from the program.[15]

During the early 1950s Formica authored two of her most widely known novels, *Monte de Sancha* (1950), set in Málaga during the Spanish Civil War with autobiographical undertones, and *La ciudad perdida* (1953), which "portrays the ill-fated foray of a clandestine anti-Franco guerrilla fighter who kidnaps a wealthy young widow [María] and holds her hostage" (Pérez, "Formica" 631-32).[16] The former was granted authorization for publication with the statement "No contiene nada censurable" (File *Monte*), absent a plot summary and interpretation of the novel. Its content would have been amenable to the censor for its narration of events surrounding the war in a story aligned with Falangist ideology.

Formica's second novel received the assessment of "Autorizada con carácter de '*tolerada*'" (File *La ciudad*, emphasis added). Originally titled *Las calles de Madrid*, *La ciudad perdida* is a crime story, in the sense that the reader witnesses the criminal acts as they unfold under cover of night in a noir-like atmosphere, replete with kidnapping, violence,

---

15 Additional information on this presentation, and its relevance to the broader context of Formica's advocacy for women's rights, appears in Kathleen J. Richmond's "The Yoke of Isabella: The Women's Section of the Spanish Falange 1934-1959" (118-19).

16 In the same year she published *La ciudad perdida*, Formica also published the short novel *El secreto* (1953), which censors likewise considered tolerable, using the phrase "dentro de los límites de la decencia," as summarized in the following report: "Es una novela de argumento bastante folletinesco. Un joven acusado del asesinato de su hermana, que resulta estar embarazada, es condenado por la justicia. Cumplida ya su condena y muerto el joven se descubre su inocencia. No hay, a juicio del lector, nada que impida su publicación, pues el relato se mantiene siempre dentro de los límites de la decencia" (File *El secreto*).

and a criminal pursuit.[17] The novel features Rafa, a resistance fighter who returns to Madrid, the "lost city," in the aftermath of World War II. Throughout the night, he attempts to save himself from armed law officers who discovered his kidnapping of the wealthy María based on a missing person's report and then discerned his whereabouts from bystander tips. His precarious positioning is further accentuated when the reader learns that his three accomplices have already been killed while committing their acts of subversion, and the police are searching for him as the remaining survivor of the group. Rafa's portrayal is both normative, in the context of his opposition to social order, and peripheral for his positioning in this order as a political dissident who is trying to evade capture. Rafa is self-aware of his ideological dissonance and disadvantageous positioning, doubly complicated by his hostage taking. The woman he kidnaps, the widowed María, holds a fixed place in Francoist aristocratic society and provides an extra layer of motivation to view the narrative within the damsel in distress trope. For its visual appeal and fast pace, it was adapted to an Italian film in 1953, directed by Margarita Alexandre and Rafael María Torrecilla—a now classic film noir, at the height of the genre's popularity—which translates to the big screen the tension between shadowed locales and character antagonism to dramatically portray what R. Barton Palmer identifies as a cornerstone of the dark film, the "exteriorization of alienation, self-destructiveness, and unruly passions" (172).[18]

---

17   The film was projected in Spain the following year, after many changes demanded by the film section of the censorship board: numerous cuts, dubbing with new dialogue, addition of characters to emphasize María's social standing, and a new ending in which the police kill Rafa (García López 52).

18   García López's interview with the film's co-director, Margarita Alexandre, reveals the complicated experience the film had in the censorship process. A co-production between Spain and Italy, the movie was first released in Italy under the title *Terroristi a Madrid* (1955). Alexandre discusses the tenuous interactions with the censorship board, the mutilations to both language and scenes, and the censors' view of pernicious moral rather than political content (García López 11-12, 37-48). Carmen Moreno-Nuño summarizes the central message of the film, which may likewise be ascribed to the novel, "as armed resistance is a dead end that leads nowhere" (91). The overt

The censor considers the articulation of potential threats to dogma, religion, morality, and the regime within the limits of acceptability. Dated 24 February 1951, the novel's assessment appears on a separate sheet of paper:

> Novela (?) de tiempo actual y lugar Madrid, en la que se refleja superficialmente distintos ambientes sociales, siendo protagonista Rafa, un estudiante rojillo emigrado, convertido en "maqui."
>   Psicológicamente los personajes no tienen profundidad y muestran sus miserias con tan decorosa timidez que no llegan a conmover. Aunque el clima pretende ser áspero y amargo, no se logra por la natural limitación de su autor que no cala hasta el meollo el paisaje moral que pinta o porque lo desconoce o porque no se atreve.
>   Rafa es el estudiante de médico, políticamente despistado e idealista, que singularmente se dió en el tiempo mediato a nuestra Guerra Civil, y Mercedes Formica logra en "Las calles de Madrid," quizás por contraste a la imbecilidad de la clase "bien" que se retrata en el capítulo IV que Rafa se gane la simpatía del lector, al igual que Ayn Rand hizo en el Andrés Taganov de "Los que vivimos." ¿Es peligroso políticamente hablando que resulte simpático un "maquis" acosado?
>   Se considera que este libro puede ser autorizado. Su tono es siempre ponderado aunque el nudo de la trama sea forzamiento de una mujer. (File *La ciudad*, emphasis original)

The opening lines deflect from the plot assessment and position the novel as an unconvincing narrative by questioning its genre classification through use of the parenthetical interrogative punctuation, by employing the phrase "se refleja superficialmente," and by focusing on the protagonist as one of the vanquished following the victory of Francoist forces at Civil War's end. Also, the quick pace of the action spanning the course of one night, does indeed offer limited time to deeply develop the protagonists' psychological impetus, but the sense

---

extinguishing of the *maquis* decenters any notion that the storyline poses risk of political threat.

of urgency heightens the readers desire to discover what happens to the fugitive and the kidnapped young woman in the end, leading to privileging the outcome over character development.

The police procedural was not a common subgenre censors encountered, and the lack of reference to law enforcement in the report despite their steady presence in the narration indicates that the censor was more concerned with Rafa's portrayal and what he represented than with the theme of law and order. The censor bases his critique in the second paragraph on the author's ability to present compelling characters and settings as part of a moral landscape on a number of possible factors, including the author's ignorance or cowardice. The first two paragraphs of the report decenter the narration as a credible literary source of political or moral decay. I argue that Formica's brevity in writing this short novel provides convenient justification for not exploring in greater detail the characters' psychological development. To do so would potentially jeopardize her ability to publish the novel or would force her to incorporate significant revisions. Formica provides sufficient textual clues to understand Rafa's history and motivations as the underdog in the story but stops short of suggesting an endorsement of his activities.

In the report's third paragraph the censor views the depiction of the *maquis* to gain the reader's sympathy as questionable, although not detrimental, to the novel's publication: however, the question reveals a contradiction, namely the ability of a character whose psychological profile is not well developed to provoke a sympathetic reading of his situation. The censor concludes the report with two sentences that further attempt to destabilize the writing by underscoring the female authorship. This viewpoint suggests that decentering the authoritative, narrative voice by designating the novel as women's work removes the threat of attack to the tenets censorship is charged with safeguarding.

Absent in the report is the overt reference to distinctions in social class and political ideology between Rafa and María, although the censor references Rand's *We the Living*. The intertextual reference to Rand's protagonist Taganov and reader sympathies he gains through his pursuit of freedom restricted by the repressive Russian state (Powell 212), as well as his frustrated romantic interest, intersect with Rafa's portrayal as a political dissenter involved with a woman who holds contrary ideological views.

The novel challenges the notion that "restitution of the vanquished back into Spanish society invariably required confession and repentance [...] for the errors committed in the past" (García López 47) through Rafa's demise at the novel's end.[19] When escape turned futile, María shoots and kills him with his own weapon to save him from eternal damnation were he to turn the gun on himself. However, even Formica remarked in her memoirs that this ending is contrived, influenced by her belief that censors would have stricken Rafa's suicide (*Espejo roto* 26). She explains in her interview with Concha Alborg that her original ending in which Rafa conveys regret for his actions would not have satisfied censors and was substituted for a perceived merciful death at the hands of María (*Cinco figuras* 111). The progression from remorse to suicide to merciful death illustrates Formica's statement on her need to regulate her writing process to adhere to censorship legislation: "yo estaba escribiendo en un medio hostil a lo que yo pensaba" (Alborg, *Cinco figuras* 111). By taking into consideration statements such as the former, what emerges is a form of compromised writing that requires the author to sacrifice textual meaning in order to gain authorization to publish. Writing under these circumstances becomes stylized to conform to censorship legislation, such that, for instance, from the lens of current day victimology, María's concern for Rafa's moral wellbeing seems contrived as well because he rapes her, yet she gives precedence to his moral salvation over criminal conviction. The subtheme in today's language of the Stockholm syndrome paradigm is entirely absent in the censor's report.

---

19 Establishing parallels between Rafa as a resistance fighter and Partido Comunista Español member Cristino García Granda who was captured in Madrid in 1945 and executed in 1946 may further tease out the historical relevance of this novel. The two men share a similar past in terms of their wartime activities and movements including Spain and France, followed by a return to Madrid, notwithstanding the differences in how their stories end. García Granda's name appears in studies on the film adaptation of the of *La ciudad perdida* in articles by Carmen Mareno Nuño and Mercedes Camino.

Also absent in the report is reference to the subtext of the *maquis* who crosses the border from France in a return to his home country on a guerilla mission to overthrow the Franco regime. His plan elides the censor's plot summary. Rafa, a young man whose medical studies were interrupted by the war, would have fought for the Republican cause in the Spanish Civil War and then against the Nazi occupation in World War II France. The history of civil war is on textual display through passages that narrate Rafa's memories, and as such the censor does not consider them worthy of explicit mention. These passages consist of Rafa's recollections of scenes of war in Madrid, death, and exile, with references, among others, that include: "Los muertos podían olvidarse, más quedaban los hechos" (54), "Nadie suele recorder la masa de muertos" (58,) and "fueron los peores meses de nuestro exilio" (80) regarding his time in France at the end of World War II. Widening the temporal-spatial gap between events in the novel's past and present, Guillermo, an acquaintance of María who makes a brief appearance only in the novel's opening as a representative of the nobility in Poland, obliquely remarks that he remembers "lo que había sucedido en su país" (39). These reminders evoke a spectral atmosphere in the nighttime shadows of the lost city.

As Rafa's aspirations of becoming a surgeon vanished with the onset of civil war, María grapples with widowhood as a consequence of the war. She reminisces about life with her now-deceased husband, Carlos, and the perils of her kidnappings bring her to the thought that she may soon be reunited with him. García López surmises that the figure of Carlos refers to Carlos Haya González, Formica's aviator friend who died in aerial combat in 1938 (50) over Puerto Escandón, La Puebla de Valverde, Teruel. The two men share the same fate, literarily described as: "su aparato cayó sobre el Ebro. Murió convertido en cenizas" (63). Parallels in the circumstances of their untimely death are another signpost of the intersection of fact and fiction. María emerges a symbol of purity, one who has respectfully honored her late husband's memory by not remarrying over a decade removed from his death. She inhabits a world of elegant dress with dinner parties in palaces where she mingles with the upper echelons of society. Rafa selects her as a victim because he views her as "armoniosa, delicada, en extremo frágil"

(46). Though she experiences desperation and angst as a kidnapping victim, her benevolence keeps her from shooting Rafa in self-defense midway through the narration even when she gained momentary access to the gun. When she had the opportunity to call attention to her plight by shouting out, she refrained from doing so, for reasons that she cannot explain. The intervention of the third-person narrator mediates a pervading sense of unease: "Ella tiene que desear la muerte. [...] Al menos todas las mujeres cristianas han deseado la muerte como una liberación" (164), where death is preferred over the psychological torture of facing the barrel of a gun and the physical abuse of sexual assault. In the moments of her kidnapping she is terrified by her kidnapper and the potential harm that he may cause her: "— Que no haga eso, suplicó a una invisible presencia. — No es posible que se comporte como un animal" (59). Sparks of resistance appear, however, in a sanitized manner of expressing her inner thoughts such as "decepcionada de si mimsa, decepcionada de no sentir por Rafa un odio feroz, una ira ciega. De no experimentar aquellos sentimientos aun cuando los desea" (165-66). She is frustrated by gender norms that dictate conforming her behavior to societal expectations.

The censor's evaluation contains words and phrases that suggest the text may not reach the threshold to gain authorization to print. We recall that the potential popularity or the quality of the prose is not necessarily a determining factor, such that phrases that appear in the report's second paragraph do not determine the outcome to authorize publication. Clues in the first, third, and last paragraphs show that the novel teeters between granting and denying authorization to publish. In the first paragraph, while the questioning of genre and the word "superficialmente" minimize the narrative rigor, the diminutive "rojillo" suggests a sense of disdain that would lean toward a decision to reject or at least accept with revisions. In the third paragraph, the censor attempts to reconcile the menacing Rafa's portrayal (resistance fighter, kidnapper) with reader sympathies. In the final paragraph the passive construct "se considera" combined with the modal auxiliary "puede ser" counter a decisive endorsement of the novel as publishable. Taking into consideration as well the novel's measured tone and female authorship, the handwritten assessment of *tolerada*, without the need for revision, allows the novel to proceed to publication.

CONCHA FERNÁNDEZ LUNA: *MARTÍN NADIE* (1954)
Concepción (Concha) Fernández Luna (1915-1999) was an esteemed writer of children's literature, garnering multiple literary accolades. One of the most noteworthy is the Premio Lazarillo in 1962 for *Fiesta en Marilandia*, included on the 1966 International Board on Books for Young People (IBBY) "Honour List" by the prestigious Hans Christian Andersen Prize Board as one of the best 15 children's books of its time.[20] She also won the Premio Sésamo de Cuentos in 1962 for her short story "El botones." The legacy of her cultural patrimony includes the annual children's short story writing contest, "Premio María Fernández Luna" in Lorca, Murcia in which between 1,000 and 2,000 students participate each year. She received the 1963 Premio Fray Luis de León de Traducción for her translations of juvenile literature, *Las gafas del león* and *La familia gorrión*, from the original "Les lunettes du lyon" and "La famille moineau" by French writer Charles Vildrac. Among the favorable reviews of her work, one uncredited book review of her time considers her "como escritora de fácil estilo y clara comprensión en ese maravilloso marco de las ilusiones y las alegrías" ("Fernández Luna" 58.)

Fernández Luna, a university student interrupted by the outbreak of the Spanish Civil War, continued her studies to graduate in 1942. According to Joan Manuel Verdegal Cerezo, she began working as a librarian in Spain's National Library in 1955, followed by employment with the National Reading Service (Servicio Nacional de la Lectura)

---

20   See "Concesión del Andersen 1966" (43). Sources have erroneously credited her with receiving the Andersen Prize, which was awarded in 1966 to the Swedish writer Tove Jansson. Other achievements of note are that Fernández Luna published a full-page interview with Elizabeth Mulder in *ABC* in 1956 (Fernández Gutiérrez 33). She also taught a class with artist Nadia Werbo offered by the Biblioteca Nacional de España on illustrating children's books (Fernández Gutiérrez 36).

in 1958 (118-19).²¹ These details build a narrative of a writer whose postwar public endeavors and institutional presence adhered to the dominant political discourse.

Fernández Luna's short novel *Martín Nadie* (1954) was published as part of the Novela del Sábado series.²² She udpates the Lazarillo de Tormes picaresque motif in her titular character who recounts his mischievous ways as he meanders through rural landscapes of southern Spain as a young man at times under the watchful eyes of adults, at times left to his own devices. Dated Madrid, 26 July 1953, the censorship file reads:

> La Srta. Fernández Luna no es precisamente una ursulina, aunque sí buena escritora. Novela tremendista y desgarrada la suya, muy estilo "Cela": fragmentos de la vida de un pícaro vagabundo. Deben suprimirse o modificarse los párrafos y palabras acotados en las págs. 1, 13, 21, 22, 25, 29, 33, 34, 37, 47, 48 y 49, según me parece. Por lo demás, puede autorizarse. (File *Martín Nadie*)

The censor indirectly contests the didactic nature of the work by distancing its author from the educational mission of the Ursuline Order, yet at the same time recognizes Fernández Luna's talent as a writer. It may be gleaned from the first part of his statement that the intended audience is adults rather than children, considering also several adult-themed plot points that include marital infidelity, sexual assault, and murder. Stated another way, despite the protagonist's presumed naiveté and a potentially perceived straightforward narration of his journey

---

21   The purpose of the Servicio Nacional de la Lectura (1947-1975) was to "promote Spanish cultural development in general and reading in particular" (Escobar Sobrino 595).

22   José María Fernández Gutiérrez recalls Américo Castro's observations on the classic picaresque schema that was updated in other novels in this series. Castro "veía el ejemplo final de las novelas picarescas como fórmula necesaria para que los judíos se pudieran manifestar sin ser represaliados. [...] ¿Es, en *La Novela del Sábado*, la formula también necesaria, para subvertir un orden político-social, en una época en la que había que guardar apariencias?" (34).

across the Andalusian countryside, these plot points move the short novel out of the realm of children's literature to position the work before the adult audience. This shift in audience may also have been another contributing factor in the story's evaluation had the censor not taken it into consideration. The label of "tolerated" applied to Fernández Luna's and Cela's novels is rooted in their picaresque qualities that convey an irreverent tone and a high degree of irony—such as the protagonist's occluded vision, both literal and figurative—to tease out social class disparities that push vulnerable populations into a world of survival amidst harsh realities of daily living.

The author then began to negotiate with the censorship board to attain authorization to publish her novel. In a letter dated 21 January 1954 in Madrid, she advocated keeping intact some of her original text and indicated where she removed or revised the problematic areas listed on the report. As she explained, she recognized "que algunas frases o expresiones merecen tacharse, pero que, en cambio, ciertos párrafos, de ser suprimidos romperían la fuerza primitiva del personaje, su clima biológico, y la trayectoria toda de la citada obra" (File *Martín Nadie*). She continues to ask for a second evaluation of her novel in which the remaining marked pages are left unchanged: "me permito rogar la revisión de dicha novela, conservando intactas las frases y párrafos originales, excepto aquellos que yo misma he tachado con lápiz azul, y que figuran en las páginas: 1, 21, 29, 33, 34, 37, 47" (File *Martín Nadie*).[23] The final decision was rendered in a handwritten note: "Puede autorizarse con las tachaduras que propone la autora. Los demás son *tolerables*," and the novel's publication is authorized on 23 Jan 1954 (File *Martín Nadie*, emphasis added).

The revision on the first page resulted in the reframing of "la guerra civil española" (Ts. 1) in the opening lines: "El hombre se llamaba Martín. O eso decía 'Martín y para qué más. Con esto hay bastante.'—Había contestado durante muchos años: la guerra española, preguntas de un lado, de otro, siempre todos preguntándole" (Ms. 6). What

---

23   Respectively, the pages in the published novel are 6, 30, 39, 45, 46, 49-50, and 60.

would appear to be an innocuous temporal reference was modified to remove the association of the term "civil" with "war."[24]

In the next example of required textual revision, the implied indecorous language, even though it only partially appears as "c..." is removed, as is the sacrilegious act of corporal desecration of a priest's body. The original "Sí, lo del cura, c..., eso sí que fue un trago. A ése le hicieron polvo" (Ts. 21) then becomes: "Sí, lo del cura..., eso sí que fue un trago. A ése le hicieron polvo" (Ms. 30). In Martín's description of how his friend "el Tingo" and other acquaintances murdered the priest, the gruesome details were removed in the printed novel to replace the original "lo mutilaron antes de enterrarlo: le cortaron sus partes, entre risas y blasfemias, que pisaron luego hasta convertir en piltrafa sucio lo que fuera vida y polen; luego las orejas" (Ts. 21) with "lo mutilaron antes de enterrarlo; luego las orejas" (Ms. 30). The references on the manuscript's preceding pages that describe the war are considered acceptable for their lack of pointing to the specific war in Spain: Martín uses the ruse of attaching himself to a military war effort in order to boast of his experience to seduce (*conseguirse*) women. He conflates women's attraction to wartime soldiers with attraction toward him: "Le sedujo, en un principio, en parte, la aventura de la guerra: además, tenía náuseas de tanta sangre mezclada a la vida cotidiana, como una costumbre de matar porque sí, sin porqués. El frente sería otra clase de guerra" (Ms. 29). However, the focus on playing a soldier as a method of seducing women shifts to the articulation of war's devastation, which falls within the realm of the acceptable because it relates to the notion of performance and is not explicitly identified as consequence of the Spanish Civil War.

---

24 Inconsistencies surrounding the use and revision of the phrase *guerra civil* emerge in the censorship reports and in the novels. To name several examples, whereas in *Martín Nadie* the censor required the erasure of the word *civil*, in Ángeles Villarta's *Mi vida en el manicomio*, the censor permitted the phrase when the ideologically conservative author explained that the psychiatric hospital was severely damaged during the war, in the "asedio de Oviedo" (29) used in the context of mental illness in a patient brought on by the death of her son in the war (74). Likewise, the censor who evaluated Formica's *La ciudad perdida* incorporated the term *guerra civil* in his report.

What the censor would also consider tolerable is Martín's interaction with a young man named Juan Ramón and his ill father who were formerly jailed "por cosas de la Guerra, ya sabes, no por nada malo" with "no por nada malo" circled in red (Ts. 29). This tolerated phrase remains in the printed novel (Ms. 31-32). Likewise tolerated is the portrayal of social class distinction, in that Fernández Luna did not revise the observations of the young man who, when asked to explain what he and his father are doing in Martín's town, explains that they are need a comfortable place to rest and are not looking for trouble. This character explains his bleak alternatives: "Ir a misa, creer en Dios, golpearnos el pecho y hundir los ojos en las losas de la iglesia, esperar, como mastines hambrientos y engrifados, la comida de ricos, esas sobras que desdeñan sus perros de lujo. Ni somos más, no valemos ya para otra cosa" (Ms. 35).

Fernández Luna adopts an irreverent tone in a casual conversation that takes place in Granada between Martín and his acquaintance, Ricardo, who points out a guard in the distance entrusted to keep order: "Bueno, pues, ahí, a poco de donde estamos, hay un niño bonito, que porque lleva uniforme está más creído que San Miguel Arcángel. Y que no le íbamos a meter leña ni na, si fuera un paisano. Nos está hundiendo el fulano ése" (Ts. 29). In this passage, although the censor circled "más creído que San Miguel Arcángel" the phrase remains in the printed novel; however, the phrase "Nos está hundiendo el fulano ése" originally appeared as "Nos está hundiendo el jodi... ése" where the censor crossed off "jodi..." (Ts. 29).

To avert an attack on dogma, the original "El que tenía dinero, lo pasaba como Dios, el pobre se hacía la pascua" (Ts. 33) was changed to "El que tenía dinero, lo pasaba de lo mejor, el pobre se hacía la pascua" (Ms. 45). Further, other references were removed to avoid attacks on religion that intersect with social class. When describing Martín's financial hardships, the narrator laments in the original typescript "que el cielo y el infierno estaban aquí, en esta vida humana, y nada más que aquí, en la tierra, que el cielo pertenecía a los ricos y el infierno correspondía a los pobres" (Ts. 34). The narrator here also describes the sexual violence Martín exhibits toward a woman named Torcuata, which, although marked for removal by the censor, remained in the printed novel: "aquella Torcuata a la que él [Martín] violó, en un bancal de trigo de mayo, alto y verde, como hedía antes y después del acto, cada vez, a sangre podrida" (Ms. 46) This act blends the harsh reality of Martín's criminal acts with the all-consuming financial hardship that marked his early years as he thinks back to his impoverished childhood: raised by his mother who was a laundry woman and his essentially absent, alcoholic father, Martín lived in caves, just as his parents and grandparents, and never washed or changed his clothes (Ms. 45-46).[25] Further, the act of sexual violence, much like the priest's murder and desecration of his body, is an unmistakable reminder of Fernández Luna's intended readership.

The next textual revision appears in the context of a conversation between Martín and four men (two soldiers, a merchant and a black marketeer) he meets on a train as he journeys toward Granada. At the beginning of their card game in which they establish the maximum bet, one of the soldiers acquiesces to a lower bet than he initially proposes and mockingly gestures: "golpeándose cómicamente en un muslo, a imitación, en voz y gesto, de los maricas" (Ms. 37, Ts. 49). Although the censor bracketed this phrase, it appears in the printed novel. In the original version, the other soldier defends his manhood, reminding him of an encounter with a woman the previous month, with brackets added by the censor: "[no hace más de un mes, más delgado que un silbido, porque una fulana se le estaba bebiendo hasta el tuétano de la sangre]. Este es un elemento de primera, hombre" (Ts. 37). In the published novel, although the phrase "no hace un mes" remains, the despective reference to the woman is removed (Ms. 49). The last textual revision requires the removal of one word the censor crossed off in the typescript, in the context of one of Martín's travel companion's question wondering why his demeanor has changed and he seems unhappy: "—¿Qué Dios le pasará a ese?" (Ts. 47, Ms. 60).

Saved from censorial revision as a result of Fernández Luna's letter, for example, are references to sexuality that represent a threat to morality. In one example of textual ambiguity, Martín imagines a sex-

---

25   The images of Martín's childhood recall the extreme poverty portrayed in Luis Buñuel's 1933 ethnofictional documentary *Las Hurdes*.

ual encounter with Rosa, the wife of one of his protectors early in his journey, without regard to consent, and without explicitly confirming whether or not the encounter took place:

> — Rosa, ay, Rosa. — Se le estremecieron los muslos y el corazón se le puso en la garganta, en las sienes. Pensó que ella estaba sola, que Ramón y Frasco no volverían hasta la tarde, casi con estrellas. "Está sola, ella sola" — le bramaba toda su sangre. "No habrá ascos a tus ojos, ni a tu cuerpo costroso; tú serás el más fuerte, el macho: le podrás; la tendrás por la fuerza, pero la tendrás. Sera tuya, quiera o no. Y tienes tiempo de sobra para volverte antes de que llegue el marido. La casa está sola; además, todavía no se sabe los vecinos que tú te has ido del todo, para no volver más." Se retorcía, de deseo animal; el aire se le estrangulaba, y se fundía con la saliva; babeaba; los ojos eran una raya purulenta. (Ts. 13, Ms. 20)

In another example, a war widow named Ascención was given a kiosk by a "protector" as a legitimate business so that it could serve as a front for black market goods. She acquired this business opportunity in exchange for sex with the "protector." The original remains untouched in the published version although the censor circled part of the text in red ink, underlined here: "me lo ofreció a cambio de que me acostara con él" (Ts. 47, Ms. 63).

After evaluating the galley proofs, the Director General de Información gives his final response on 25 August 1953:

> Visto su escrito de fecha 22 de los corrientes en la que solicita revisión de las supresiones que le fueron indicadas para hacer en su obra, titulada "Martín Nadie." Esta Dirección General de Información a propuesta del Servicio correspondiente, ha resuelto comunicarle, que dichas tachaduras quedan reducidas a las indicadas en lápiz azul, en el original adjunto, y en las páginas 1, 21, 29, 33, 34, 37 y 47. Una vez así realizado, a petición y previa a la presentación de la galerada impresa, y haciendo referencia al número de expediente y fecha de este oficio y con las supresiones efectuadas, se

procederá por esta Dirección a extender la tarjeta de autorización definitiva. (File *Martín*)

Through a combination of selective editing and communication with the censorship board, Fernández Luna's experience in publishing *Martín Nadie* exemplifies the transactional nature of the censorship process. She was purposeful and respectful in her letter, and the censorship process reveals the boundaries of tolerance. References that paint a picture of squalor to describe Martín's life offer an overall testimony to the financial hardships in postwar Spain that certain social groups experienced, much in the same way that Camilo José Cela's *La familia de Pascual Duarte* (1942)—as mentioned above, censors also regarded this novel as *tolerable*—underscores the poverty that enveloped rural areas in the aftermath of the Civil War. The *tremendista* undertones of Martín's surroundings combined with his picaresque behavior evoke two literary traditions that Fernández Luna modernizes in her story that sees publication after select revisions position the novel in the category of publishable as a tolerable text.

Observations

As controversial as some of the content was considered in the novels presented in this chapter, they underwent little if any revisions. They did not stray far from censorial restrictions and exemplify the threshold of acceptability. Tolerated texts, although few in number, reveal the bounds within which the censors judged suitability for public consumption. Authors in this category, with the exception of Fernández Luna, had gained certain degree literary renown through previously authorized published works, which situated their writing on the whole as non-threatening to the tenets on the censorship report. The censors remark upon the writer's stylistic techniques that rescue the texts from falling in to the category of publishable with edits or non-publishable (Conde, Quiroga). When a young protagonist acts altruistically to effect meaningful change in her community, even though her endeavors clash with totalitarian initiatives—for example Carola's contributions to the Misiones Pedagógicas of the Second Republic in *Perdimos la primavera*—the novel is tolerated because the author transacts her protagonist's death soon after childbirth as a textual indictment against what would be subversive political action combined with the prospect of unwed motherhood. The theme of political subversion plays a central role in *La ciudad perdida*, but the male protagonist's death in the end underscores what censors would deem a fitting punishment, even when the female protagonist is responsible for killing him, not overtly in self-defense but as a way to save him from the sinful act of suicide, in a textual maneuvering that, although narratively unconvincing, satisfied the censorship board. Fernández Luna portrays the social outcasting of a young man who wanders through rural spaces against the picaresque subgenre and *tremendista* esthetic as a way to justify the nuanced irreverences that place the tenets of religion, morals, and political institutions against the backdrop of postwar angst, on the border of what censors consider tolerable. Novels in this category rest upon the perimeters publishable. The variance in the development of plots, themes, and characters highlights multiple ways the authors test the limits of censorship's bounds.

Chapter 4.
Texts Authorized with Revisions and Excisions

> She had to possess the courage to enter, through language, states which most people deny or veil with silence.
> - *Adrienne Rich*

WHEREAS TEXTS THAT FEATURE characters and themes that fall within the bounds of material censors deemed acceptable or tolerable appear in the previous two chapters, this chapter examines novels that required revision in order to gain authorization for publication. These novels presented challenges primarily based on threats to morality or political ideology and feature characters that Arias Careaga describes in the following manner:

> Algunos de los personajes femeninos que reflejan estas novelas [de las primeras décadas de la posguerra] abandonan esas fronteras y cuestionan con rebeldía y fuera del hogar, el papel mítico que la sociedad de posguerra les ha asignado; cuestionan el ritualismo religioso impuesto por la Iglesia Católica integrista cuyo mito más obvio es que la felicidad de la mujer está ligada a la dependencia del varón y sumergida en el hogar. Algunos de estos personajes femeninos conseguirán romper ese cerco y escapar. (155)

Some studies posit that women's texts were most commonly censored for reasons dealing with morality more so than political issues, a point DiFrancesco summarizes as: "Some scholars suggest that these authors' emphasis on developing women's interior lives and friendships safeguarded their works from appearing particularly threatening to censors" (170). While this is certainly true of many novels, evidence exists of numerous texts that push the boundaries of acceptability regarding their portrayal of institutions and the regime.

From a revisionist standpoint, censors allow publication when authors modify their texts by deleting or revising incendiary words, phrases, or passages, or by reframing for instance the views their character espouse or traits that define them. At times, writers offer a moral or ideological corrective of those traits. The two primary categories of suspect text relate to moral or ideological concerns. When censors respond affirmatively to the guiding questions on the report (regarding threats to dogma, morality, the Church, the Regime, its institutions) they indicate where writers must incorporate changes in order to see their works published. This process, however, is subjective—determined at the discretion of a particular censor—and opens the possibility that certain textual maneuvering elides censorial restriction. For example, when characters engage in behaviors censors would deem threatening to social order, in the end textual revisions may not be required if these characters suffer pain, violence, or even death, whether implicitly or explicitly related to their behavior. Characters may also display behaviors contrary to moral codes of conduct, but by novel's end they experience a moral conversion, display contrition or remorse, or are offered the possibility to confess their sins.

This section features novels by Elisa Brufal, Isabel Calvo de Aguilar, Carmen Kurtz, and Concha Alós by examining the ways the censorship process altered the original manuscripts. The novels examined here showcase the textual features that censors scrutinized and subsequently required revision, whether by altering the text or excising the questionable content. The analysis illustrates the ways censors evaluated these features, including word choice, character development or behavior, thematic elements (particularly as they relate to the Spanish Civil War) against the guiding questions on the censorship report.

ELISA BRUFAL: *SIETE PUERTAS* (1964)
Biographical information on Elisa Brufal (1919-1996) is scant, and her only published novel has heretofore escaped critical commentary. Journalist Ismael Belda provides minimal details on Brufal's life that reveal her professional ties with the intellectual circles in her home town of Elche, including her participation in the *Trastienda,* a *tertulia.* The host of this tertulia was Sixto Marco (21), the Valencian artist who would go on to form the culturally significant Grup D'Elx in 1967. Belda traces Brufal's experience of obtaining runner-up recognition of the Premio Planeta for *Siete puertas,* the year that Emilio Romero won the prize for *La paz empieza nunca* (1957). According to Belda, Brufal became disillusioned with the obstacles to her publishing and, although had envisioned *Siete puertas* as part of a tetralogy, the remaining three novels, if written, remain unpublished (21).

Completed in 1954, *Siete puertas* was not evaluated by the censorship board until 1961, four years after its submission for the Planeta Prize. It underwent three censorial reviews (1 November, 12 November, and 12 December) and saw publication in January 1964. No explanation appears in the file of the decade-long span between the novel's completion and publication. However, in the gap between the final review and publication, the author arranged for the self-financing of its printing with a local publisher after exhausting other avenues.

The novel's appeal rests in its nuanced portrayal of the protagonist across time and its representation of the author's hometown of Elche.[1] The town's physical remove from Madrid underscores the sense of marginality the protagonist experiences away from or outside of Madrid's hegemonic cultural and urban anchoring. The novel's *costumbrista*-like setting in Elche shelters the protagonist from a grander social imperative to behave in accordance with culturally prescribed gender norms. In this way, she is free to explore both her physical surroundings and her sexuality during her transition to adulthood. As she experiences the vicissitudes of a subject clamoring to adopt the cultural norms of the hegemon, she also experiences a coming of age before marrying,

---

1   Among the novel's scant critical study, Vicente Ramos observes its "simbolismo sencillo, elemental, y armónico" (7).

exhibiting her embrace of normativity. For Vicente Ramos, the protagonist's rebelliousness against moral imperatives directly relates to the historical context of Francoist Spain surrounding the novel's publication: "La historia de la protagonista se destaca por una entereza y rebeldía personal que, a todas luces, resulta heroica durante los primeros años de la posguerra" (15).

The novel's first-person narrator passes through seven metaphorical doors as she experiences the right of passage from adolescence to adulthood. Each uniquely colored door represents her interactions with seven men from her teenage years to young adulthood in a guesthouse in Elche. The now-adult narrator, whose name readers never learn, recounts her experiences with the men as she journeys toward adulthood and navigates the circuitous path laden initially with timidity and ultimately with transgression, before settling in on a comfortably normative outcome. To summarize the plot, set initially in the postwar years, the adolescent girl lives with her mother in Elche where they run a *pensión*, renting rooms in their home as a way to generate income, following the death of the narrator's father; mother and daughter occupy the garden house adjacent to the main house, tending to the daily operation of the business until the latter died and the daughter assumed this responsibility. As a result of the loss of her family structure, the freedom associated with her financial agency in turn allows for an exploration of her sexuality in ways that social mores would otherwise restrict.

The novel's premise, that the girl's future husband will walk through the door, plays out as she explores relationships with the men within and beyond the dictatorial confines of prescribed gender roles. Her testimony details the route that led to her securing a normative position in society now that she has married, as revealed in the epilogue. Her incorporation into society as a stable, i.e. married, woman, however, may have appeased the censorial requirement that the narrative adhere to an acceptable moral code, but in doing so this plot point fails to honor the protagonist's sense of agency legitimately acquired as part of her life experiences.

Each of the the novel's three censorship file highlights the narrator's transgressive nature while ignoring the redeeming quality of her marriage to the man associated with fifth door after he returns from an extended period away from the protagonist.

The first two censors excoriate the novel on the grounds of its immorality. The first censor rebukes the novel:

> Novela brutalmente lujuriosa, pornográfica, plagada de obscenidades, con escenas vergonzosas, cínicamente presentadas, de la vida de una golfa sin asomos de pudor. TODA ELLA RECHAZABLE. Como botones de muestra las tachaduras arriba apuntadas. (File *Siete puertas*)

The stricken passages to which the censor refers appear on the pages following the question, "¿Ataca a la moral?," and are listed as "21, 84, 94, 103, 109, 120, 121, etc. etc." The "brutally lustful" nature of novel, for this censor, reaches the level of pornography, despite the absence of explicitly graphic details of the relationships the narrator has with several of the men. Indisputably, the seven men that entered the narrator's life play a role in her sexual maturity to varying degrees. In this report, the censor casts the female protagonist in a negative light by criticizing her character as "golfa sin asomos de pudor," thereby absolving the men of irreproachable conduct. Although the scenes are described as shameful, the censor implicitly encodes gender in the report by focusing on the novel's portrayal of the unchaste young woman that aligns with the aforementioned attention sinful actions over criminal acts (Ruiz Bautista, "La larga noche" 95-96).

In the second report, the censor reproaches the sense of impropriety the author conveys with the relationships between the narrator and the men because the she exhibits amoral-forward actions and is not repentant of her lascivious behavior:

> Siete episodios en los que la autora nos cuenta sus aventuras amorosas sucesivas con siete hombres. Desde el episodio o puerta cuarta siempre hay relaciones íntimas o al menos provocación directa por parte de ella como sucede en el séptimo. No hay propiamente relatos pornográficos pero las relaciones sexuales aparecen como algo natural entre los novios excitados a ello simplemente por la

pasión. No hay ninguna consideración de esta conducta, aún más se aprueba explícitamente de suerte que aparece como nada censurable, pág. 126, por lo que no se debe permitir su publicación. (File *Siete puertas*).

The censor decries the lack of contextualization of the attitudes toward sex ("ninguna consideración") and the representation of condoned behavior ("se aprueba explícitamente"). For example, had the protagonist interacted with a priest, taken stock of her actions in remorse, or experienced some sort of tragedy, she would have suffered textual consequences for her actions, instead of, ironically, ending up happily married within normative bounds. Contrarily, the narrator's question and response in the novel's opening pages confront domestic passivity: "¿Sentir arrepentimiento? No" (24-25). What also stands out in this report is the author-protagonist coalescence: "la autora nos cuenta sus aventuras" (File *Siete puertas*). As an unknown writer in Madrid's literary circles, censors would not likely have been familiar with Brufal. Indeed, although the creative description of the Huerto de los Toros evokes the author's Hort del Bou, character portrayal diverges in that the author, unlike the narrator, was not an only child. Social class standing differed as well in that the author's father, who was an Elche council member as late as 1930 when the author would have been 11 years old, would diverge from the character's father whom she barely remembers and who spent his spare time gambling and chasing women (18).[2] Further, physical appearance also separates the author from her protagonist. Brufal's appearance as shown on book jacket and in a photograph that accompanies Belda's article show her to be dark haired, whereas the literary character is a fair-skinned, light-haired woman (18).

The second censor's recommendation that publication not be permitted falls short of formally declaring it is unsuitable for publication. Because of the discrepancies between the two reports, the manuscript underwent a third evaluation one month later, yielding the following

---

2   Future inquiry may uncover biographical details that aid in contextualizing the novel's father-daughter relationship.

report dated 24 November 1961 and authorizing publication as long as questionable passages were removed:

> Las siete puertas a que se refiere el título son siete hombres que aparecen en el horizonte sentimental de una mujer que espera su oportunidad. Juega con ellos un juego peligroso y no muy cargado de escrúpulos. Caben reparos, pero todos ellos serían de no excesiva monte. PUEDE AUTORIZARSE. P. [Saturnino] Álvarez Turienzo (File *Siete puertas*)[3]

The novel was authorized after Álvarez Turienzo's final evaluation as the deciding voice, despite the eight infractions to moral propriety the first censor identified and the general tone of reproach in the second report. In the published novel, these passages appear in their original form except for one deletion relating to page 126 referenced in the second report, even though the censor who proffered the third evaluation did not explicitly require its removal.

Of the doors, the narrator reveals in the prologue that rather than symmetrical in size, they are unique yet linked together. She takes stock of the doors: some revealed to her joy, some bitterness; one led to nowhere; one both frightened her and supported her when she thought she would fall; one was left only ajar; one behind which was a vast nothingness; one that opened to a winding hallway and then to the outside; one that led to surprises. She elaborates that sometimes she made the conscious decision to open the door, but others she impulsively opened, and in their totality: "fue lo que me formó, haciendo

---

[3] As an operational practice, when the first reading rendered an outcome to reject publication or an inconclusive outcome, this generated a second reading, often by a censor who specialized in writing styles or were considered ecclesiastical or political censors. For example, "Father Saturnino Álvarez Turienzo (La Mata de Monteagudo, León, 1920), especially well regarded in the higher spheres of the Francoist authorities and a great scholar of the philosophical currents of the time due to his studies in France and Germany, [was a] specialist in second evaluations (Larraz, *Gender* 180). He was also a "Religioso agustino y catedrático de ética en la Universidad Pontificia de Salamanca" (Laskaris 212).

que mi vida se encauzara como es ahora. De lo contrario, de un modo u otro, quizás ya no estaría aquí" (25). The protagonist's restricted movement in the environs of her home and garden, where the visitors come from various places, may be projected onto the author's desire to escape a repressive environment, which inspired Brufal's numerous trips following the publication of *Siete puertas* to Sweden, Morocco, England, Belgium, and ultimately France, where she died in Paris in 2006 (Belda 21).

The section that follows discusses content on the seven pages listed in the first censor's report, which remained in the published novel. Because the first censor identified these passages as contributing to a highly scandalous representation of femininity, and thereby a threat to upholding moral conduct, their analysis points to the threshold of staying within the legislative bounds of the censorship process, mediated here by the ecclesiastical specialist. This process demonstrates as well an attempt to mitigate the subjective nature of the censorship evaluations. To note, all of this content appears in the published novel, despite presenting potentially suspect content. The second censor's remark calling attention to page 126, as will be shown, is the only section that Brufal removed in the printed version. The first passage marked in the manuscript calls to question moral conduct and deals with the teen-aged narrator's first kiss from the older man associated with the first door, in the privacy of his room:

— Necesito besarte — dijo.
— Déjame — y su voz era de un tono que antes jamás le escuchara. Pensé, que no debía decírmelo, pues también yo deseaba que lo hiciera. Y le miré fijamente, sin pestañear; estaba muerta de ansiedad. Él cogió mis brazos y se fue acercando despacio; su mano izquierda pasó por mi espalda hacia el hombro y la derecha soltando el brazo subió por mi cuello y abierta me levantó el rostro y me besó. Sentí mi boca aplastada por sus labios y creí ahogarme, pues me faltaba la respiración, pero.... ¡Me estaba besando!

Cuando se apartó, escrudiñó mi rostro, pero no me soltó y de nuevo sus labios se acercaron a los míos. Ahora sentí los latidos de mi corazón y cerrando los ojos me olvidé de todo. (Ts. 21, Ms. 56)

The reproachable behavior lies in the narrator's desire and her failure to reject the kiss. The cinematographic description of the man's assertive movements in drawing her into him also points to a level of physical contact that would have encroached on a sense of moral propriety, especially given the age difference between the two.

The second passage under question describes the protagonist's physical encounter with a traveling salesman that moves from the kitchen to living room to bedroom:

— Soy la más dichosa de las mujeres [...].
— Ven — dijo él entonces levantándose, y cogida de la cintura me llevó hasta el centro de la sala.
Me abrazó fuerte, y yo, dando un suspiro, me eché hacia atrás y le miré. Él, que no me había soltado, me seguía sujetando, y nuestra mirada, la una en la otra, me fue serenando. Y de pronto supe con claridad meridiana, que él me deseaba, y que yo deseaba ser suya.
En sus ojos había una pregunta, y sin que sus labios dijeran nada, los míos formularon:
— Sí quiero — y añadí—. Aunque no te vuelva a ver nunca.
— ¿De veras?
Asentí sin palabras, y entonces, acercándose, me acarició. (Ts. 84, Ms. 196-97)

The next lines offer further contextalization of the implicit interaction between the two followed by a metaphoric erasure of that interaction:

— ¿Vamos? — dijo junto a mi oído, y yo le seguí.
Se marchó temprano, cuando aún era de noche. Entonces bajé a mi cuarto; pero en la casa de arriba no quedaba huella de lo ocurrido. Escondí la botella y luego de retirarlo todo, mis ojos miraron bien, por si descuidaba alguna cosa; mas todo daba la impresión de que

allí no había ocurrido nada; en apariencia, nada había ocurrido, pero yo nunca volvería a ser la misma. (Ts. 84, Ms. 197)

That this encounter happened when the housekeeper was away from the home means it was shrouded in secrecy, thereby accentuating taboo implications. It is perhaps this combination of concealed interaction in the private space that rescued this excerpt from deletion or revision.

The third marked passage narrates the visit of Antonio, an industrial engineer who was in Elche to set up machinery for a shoe factory and who would eventually become the narrator's husband. It is part of an extensive passage that appears on pages 217 to 219 in which the two characters negotiate the terms of their friendship-turned-romance that includes the following exchange, beginning with Antonio's affirmation:

— Necesito tenerte.
  Por favor, pedí asustada intentando soltarme —. Quiero irme;
— pero él me tenía cogida y supe que todo era inútil; en realidad no lo sentí. [...]
— Soy un hombre, y tú una mujer. ¿Es que no lo has comprendido? — y como yo estaba pensando lo mismo, ya no me resistí. (Ts. 94, Ms. 218)

Despite not loving him and knowing that he only be in town for about a month, this encounter happens because she felt that "a su lado era feliz" (219).

The next two sections identified in the censor's report refer to interactions with Michel, the French nephew of one of the houseguests. The censor underlines: "me hundí hambrienta en la maravilla tersa y clara de su cuerpo," despite ignoring as infringing on moral values the lines preceding this section: "noté como se soltaban los cierres del vestido. Siempre ocurría, y sentí mi carne descubierta" (Ts. 103, Ms. 238). Then, the following description continues in the outdoors when the narrator was lying down with Michel kneeling next to her at the edge of a stream: "La tierra estaba cálida y mi cuerpo se estiró voluptuoso.

Levanté los brazos con las palmas abiertas echándoles atrás y la sonrisa quedó quieta en mis labios al ver que se iba acercando; cuando fue a besarme, brusca, volví el rostro y entonces sus labios tocaron mi oreja" (Ts. 109, Ms. 251).

The last segments the censor noted pertain to the character associated with the seventh and final door, an Austrian archeologist. His platonic disposition toward the protagonist and her failed attempts to seduce him prompt her questions: "¿Es que no le interesan las mujeres?" (Ts. 120, Ms. 278) and "¿Es que jamás ha sentido deseos de poseer a una mujer?" (Ts. 121, Ms. 279). His revelatory silence dashes her hopes of a relationship with him. Lastly, the censor's red pen crossed off the author/narrator's declaration that would remove any doubt about the archeologist's sexual identity, which was excised in the final version of the text: "No le interesan las mujeres en absoluto" (Ts. 126). The posing of questions that remained unanswered, although provocative in the censors' view, veiled the implications of homosexuality enough to remain in the final text whereas the explicit affirmation was too overt and therefore excised.

The novel's route to publication consisting of three evaluations led to eventual authorization to publish after the third censor made the definitive determination. This path demonstrates the context in which multiple readings occur, as testimony to a dialogue internal to the censorship bureau. A novel identified as a potential candidate for the label of "deny publication," in this case on grounds that it poses a threat to morality for the specific actions of the protagonist, received a customary second read, in which that censor concurred with the first. With two recommendations to reject the possibility of publishing, it is the third censor's reading that salvages the novel, as he is an authority on ecclesiastical interpretation entrusted to uphold tenets of moral propriety.

ISABEL CALVO DE AGUILAR: *LA DANZARINA INMÓVIL* (1954)
Novelist, short story writer, and journalist Isabel Calvo de Aguilar (1916-1986) was best known as a mystery writer who set her creative works outside of Spain. She edited *Antología biográfica de escritoras españolas* (1954), one of the first anthologies of its kind, which disputes

the notion summarized by Pilar Sáenz that there were no important women writers in mid-20th century Spain ("Isabel Calvo" 87). [4] The scores of writers that appear in her anthology attest to a vibrant and nuanced literary scene of the time, and the collection opens the door to continued efforts to recover the literary memory of Spanish women writers of the mid-twentieth century. Calvo de Aguilar appears in several literary bibliographies, but critical reception of her work is scant. She was also the founder of the Asociación de Escritoras Españolas, serving as its president for six years (Sáenz, "Isabel Calvo" 87). *La danzarina inmóvil* is the author's third novel, one of four detective novels she published that included also *Doce sarcófagos de oro* (1951), *El misterio del palacio chino* (1951), *La isla de los siete pecados* (1952), and *El monje de los Balkanes* (n.d.).[5] Dubbed the Agatha Christie of Spain, Calvo de Aguilar cultivated primarily the subgenre of crime fiction. According to Shelley Godsland, women's detective fiction in mid-century Spain can be read as fundamentally feminist writing that articulates the authors' concerns about the "straitjacketing of women, their intellects, and aspirations, under the Franco regime" (*Killing Carmens*

---

    4   Calvo de Aguilar's critically overlooked anthology provides introductory biographical information followed by a selection of literary works of 85 authors of her time, including Mercedes Ballesteros, María Beneyto, Rosa María Cajal, Carmen Conde, Concha Espina, Mercedes Formica, Gloria Fuertes, Eulalia Galvarriato, Carmen Laforet, Luisa María Linares, Concha Linares-Becerra, Carmen Martín Gaite, Carmen de Icaza de Montejo, María de Gracia Ifach, Ana María Matute, Julia Maura, Dolores Medio, Elizabeth Mulder, Elena Soriano, Pura Vázquez, Ángeles Villarta Tuñón, and Concha Zardoya. The anthology points readers to lesser-studied writers such as Eugenia Alsina de la Torre, Josefina Carablas, María del Carmen Barberá, María Dolores Cuétara, María Luisa Gefaell, Gabriela Insúa, Josefina de la Maza, Blanca de los Ríos, Mercedes Tapiola Bualous, and Ana Voyson. The writers featured in the anthology cultivate genres of prose and poetry and adhere to various political ideologies. The featured writing spans the 1940s to the early 1950s.
    5   Further research is needed to locate this text, which does not appear in database indexing. Sources identify an alternate title, *El numismático*, which is identified as a short story in the journal *Meridiano* (vol. 1, 1958, pp. 30-36).

3).[6] For Calvo de Aguilar's choice in setting the majority of her novels outside of Spain, Conde Peñalosa observes that "las escritoras españolas, en los años cincuenta, exploran caminos narrativos en los que no solían adentrarse las autoras que les precedieron y uno de ellos es éste" (125). For Nicolás González Ruiz, Calvo de Aguilar's crime novels:

> están llenas de facilidad de expresión y rica fantasía que hace que se hallen al alcance de todos los públicos, ya que armonizan el interés y la intriga de cada una de sus obras con la aventura en paisajes a veces conocidos del lector, por tratarse de España y de África, o soñados, como los de China y la India. Baraja el amor y el odio, lo religioso y lo psicológico, haciendo de esta mezcla libros muy interesantes. (881-82)

Calvo de Aguilar's novels provide the opportunity to move beyond the first read in which the love story emerges, in order to examine a destabilized narrative of femininity that locates actions away from Spain as a way of testing thematic innovation and exploring alternative depictions of the traditionally domestic female protagonist.

The book jacket of *La danzarina inmóvil* includes the following description of the text: "Novela del género policial y de intriga precursora de la petrificación en los cadáveres, enero de 1954." The editor's note announces with this publication the inauguration of the collection Júpiter y Danae as an offering of the Madrid-based publisher, Rumbos:

> Nuestra idea es dar una muestra literaria de cada matiz, por la pluma maestra de los consagrados, cuyas obras completas no son asequibles a todas las fortunas, a la par que presentar nuevos valores, nuevos e indiscutibles valores como aquellos que por su propio

---

6   Godsland and White reference Calvo de Aguilar's cultivation of crime fiction as an introduction to their analysis of three Catalan detective writers (María Antònia Oliver Cabrer, Isabel-Clara Simó and Assumpta Margenat) and a selection of their novels published during the 1980s and 1990s. Calvo de Aguilar "reworked the classic English whodunit for a Spanish readership and enjoyed considerable success in the 1950s" (219).

mérito, llegaron al final de reñidísimos concursos, sin logar el galardón definitivo.

However, the collection only produced six additional titles through 1955.

In his *ABC* review of *La danzarina inmóvil*, Melchor Fernández Almagro notes the influence of Edgar Allan Poe for its blend of mystery, horror, lyricism, and psychology, but in a thinly veiled compliment he states that the author "al poner a máxima tensión sus recursos imaginativos, procura mantenerse en la línea legítima de la novela. Pero la verdad es que no siempre acierta a eludir los riesgos del folletín" (39). Fernández Almagro attributes much of the interest in this book "al hábil movimiento de la acción; a la rapidez, un poco esquemática, de los episodios, con salida y entrada de personajes al modo de los 'guiones'. Lo que en esa jerga llamaríamos 'secuencias' las referentes a Elisabeth, acusan fino tacto. Pero a veces la emoción literaria se le escapa de las manos a la autora demasiado atenta a la mecánica del relato" (39). The *folletín* characteristics observed upon the initial reading provide background plot movement rather than occupying a primary axis of the narration and include elements such as marriage as a cure for the male protagonist's psychopathy, the 26-year age difference between husband and wife, and differences in the protagonists' countries of origin as a way to dramatize the love story.

Toward the opening of the novel, the protagonists fall in love in Paris and move to New York, he a taxidermist from Argentina and she a ballerina from Russia. The talented ballet dancer's promising future is cut short when her husband murders her. The narrator, a writer-turned-private investigator, elucidates the crime committed by Alberto, so infatuated with his wife's physical beauty that he kills her in order to preserve her perfectly shaped body in taxidermy form.

For a brief plot summary and an evaluation of the novel's suitability for publication we turn to the novel's censorship file:

> Novela dramática. Alberto Castillo, taxidermista o disecador ya cuarentón, se ha enamorado de la bailarina Niska Pavlova [sic] casándose con ella. Se trata de un vesánico que, maestro en su profe-

sión de anatomista y disecador, concibe la criminal idea d petrificar la belleza y el arte de su mujer, convirtiéndola en estatua. Ello da lugar a la intervención de la policía cuando descubre el crimen. Alrededor de esta acción general se mueven unos cuantos personajes dando vida a este drama. La novela está bien construida. Deben desaparecer las líneas tachadas en las páginas 88, 95 y 96, demasiado realistas. (File *La danzarina*)

Calvo de Aguilar creates suspense through the curious objectification suggested by the antithetical title *La danzarina inmóvil*, contradicting the fluidity of a ballerina's gracefulness with a perpetual state of motionlessness. Calvo de Aguilar sets up the metafictional narration produced on the authority of a North American writer's sleuthing in which the opening scenes take place during Alberto's trial. The trial serves as a frame for the flashback narration recounted by the detective novelist who had served on a secret police force in the United States and then gave up that profession to obtain a degree in literature, "especializándose con gran éxito en el género policíaco" (16-17). This narrative strategy advances the novel's mystique by identifying the antecedents of the crime with its settings in locales foreign to Spain: Paris and New York. The macabre atmosphere is accentuated by the taxidermist's work aimed at the lifelike preservation of dead figures that not surprisingly include animals but in a chilling twist extend to human beings as well, first a young boy and then the titular character. The third-person narrator represents another wedge that distances the reader from the horrific crime against the young dancer.

Unlike hard-boiled detective fiction in which the male gumshoes discerns the identity of a cold-blooded killer, Calvo de Aguilar's novel is a very early forerunner of the cozy crime genre, a type of mystery novel that began circulating in the early 1990s. Marilyn Stasio summarizes that in the cozy crime novel, gore, and sex are kept to a minimum, characteristics that bode well for censorial approval (42).

The narration results from the detective's interviews with the subjects who provide evidence in the case that the perpetrator refuses to detail. As the novel progresses, the (meta)author focuses the plot on the relationships among the characters and the commentary on social and psychological malaise: "By oversimplifying the plot through the elimination of its trickier puzzle elements, cozy authors have also reduced the complexity of the crime-solving process and diminished the detective's intellectual role in that cognitive process" (Stasio 43). This simplification would align with the censor's observation that the novel is well-constructed, as the writer-detective has pieced together the puzzle for the reader.

The censor judges three sections as inappropriate, which ultimately the author removed in the published version. The first portion appears immediately after Alberto asks for Niska Poltova's hand in marriage. While a long kiss goodnight before turning out the lights receives the censorial nod, references to more overt physicality in their relationship, despite their implicit nature, were struck in the original typescript. These lines begin the morning after that kiss. Alberto has just proposed to Niska, with censor strikethrough here bracketed:

> — Nos casaremos. La primera visita a la ciudad será para unirnos en matrimonio ante el juez. [Déjame que te estreche otra vez.
> — ¡Alberto! Bésame y ve a tu trabajo.
> — Estás rendida, pequeña mía, de tanto amor. Tus ojos tienen huellas de la noche en vela y tu piel es como una azucena que hubieran estrujado bárbaramente mis manos. Perdóname]. (Ts. 80)

This exchange is replaced in the published novel with an ellipsis after the phrase "ante el juez" in the novel plus the following:

> — Nos casaremos. La primera visita a la ciudad será para unirnos en matrimonio ante el juez...
> — El hombre es bárbaro, y solamente cuando ha hallado la nitidez de la flor, es capaz de percibir su aroma. ¡La piel de azucena está herida, Niska, y la herí yo! Te herí para beber tu alma entera.
> — No me digas eso. No hables así. ¡Es tan dulce y maravilloso todo ahora en la vida! Baja a tu trabajo... Por favor... ¡Por favor! ... (Ms. 150)

The metaphoric language of the interplay between the flowers and the characters, in addition to adding a *novela rosa* undercurrent, align their relationship with acceptable moral values of decency and decorum.

In the second and third portions in question, Alberto refuses to accept Niska's pregnancy by telling her in the original typescript: "No, Niska, no permitiré nunca que la maternidad destroce tu bella escultura. Jamás. Tú serás siempre el ídolo puro de arte" and also the more inflammatory: "Hay que evitarlo" (Ts. 95-96). The published version underwent considerable modification: Niska ironically must console Alberto for his reaction to this news, as he experiences a sort of anxiety attack that has recently begun to suffer, by falsely denying her maternity to him. Her interior monologue reveals that she will avoid future pregnancies but under no circumstances will she terminate the current pregnancy. In terms of censorial authorization, Niska's benevolent attitude toward her unborn baby would have outweighed Alberto's request to terminate, positioning her as the redeemed good wife and future mother. The three instances of censored material are central to thwarting the protagonist's agency despite limitations her husband places on her throughout the novel, echoing Godsland's remarks on the symbolic straitjacketing of women.

In the end, the death of the mother translates to the death of the unborn child. The restored social order through Castillo's conviction is of small consequence. Aggression against the female body attacks both marriage and maternity, perpetuating a narrative of confinement of the female character that aligns with Francoist discourse.[7] However, in order to restore social order disrupted by these heinous acts, the trope of the detective story provides the opportunity to criminalize Alberto's actions, thus accentuating his transgressive behavior as a

---

7   Aggression against the female body is a thematic thread that serves multiple purposes. In *La danzarina inmóvil*, aggression as a vehicle to the confinement of the female body is a measure of extreme violence, though it yields to justice in the husband's court-sanctioned culpability. In *En manos del silencio*, Cristina's miscarriage and eventual fatal car accident is punishment for her transgressions. María's rape in *La ciudad perdida* marks the vulnerability of an innocent, wealthy woman unable to protect herself from the atrocity committed by a political pariah, whereas Torcuata's rape in *Martín Nadie* is testimony to violence women experience in a harsh environment.

metanarrative construct that contests the restriction of feminine subjectivity.

CARMEN KURTZ: *AL LADO DEL HOMBRE* (1961)
Carmen Kurtz (née Carmen de Rafael Marés, 1911-1999) published her first novel *Duermen bajo las aguas* in 1954, winning the Planeta Prize for her next novel *El desconocido* (1956). That same year also saw the publication of two more novels, with six others in the 1960s. Kurtz continued publishing novels through the 1970s and published short stories throughout her literary career, many of them prizewinning, until the early 1990s. Because she was living in France at the time of the Spanish Civil War and returned to Spain in 1943, "although she often writes about the impact of the war, she does so from a social rather than a political point of view" (Gordenstein 326). According to Antonio Iglesias Laguna, Kurtz self-identified as a member of the middle class whose reflective voice championed the bourgeois reality (242). As Montejo Gurruchaga explains, Kurtz's work, like that of other women authors of her time, eluded critical study; it was not until the 1980s that her writing gained traction in the critical arena, whether as the focus of a specific study (Pérez, *Contemporary Women Writers*) or in studies that situated her work within the literary panorama of her time, such as those by Concha Alborg and Ignacio Soldevila Durante, or that included her in literary biographies, for example, those edited by Galerstein or Gould Levine ("La narrativa de Carmen Kurtz" 408).

Kurtz's fifth novel, *Al lado del hombre* (1961), features the extended conversation between protagonists Carla, a 23-year-old single woman, and an unnamed married man in his forties, which for its premise would appear to place the work in the *novela rosa* subgenre. The action takes place almost exclusively aboard a train as the protagonists journey from Bilbao to Barcelona seated next to one another to provide a safe context that allows for their extended conversation to unfold. However, analysis of the narrative structure combined with Carla's articulation of ideas that challenge gender-prescribed identity allow for a nuanced reading to resist the *novela rosa* label.[8] This section builds upon Montejo Gurruchaga's critical interpretations and analysis of the novel including its censorship reports (*Discurso de autora* 73-77).[9] As Montejo Gurruchaga explains, numerous passages were slated for alteration and excision, but Kurtz decided to remove them entirely rather than engage in a back-and-forth exchange with the censors. According to Montejo Gurruchaga, the suppressed passages "son significativos porque atañen a la férrea asignación de roles establecida a mujeres y hombres y a la reflexión sobre la necesidad de romper con los límites de género impuestos" (*Discurso de autora* 76). The deleted sections include those that legitimize divorce (focalized from the point of view of Carla), encourage a young woman to experience intimacy with men before marriage (focalized from the point of view of her travel companion), and portray the Spanish Civil War as one of fratricide. With Carla's protagonism, Kurtz poses an alternative to the domestic woman through her textual positioning exclusively outside the home. Carla's exploration of sexuality through words and actions resists and questions the patriarchy.

The novel received three evaluations before gaining authorization to publish. In a report dated 22 October 1959, the first censor judges the quality of the novel's themes, concluding that the minimal sub-

---

8   Montejo Gurruchaga refers to *Al lado del hombre* as a *novela rosa* ("La narrativa de Carmen Kurtz" 412), written "bajo los moldes de la novela rosa" (*Discurso de autora* 73), while at the same time recognizing that "resulta ser una transgresión del canon de esta tendencia; cuestionará los comportamientos sexuales masculino y femenino, presentará fantasías femeninas de poder y libertad sexuales, discutirá la pasividad característica de la heroína de la novela rosa, cambiará el final cerrado por un final abierto y pondrá en cuestión otros mitos y herencias de la tradición patriarcal y eclesiástica" ("La narrativa de Carmen Kurtz" 412).

9   The primary sources of this analysis appear in Montejo Gurruchaga's *Discurso de autora: género y censura en la narrativa española de posguerra* (2010), and "La narrativa de Carmen Kurtz: compromiso y denuncia de la condición social de la mujer española de posguerra" (2006) and "Realismo, testimonio y censura en la obra de Carmen Kurtz" (2005).

stance does not meet the threshold for publication due to the threat to morality:

> Es lamentable que la señora Kurtz tan acreditada por su talento novelístico haya escrito esta novela que revela claro es sus condiciones de fantasía y de observación, pero en este caso para nutrir la sustancia de su narración, que ocupa unas brevísimas páginas, y todas ellas deshonestas e inmorales. Porque se trata de un viaje donde se encuentra un caballero con una señorita decente. (File *Al lado*)

If by *fantasía* he refers to imagination, and this combined with observation, then the censor is simply describing the creative process that could be applicable to a vast majority of creative writing. The *brevísimas páginas* contain Carla's thoughts that Kurtz sets apart with parenthetical and italicized text, usually several pages long, and usually a few times per chapter, in chapters ranging from 30 to 50 pages in length. The encounter between the protagonists is based on random seat assignment; the phrase "señorita decente" means that she is virginal, even though a multitude of her thoughts push the boundaries of moral decency.

The report continues:

> La consecuencia del viaje estriba en que llegados a la capital ocupan el mismo hotel, y luego de cenar y de darse un breve paseo, al retornar el señor al hotel, ve en la habitación que ocupa la señorita una llave, y abriendo oye la voz de la mujer que desde la cama le dice: "te esperaba." Por lo visto se acuesta con ella: y ella al final "sigue con sus manos el cuerpo del hombre como si quisiera retenerlo en su memoria." Téngase en cuenta que se trata de una "señorita decente," a quien nadie ha tocado. Donosa novelística que encuentra solo por sus temas "humanos" tales especies. NO DEBE PUBLICARSE. (File *Al lado*)

Textual ambiguity leads the censor to infer the intimate relations between the two characters through his own language that refrains from plainly naming the action—by employing the term "por lo visto" and then quoting directly from the manuscript—although he clearly conveys that the encounter was mutual.

Montejo Gurruchaga explains that the publisher (Planeta) requested a second read upon learning of the initial assessment ("Realismo, testimonio" 219). In a report dated 28 March 1960, the second censor disregards the novel's parenthetical text, which includes many of the problematic areas the first censor identified, and euphemistically explains the novel's ending, before authorizing publication on the condition that areas considered threatening to morality on pages 97, 111, 144, and 145 be addressed:

> Una novela no puede llamarse precisamente ejemplar, y casi no novela. En efecto, se trata pura y simplemente de la conversación—sobre todo lo divino y lo humano—de dos personas, hombre y mujer, en un viaje desde Bilbao a Barcelona. Al fin, en un hotel en Barcelona, ella y él "se conocen" en sentido bíblico. Novela discursiva, hay algunas afirmaciones que llegan a lo inconveniente. De entre ellas, es necesario expurgar las anotadas arriba. Con dicha salvedad, PROCEDE LA AUTORIZACION CON LAS TACHADURAS ANOTADAS. (File *Al lado*)

In order to definitively determine viability to publish, the novel proceeded to a third evaluation. In the last report, the censor identifies infractions dealing with morality and adds another layer of contention by calling to question the portrayal of the Spanish Civil War:

> Novela. Una soltera y un casado viajan juntos desde Bilbao a Barcelona, intercambiando puntos de vista sobre diversos motivos, pero especialmente sobre el matrimonio. La conversación deriva a la relación afectiva con concesiones de hecho a la inmoralidad, tanto más censurables cuanto que la actitud general es de franca indecisión y ambigüedad en los principios. Se critica por anticuada la regulación del matrimonio y su indisolubilidad, y se insinúa como solución un posible "ensayo" previo. Por otra parte, se confunde la conciencia con la costumbre y la Cruzada española, con

una vulgar guerra civil. Por ello, debieran suprimirse o modificarse los subrayados de las págs. 47, 61, 97, 102, 103 y 145. (File *Al lado*)

In addition, the numbers 111 and 144 are handwritten on the report in red ink. The third read was indeed a careful one in that the censor noticed the phrase *guerra civil*, calling it *vulgar* and replacing the term in his report with *Cruzada española*, showing that even two decades after the conclusion of the war, its naming mattered, reflecting the principles held by the winning side.

Questionable text that Kurtz removed in the printed novel refer to marriage as an antiquated rite of passage joining people based not on love but rather on the concept of social contract, which would have appeared following Carola's statement: "Quizás sea la decisión más importante de la vida. Es como jugársela a cara o cruz. Como una lotería" (Ms. 67). Kurtz removed the part of the male protagonist's reaction in response to the censor-stricken passages below that appear in brackets:

> — Exactamente no es eso. En la lotería no se pierde — en caso de no ganar — más que aquello que se ha apostado. En un matrimonio fallido, la mujer y el hombre lo pierden todo. [Pero es difícil luchar contra las costumbres. Los pueblos instituyeron ceremonias y leyes de matrimonio antes de conocer el amor. El amor es un sentimiento totalmente civilizado. Pero esas ceremonias y esas leyes siguen en vigor y han sido reforzados antes de haber sufrido una natural reforma]. (Ts. 47, Ms. 67)

In another instance, the married man reminisces about his previous sexual encounters, including with his wife, Laura. The text bracketed here appears in the typescript with a red line through it and is omitted from the published version for its portrayal of a woman's entering into matrimony as a rote response to social imperatives:

> Podía decirse que éste seguía la trayectoria de la entrega de antemano prevista, pero sabiamente regulada para que él, *el hombre*, quedara bien asentado en su papel de seductor. [La entrega de Laura había sido sencilla, sin ruegos, sin frases, sin condiciones, sin falso pudor. Se entregaba como una prueba más de confianza hacia él,

pues Laura era inocente y aquel paso en su vida lo dio tan segura, tan auténticamente como daba otros. Recordaba su frase, eso sí: "Para siempre." Para siempre]. (Ts. 97, Ms. 131, emphasis original)

Because censors considered the war a crusade, or *una guerra de liberación*, they rarely accepted the qualifiers *civil* or, in the case of *Al lado del hombre*, *fratricida*, requiring the removal of the phrase the male protagonist employs, which the censor crossed off in red ink:

— [...] Si es cierto que a las chicas de hoy no les interesa la guerra de ayer, es lamentable. [...] Pero sin olvidar que las chicas de hoy son hijas de padres que hicieron esa guerra, una guerra fratricida cuyas consecuencias sociales son de tal índole que Francia necesitó cincuenta años para consolidar la suya. (Ts. 102-103).

However, this fragment does not appear in the published novel when the two characters are discussing the young woman's age compared to the age of the male passenger's wife.

The excised reference to fratricide shifts focus away from the reminder that the war destroyed families when Francoist messaging emphasized the importance of protecting the family and preserving its patriarchal structure: "The social project of the Franco regime may best be defined as paternalism, an extraordinarily pervasive and long-lasting ideology. [...] The prospect of domesticity, a belief in paternal authority, appeals to the 'natural' order" (Vincent 168).

The following passage referring to the war appears in the typescript and was removed from the published version, with the text bracketed here struck through with the censor's red ink:

— ¿En qué lado combatió usted?
— Eso no tiene importancia, créame. [Todos combatieron en el lado que les cupo en suerte. Lo único importante es el hecho.
— ¿Y qué opina usted del hecho?
Se quedó mirándola fijamente, en silencio. Luego repuso:
— Que todas las injusticias y todos los errores cometidos en una guerra civil son siempre superiores a la justicia que haya podido alcanzarse.] (Ts. 145, Ms. 192)

Carla's forward behavior toward her fellow passenger resists the regime's social project that called for the passive or submissive model of femininity as a way of exhibiting her opposition of this dominant power structure: "The reassertion of the family had also to mean a recovery of domesticity" (Vincent 169). Carla's resistance of this posturing can again be gleaned from her actions at novel's end. The novel concludes as the man is about to leave but heeds to Carla's asserted sense of agency. The original ending reads:

— ¿Dime?
    Ella negó con la cabeza mientras con la mano le indicaba que se fuera en silencio.
    La contempló *aún* por un instante. Luego, cerró la puerta. (Ts. 248, emphasis added).

The printed version replaces "aún" with "indeciso" (Ms. 289), a subtle yet significant revision, to imply that his final interaction with her was met with a question instead of a lingering gaze.

In *Al lado del hombre*, Kurtz relies on the dialogic interplay between the protagonists to create an alternative narrative to domesticity. Kurtz allows a young woman who travels unchaperoned to articulate her agency through both verbalized conversation and interior monologue. She navigates in a public space outside the confines of her family's watchful eye. The censors' requisite revisions smoothed Carla's distancing from normative portrayal, but her independent spirit and actions liberate her from that normativity. The censorship process of this novel was a bit unusual because of the second and third readings after an initial rejection, as an example of the explicit negotiation through correspondence between the author and the censorship board in order to reach an agreement on the terms of publication.

Concha Alós: *El caballo rojo* (1966)

Concha Alós (1922-2011) published nine novels and a short story collection in the period spanning 1958-1986. She is among the writers of her time who have gained literary acclaim for her social realist writing not at the time of publication of her work but beginning in the mid-

1980s.¹⁰ Alós sets the action of her fifth novel *El caballo rojo* (1966) during the last year of the Spanish Civil War and its immediate aftermath. Although, as Juan Carlos Martín states "The 1966 Press Law decreased censorship, facilitating an increase of civil war literature from the perspective of those who lost the war" (208), *El caballo rojo*, evaluated in May 1966 was likely written before the April passage of this law and clearly exemplifies this shift in writing as it adopts the perspective of the vanquished. Because it does so from the perspective of the suffering and hardships the Republicans endured, rather than presenting them in a heroic or glorified light, censors saw fit to authorize its publication as long as Alós incorporated a handful of revisions.¹¹

---

10   Montejo Gurruchaga summarizes the gradual entry of Alós's work in the critical space ("La narrativa realista de Concha Alós" 176-77) and contributes to the evaluation of the Alós as a social realist author through an analysis of her first five novels.

11   Juan Carlos Martín gives the example of *Las ultimas banderas* (1967) by Angel María de Lera as a text featuring the perspective of "those who lost the war" (208), but it is important to turn to the novel's censorship file to contextualize how this occurred. The novel gained reluctant authorization after edits were incorporated as the censors expressed a sense of exigency that forced them to this approval because the novel had won the Planeta Prize. A portion of the novel's file reads:

> Novela literariamente deficiente, tanto por el escaso interés argumental, como por la falta de auténtica vida y vigor en los personajes, y sobre todo por el más grave defecto del mal conocimiento del idioma. [...] El escaso argumento novelístico se refiere a las actuaciones de los protagonistas en la épica de nuestra Guerra de liberación y fundamentalmente en la zona roja, y como todos los personajes, al menos los principales, son partidarios adictos al Frente popular, sus acciones y pensamientos en la novela responden a esa tesitura, que es la que en el fondo viene a ser la que le simpatiza al autor, y así se trasluce de tal modo en la lectura, que el personaje principal, el Federico, se halla en ese sentido tan idealizado como héroe principal, que parece responder a experiencias y a tendencias sentimentales del propio autor, dándole cierto tinte autobiográfico al citado protagonista.
>
> [...] se expresan juicios de valor claramente inaceptables, por cuanto pugnan por los principios que informaron nuestra Cruzada y por tanto

The novel narrates the Alegre family's abandonment of city of Castellón, their life as refugees in Lorca, and then their return to Castellón upon the conclusion of the war. Félix Alegre and his family were forced to abandon their home in Castellón because of the ravages of war, escaping during a dreadful bombardment that killed Félix's infant son. The title refers to the café where Félix worked that served as a meeting space for displaced Republican sympathizers who as patrons represent a social collective. The novel's young protagonist is Isabel Alegre, Félix's daughter who is compelled to make sense of the chaos and confusion surrounding her family and their new environment.

The portrayal of the different characters that frequent the café contributed to the critical interpretation of the novel as a portrait of the social panorama in Lorca during the last year of the civil war, what Arias Careaga calls "a mosaic of characters" (148). In spite of the multiple characters—Janet Pérez affirms that the novel lacks a central

> contrarios al Movimiento Nacional, tal como el concepto viene expuesto en el preámbulo de la Ley de Principios de Movimiento.
>
> [...] Dado el carácter de premio público concedido a ésta y en evitación de la propaganda que se le pudiera hacer con una denegación, consideramos indispensable se líen, atenúen o borren tales conceptos y expresiones indicándolo así, pies de lo contrario creemos que la novela y su autor son denunciable con arreglo al art 165 bis b) del Cod. Penal. (File *Las ultimas banderas*)

One of the excised sections of the novel would have appeared on page 375 of the edition consulted:

> Todo el país está en el podrido de odio: el aire, la tierra, las gentes... ¿Y qué hará la iglesia cuando esto termine? Hasta ahora no ha hecho más que azuzar, bendiciendo a unos y aludiendo a otros. ¡Qué obispos más terribles! Pero tal vez los curas hayan aprendido algo. ¿Cuándo se enterarán de que el pueblo no los odia por curas, sino porque se siente traicionado por ellos, precisamente porque los querría tener consigo, a su lado? Para nuestro pueblo, una revolución con curas, toques de campana, procesiones delirantes, sería la ideal. Nuestro pueblo odia a los curas por despecho. Si muchos asaltaron las iglesias y se llevaron luego imágenes a sus casas...Si el nuestro es todavía un pueblo beato.

protagonist (112)—Alós focalizes much of the narration on Isabel. She inhabits a doubly hostile world first for the historical period and second for the subaltern positioning of femininity that classifies the woman in traditional terms: the woman as a good mother, wife, nurse, and daughter, or the materialistic and superficial woman allied with a soldier solely for convenience, showing no signs of her own identity except in her subaltern relationship with a man, as observed by the third-person narration. Alós belongs to the group of writers who published in the second phase of censorship legislation (post 1962) "with no visible quarrel with the regime [who turned] to retelling the Civil War and mulling over the nature of (middle-class or picturesquely peasant) social relations in the twenty-five and more years of 'Peace' (Perriam et al. 19). Perriam et al. posit that women's writing during this time often "combines lyrical subjectivity and social critique in novels which focus on psychological analysis and emotional probing of characters through narrative devices such as introspection and retrospective recall, multiple perspectives, and stream of consciousness" (19).

The detachment of the selfless omniscient narrator who portrays models of the traditional woman of her time, in turn, situates that narrator as the spokesperson of an objective author who comments on the reality that surrounded her during the span of the year. Giving voice to the different scenes that Alós's narrator describes reflects tangentially a political stance, and this subtlety in part would likely have contributed to the approval of the censors. Along with the description of the domestic tasks of the female characters, Alós allows subversive elements to enter the narration. For example, Elizabeth Ordóñez has observed that secondary character, Nanín, married to a soldier so as not to go hungry during this difficult period, throws away birth control pills hidden from her husband (42). In addition to the power that a woman may exercise over her body, Isabel, who has the most biographical connection with the author, tries to improve her situation through education. However, the decrepit educational system and the scarcity of resources impede her plan, and the young woman loses the courage to study. A marked predilection for the acquisition of knowledge surfaces in references to both the books that inform her thoughts and her frequent moments of contemplation. Women who overcome their circumstances, such as the sisters Amparo and Serafina, reveal a spirit of resistance in the patriarchal environment of the dictatorship, Amparo for her rejection of marriage and Serafina for her frequent absence in her mother's knitting circle. The symbolism of birds and cages overlayed on characters who are confined—in hiding to avoid political persecution based on ideology or in shelters to avoid bombings—accentuates the subalternity of Republican refugees in Lorca during the war.

The censorship report reveals that the novel in its original form constituted a threat to dominant ideology. The censor considered the use of the word *fascistas* excessive and called the text's favorable rendering of Republicans dangerous. The reason—"ello puede crear entre los jóvenes lectores una peligrosa identificación política con sistemas pasados" (File *El caballo rojo*)—reveals the sense of ideological division the regime would have wanted to suppress even 25 years after the war. The resulting substitution of the term *nacionales* for *fascistas* softens considerably the author's message intended to highlight the difficulties of Republican refugees as a result of political rife during the Civil War. The substituted term also connotes the idea of nation or nation building as an ideological campaign central to the regime's discourse. The censor's annotation, however, does not take into account the injustices the family and their acquaintances suffer for their identification as Republicans. Alós's displaced Alegre family withstands, for example, the mother's mental illness as a result of the grief she experiences in the aftermath of her infant son's death in the bombardment in Castellón that forced their move. The havoc wreaked on the broken family also negatively impacts the adolescent Isabel, illustrating the scope of war's destruction that extends beyond the battlefield. The positioning of Republicans who endure numerous hardships as a direct consequence of their political ideology perpetuates the notion of their subalternity, which firmly anchors the prevailing and predominating Nationalist ideology.

This novel received evaluation by two censors who both authorized publication with revisions to tidy up the ideological references that cast the Nationalists in a less-than-positive light. The first report summarizes the novel's temporal-spatial referents:

La presente novela, ambiente bélico, se sitúa en el pueblo de Lorca y se vive durante el último año de nuestra Cruzada. Se traslada allí una familia compuesta por un matrimonio y una hija, como evacuados de Castellón de donde huyen para evitar caer en manos de las fuerzas nacionales. Se viven numerosas escenas propias de la época presididas siempre por la escasez de alimentos, dificultades de hospedaje y de trabajo y demás miserias propias de la situación. El final de la obra termina con el regreso de la familia a su Castellón. (File *El caballo rojo*)

Conservative sympathies permeate the report, from identifying the Spanish Civil War as *nuestra Cruzada* to the normalization of the refugees' poor quality of life, which comes across as just consequences of falling on the wrong side of the ideological conflict.

The report continues:

Aunque la obra está escrita desde el lado republicano, no trata de hacer política negativa, se impone la objetividad y ridiculizan algunas consignas rojas ("Resistir hasta el final," "No pasarán, etc.") viendo el final victorioso Nacional entre las aclamaciones del pueblo por el ansia de una paz definitiva. (File *El caballo rojo*)

However, the mere act of portraying the difficulties of the Alegre family and their fellow Republican refugees is testimony of the negative political representation. The censor proceeds to indicate how Alós is to amend her text based on its political messaging:

No obstante, creemos contraproducente el excesivo empleo de la palabra "FASCISTA" para designar las tropas nacionales, aun reconociendo que es puesta en boca de diálogo de personajes del pueblo y que ese vocablo era el comúnmente usado en aquella zona (págs. 6, 11, 13, 37, 51, 99, 111, 157, 199, 206 y 211); ello puede crear entre los jóvenes lectores una peligrosa identificación política con sistemas pasados. (File *El caballo rojo*)

For this censor, the novel outlines what would be considered the correct natural order of the Nationalist victory. Although the objective tone may be understood as simply one that conveys the facts in Alós's fictional world, the result is that this Civil War narrative speaks to the large-scale displacement of families forced to abandon Castellón during the Ofensiva de Levante between April and July 1938. The novel, divided in sections corresponding to the four seasons, begins soon after the family had moved to Lorca in July, with a clear distinction of the two ideological sides. The censor notes the overuse of the word 'fascist' not explicitly because it is a misrepresentation, but because young readers in a time about 25 years after the war ended—a generation removed—may misapply the meaning given the historical significance of the term during World War II and its aftermath.

This first report's concluding paragraph references suspect material in need of removal and grants authorization to publish: "Por otro lado, hay dos alusiones que estimamos deben ser suprimidas: Página 37 y página 69, alusión inequívoca a Queipo de Llano.[12] Consideradas estas objeciones, no existe inconveniente en que sea PUBLICADA" (File *El caballo rojo*).

The second report makes note of the overlap between the author's portrayal of personal circumstances as fictional representation, suggesting that the censor would have been aware of the author's biographical profile, which is plausible given that *El caballo rojo* is the Alós's fifth novel and that her her fourth, *Las hogueras*, generated a fair amount of press as the Planeta Prize recipient in 1964.[13]

---

12   Gonzalo Queipo de Llano (1875-1951) was a Nationalist military leader responsible for tens of thousands of executions in his efforts to take over the city of Seville during the early phase of Spanish Civil War.

13   The censorship file on *Las hogueras*, which includes the report and a separate paper with the heading of "Ampliación del informe," identifies the theme of the adulterous female protagonist and also notes that the action is removed from Spain's cultural epicenter. The decentralized location of the narration is a strategy authors employed to locate characters' transgressions as occurring in spatial periphery: "Sobre el fondo de un lugar de la isla de Mallorca, Sibila, la joven y elegante mujer del maduro Archivald, pasa su aburrimiento añorando los días en que triunfaba en París como la modelo más cotizada. Ella, que no es feliz con su marido, quien además por razón de enfermedad, la tiene un tanto abandonada, busca el amor cerca del "Mon-

> Novela con influencia autobiográfica de nuestra guerra, relatada desde la zona republicana. A través de un café—que da el título—y varios grupos de personajes, se narran los postreros días de la resistencia roja en la región valenciana. Llegan a Lorca refugiados de Castellón y otros lugares, teniendo que acogerse donde buenamente pueden y pasar las calamidades de la guerra. Esta sólo se ve y se refleja en la población civil, por lo que carece de exposiciones ideológicas o militares. (File *El caballo rojo*)

The autobiographical referents capture the author's family situation during the war and position the protagonist as several years younger than the author would have been at the time the events occurred. The censor then proffers an analysis of the author's poor quality of writing style and attributes the narrative jumble to her faulty recollections of events over two decades removed. By questioning the rigor of the author's narrative expression, the censor in essence locates her outside the upper echelons of the Spain's literary community, and therefore she poses no threat to dominant ideology.

> El relato es bastante incoherente y mal escrito, como resultado de una memoria imperfecta de los acontecimientos. No tiene fuerza dramática ni arquitectura literaria digna. Aquí y allá se denominan "fascistas" a las fuerzas nacionales, pero sin intención peyorativa: simple vocabulario en gentes que vivían en aquella zona. En págs.

---

egro," tosco trabajador, con el que proyecta huir y emprender una nueva vida en París. Fracasado el proyecto, después de este breve y desesperado vuelo hacia la felicidad, Sibila propuso el matrimonio queda encallado en la "diaria y baja rutina." En resumen, se trata de una historia más de adulterio, narrada literariamente. PUEDE AUTORIZARSE" (File *Las hogueras*). The expanded report concludes that "De ninguna manera puede considerarse que en la presente novela su tesis sea la defensa o apología del adulterio" (File *Las hogueras*). This classification shifts the interpretation of *Las hogueras* as a *novela rosa*, a convenient insinuation that would solidify the chances that the novel is accepted for publication. Although it would not reach the public eye, this internal consideration derails chances the novel would be taken seriously by critics, and under the censorship purview this writing is non-threatening to the regime.

69 y 71 hay menciones poco respetuosas de Queipo de Llano y de Yagüe.[14] En la p. 157 un juicio menospreciativo, pero propio del personaje. Nada de esto, sin embargo, parece condenable a la luz del criterio actual, pero la Superioridad decidirá. (File *El caballo rojo*)

The censor grants authorization to publish under the following conditions handwritten in red ink:

Suprimirse pág. 37, 69, 71
  Y sustituir la palabra "fascista" por "nacionales" cuando no se trate de un diálogo.
  Puede autorizarse. (File *El caballo rojo*)

Regarding semantics, both reports accept the use of *fascista* when it appears in dialogue but insist on replacing the term with *nacionales* elsewhere, as hand-marked with brackets in red ink, changes that appear in the final print. This happens with the example of page 37 in the typescript that refers to the level of destruction in the city of Castellón in the aftermath of the Nationalist strike on the Republican stronghold: "Por aquellos días toda la ciudad levantina estaba atesada de gente trashumante y desastrada; eran los que habían huido de los pueblos que iban conquistando los fascistas" whereas the last word became *nacionales* in the printed novel (Ms. 48). Indeed, descriptions of the difficult living conditions abound in the novel, both of the displaced refugees and also the strain their presence puts on the city of Lorca, articulated by a local resident observes as one of numerous examples: "Los refugiados. [...] Pedigüeños. Siempre pedían. Andaban por el pueblo muertos de hambre, mal vestidos, realquilados" (Ms. 84-85). Further, on page 37 of the typescript, this dialogue keeps the permitted use of *fascistas*, but requires removing the reference to them as *verdugos*. The fragment under consideration conveys Alegre's

---

14 Juan Yagüe (1891-1952) was a Nationalist military leader. After joining Queipo de Llano in Seville he advanced to Badajoz where he headed the 1936 Battle of Badajoz and then ordered the execution of 2,000-4,000 citizens (Preston 270) in what came to be known as the Massacre of Badajoz.

response to a late-night knock on his door by the military patrol who are searching for members of the Fifth Column. He responds, in the typescript: "Somos de Castellón — les dijo — y hemos venido a Valencia huyendo de los fascistas, porque no hemos querido caer *en manos de esos verdugos*" (Ts. 37, emphasis added), which is replaced with the more overtly tempered "Somos de Castellón — les dijo — y hemos venido a Valencia huyendo de los fascistas, porque no hemos querido caer en sus manos" (Ms. 49).

Historical references casting two prominent Nationalist leaders, Gonzalo Queipo de Llano y Juan Yagüe, in unfavorable light require modification. The textual references to Queipo de Llano occur in the context of two patrons of the café who are discussing the possible end of the war with a victory for the Republican side:

— Si Radio París no nos engaña, el asunto se va poniendo bien. Otro invierno apretándonos el cinturón y España será nuestra.
— Pues Queipo dice que no. ¿Qué sabe Queipo?
— ¡Un borracho es ese! ¡Un borracho, sinvergüenza! (Ts. 69)

In the printed novel, however, the phrases "¡Un borracho es ese!" and "¡Un borracho, sinvergüenza!" do not appear. The patrons continue discussing the present state of affairs, and at the behest of the censors, the original text was revised:

— ¿No han oído lo del discurso de Yagüe?
— No. ¿Qué pasa?
— Yagüe soltó un discurso en que los italianos eran unos cagones y que los únicos que los tenían bien puestos y sabían luchar eran los soldados republicanos. (Ts. 71)[15]

---

15   Reinforcing the themes of social justice, forgiveness, and reconciliation, Yagüe delivered his speech in Burgos on 19 April 1938 in response to the Republican president Manuel Azaña's speech the day before in Barcelona titled "Paz, piedad, perdón." Yagüe's speech conveyed in terms that were considered detrimental to Franco's campaign his vision for a path away from war. Guillermo Valiente describes the speech as "la máxima muestra del deseo de unidad que él había albergado desde el inicio de la guerra y está

In the novel, the last lines read: "Yagüe soltó un discurso cargándose a los italianos y a los alemanes y diciendo que los republicanos somos unos tíos luchando" (Ms. 88), an evident softening of the verbiage. María Álvarez and Cristina Somolinos Molina's claim that these previous two excisions "no modificaban el significado de la novela" (189) merits attention. Is it true that the novel's meaning was not changed? If they do not change the novel's meaning, why did the censor require their removal? In response to the first question, the intention of censorship is not merely or only to change the entire meaning of the text but to identify threatening passages, even if they refer to events that transpired decades earlier. The portrayal of Nationalist soldiers as executioners, the unflattering portrayal of Queipo de Llano, and Yagüe's exaltation of Nationalist soldiers clash with the censors' concept of historical memory intent on preserving the dignity and righteousness of the Nationalist cause.

A fourth revision between the typescript and printed novel was made, although it was not required per the censorship report, and appears to reflect an act of self-censorship, in an effort to align with other revisions that were deemed necessary. The phrase provided by the third-person narrator reflecting the fear instilled in one of the characters would have appeared on page 216 in the printed novel but is (in)conspicuously absent: "Corrían voces de que los fascistas metían gente en la cárcel" (Ts. 199). With this textual removal Alós sidesteps any insinuation that her perspective casts the victors of war in a negative light.

The novel's treatment of the characters for their collective portrayal adds a level of distance between the third-person narrator and the events described. Isabel, similar to the other female characters, experiences adverse conditions on two fronts: her hostile world marked by wartime turmoil and the subjugation of women as wife/mother/daughter precluded from exercising agency and dependent upon men

---

fuertemente influenciado por el ideario nacionalsindicalista que profesaba, algo que se pone de manifiesto en la petición de piedad para los falangistas presos. No sólo se limita a pedir perdón y comprensión hacia los enemigos, sino que incide también en la importancia de la justicia y del bienestar de los más necesitados" (79).

for their well-being.[16] For Genaro Pérez, the novel reconstructs "incidentes [que] se cuentan por medio de un punto de vista omnisciente que se desplaza de un personaje a otro recogiendo pensamientos, recuerdos, e incidentes y poniéndolos en contrapunto" (44). This distance also serves the purpose of lending objectivity to what is a tangential memorialization of past events as testimonial rather than critical of those events. The novel's careful attention to the characters' psychological development offers the possibility to study thematically, for example, how post-traumatic stress disorder manifests in Isabel's mother following the catastrophic death of her child as a result of wartime bombings, as well as the refugees living conditions. *El caballo rojo* resists the notion that women's writing of Alós's time elides politically charged content. Although the narrative strikes censors required may appear to be minimal, they nonetheless preclude Alós from conflating fascism with nationalist ideology, a distinction censors insisted on making. Naming the war *Cruzada* further accentuates the religious undertones of Nationalist ideology and emphasized war's opposing sides that consisted of a morally superior faction that needed to squash the morally or ideologically bankrupt Other.

OBSERVATIONS

Brufal, Calvo de Aguilar, Kurtz, and Alós present female protagonists who resist or question the models of domesticity configured by patriarchy. Their novels experienced between one and three censorship evaluations because of concerns that sections relating to morality, religion, or the regime breached the bounds of official discourse. Although a first and even a second evaluation may not endorse publication rights, the third censor made the final determination to authorize, except for Calvo de Aguilar's novel, which received one evaluation. The type of edits required in her novel, minimal in number yet nonetheless text altering, combined with her previous record of publication were sufficient for attaining authorization based on one evaluation. The sole

---

16   Thematically speaking, the lack of access to education is one of underlying issues in many novels of the period under study that precludes women from participating in social, political, economic, and professional engagement beyond domesticity.

censorship report includes the praise that the novel is well-constructed, unlike the other three in this section, which use various terms to delegitimize the quality of the writing. This ranges from scenes "cínicamente presentadas" (File *Siete puertas*), to certain pages considered "todas ellas deshonestas e inmorales" (File *Al lado*), to a story that is "bastante incoherente y mal escrito, como resultado de una memoria imperfecta de los acontecimientos" (File *El caballo rojo*).

The revision of text related to intimacy between a married couple and the termination of pregnancy moves the contents of Calvo de Aguilar's novel away from threatening morality and religious dogma. However, despite what were initially perceived as the protagonist's behavioral transgressions in Brufal's novel, the only one of eight questionable passages that the author removed dealt with an explicit reference to one of the characters as homosexual, whereas implicit references to premarital sexual activity remained in the novel. Because *Siete puertas* is the author's only published work, the question remains as to the level of censorial scrutiny she would have subsequently faced.

In *Al lado del hombre* Kurtz must retract her statements that infringe upon the sanctity of matrimony and must also reframe the perception of the war to describe it simply as such, a war, not a fratricidal war. Meanwhile, Alós must reorient her text so that readers avoid exposure to critical portrayals of Nationalist military generals, and she must temper her use of the word *fascistas* by replacing it with *nacionales* or by excising it when not embedded in a dialogue. Censors praise her objectivity in presenting the Republican refugees as marginalized subjects who endure hardships, a narrative strategy Alós incorporated as a way of rescuing the text from the need for an ideological shift in tone.

I leave for future inquiry the continued recovery of women writers' voices to situate the following authors and their works in their literary context, guided by the premise that censors demanded revisions of varying degrees of their work, according to excerpts from the respective censorship files:

> Carmen Barberá, *Las esquinas del alba* (1960): "El drama material y sicológico de una mujer casada y que por complejos siente

aversión al marido y al mismo tiempo se considera insatisfecha conyugalmente, hasta llegar a un intento de suicidio."

María de Jesús Echevarría, *Las medias palabras* (1960): "Novela realista en la que sin argumento central se describen una serie de tipos en el ambiente madrileño de clase media mezclada con mesocracia. 'La niña' [...], 'el médico' con aires de gran señor y el manco que metido en negocios de mercado negro da con sus huesos en la comisaria, son los tipos principales que maneja la autora en este guiñol de la vida real, que se centra efectivamente, a 'medias palabras.'"

Liberata Masoliver, *Un hombre de paz* (evaluated in 1969, published in 1970): First report: "Un médico de ideas izquierdistas residente en Barcelona cuenta su vida desde la indicación de la terminación de la guerra civil española. Sin pretensiones literarias el autor relata llana y sencillamente los sucesos ocurridos en Cataluña durante los años 1936 a 1939. El mayor mérito a mi juicio que tiene esta novela es su propio contenido, donde los desórdenes y penalidades para poder subsistir están tratados con un fiel reflejo de lo que fue la realidad." Second report: "El autor [sic] va narrando el ambiente, acontecimientos y sobresaltos de la vida en la zona roja durante nuestra guerra de liberación. El protagonista, un médico de Barcelona de ideas simpatizantes con las izquierdas de aquel entonces, vive todos los horrores y angustias motivados no solo por las consecuencias de una situación de guerra civil, sino por el caótico estado de anarquía y criminalidad en que se vio sumida la zona roja sin que el Gobierno de la República hiciera nada por evitarlo. La obra dibuja con realismo la situación en aquella Barcelona caída en el lado republicano y las atrocidades cometidas contra víctimas inocentes. Contiene algunas frases o párrafos señalados en las pags. 1, 9, 21, *39*, *66*, *67*, *68*, 146, 149, *195*, 197, 202, 204, 207, 208, *212*, 222, 231 y 232. Estimamos que con estas tachaduras el libro ES AUTORIZABLE, conteniendo incluso el aspecto positivo de exponer y dar testimonio de lo que fue y en lo que derivó el régimen republicano en España, contado además por un narrador izquierdista" (emphasis original).

Carmen Mieza, *Una mañana cualquiera* (1965): "Deben ser suprimidos los párrafos indicados en la página 82 que se refieren a la decisión de ceder bases a los americanos."

Marta Portal, *A ras de las sombras* (1968): "El protagonista, engañado por su mujer y su amigo, y postergado por su padre, se encierra en un sumo egoísmo totalmente indiferente a la vida, aunque esta pueda volver a brindarle una esperanza. La obra, carece de valores morales, y abunda en las necesidades del sexo, aunque *no con base pornográfica*, ni como tema central de la novela, que aunque no carece de algunos incontinentes, tampoco es impublicable" (emphasis original).

Anunciación Rivera Tovar, *La otra guerra de la postguerra* (1968): "Parece ser que el intento de la autora es buscar la paz entre los espíritus. Intentar crear un clima de convivencia entre los españoles. Pero logrados estos intentos hace muchos años, repetimos su inoportunidad."[17]

---

17   Also on this list is Consuelo Álvarez's, *Puente sobre el deseo*, a book that was presented to the censorship board in 1966 but does not appear to be indexed in bibliographic sources. The first report reads: "Novela de adolescentes con pretensiones psicológicas. En cuanto a la moralidad, existen algunas palabras o frases—(págs. 39, 195, etc.)—y alguna escena escabrosa (132). En general la obra no tiene nada de particular, aunque deben tacharse, los crudos vocablos de la págs. 407, 422" (File *Puente*). The second report contains the following: "Sucesión de cuadros de costumbres de la vida en Barcelona actual sin más unidad ni argumento que la persistencia de los personajes. No hay pues verdadero argumento. Obra de realismo extremado que frecuentemente se hace verdadero naturalismo con crudezas groseras e insistencia en lo sexual. Lo cotidiano y vulgar llena toda la obra, sin que aparezca un solo personaje generoso" (File *Puente*).

Chapter 5.
Rejected: Suppressed Texts:
From Moral to Ideological Threat

Truth for authority, not authority for truth.
- Lucretia Mott

THE WRITERS UNDER STUDY in this chapter experienced the harshest censorial stricture in that censors deemed their works too threatening to social or political order to be published. This outcome is reserved for a small number of texts relative to the overall number of censorship files I evaluated. However, one may question the ability to ascertain exactly how many novels written by women in the 1950s and 1960s, or which ones, were denied publication if indeed they were never published or if there is no record of their existence. This is a valid query. I attempt to assuage the concern that there is a plethora of censored novels whose existence is unknown by undertaking an exhaustive search of the censorship files in the Archivo General de la Administración database. I cross-referenced authors' names—including those with alternate spellings such as Carmen Kurz for Carmen Kurtz—with the titles of their submitted manuscripts to uncover those titles that would have been submitted but not authorized to be printed, this to potentially locate novels authors said they wrote when they were interviewed. Although this present study examines the works of 19 writers, the number of files I consulted exceeded 200 on over 75 female writers over the course of eight visits to the AGA that ranged in duration from four to 14 days. Further, I compared the lists of novels published by the women, including under their pseudonyms, against the titles that appear in the database to ensure that all known titles were accounted for.[1] Additionally, I searched for titles submitted under authors' known pseudonyms.[2] I also encountered names of authors in the print news of their time who submitted their works for literary prizes, but who were not selected as winners, to deepen the pool of names and titles. Based on the parameters of this study, I have exhausted avenues to uncover additional titles; identifying a work whose existence is currently unknown is a remote possibility, though the work would not have been submitted by a candidate for a literary prize (and not shortlisted), or would have been written either by author not currently listed in a bio-bibliographic reference, or by an author who submitted a manuscript under a pseudonym not readily associated with her name of fame. Should these works exist, I leave their discovery for future lines of inquiry.

The purpose of this chapter is to discuss four works whose publication censors denied, prompting their circuitous route to eventual publication. In this chapter, it is necessary to expand slightly the parameters of the study to include one novel of husband and wife coauthorship to further demonstrate nuances in studying the censorship process, particularly in the category of works not initially granted authorization for publication.[3]

---

1   Exception(s) to this include hundreds of *novela rosa* entries as their thematic contents and portrayal of character dynamics fall outside of this study.

2   A useful source for identifying pseudonyms appears on the "Seudónimos" page of the *Catálogo de escritoras en lengua castellana* housed in the website mujerpalabra.net.

3   Categorized as "not authorized for publication" is a non-fiction work by Eva Forest (1928-1997), *Los nuevos cubanos: La vida en una granja del pueblo*, published decades later in 2007. Based on Forest's four-month experience in a commune in Cuba in 1966, her transcribed interviews of over 90 subjects captures the multiple voices that constitute life in a "granja del pueblo." The oral histories attest to life on the cooperative provided by a cross-section of its inhabitants, including Che Guevara, who represent the titular 'New Cubans' in the face of a post-revolutionary Cuba. Forest gives voice to the descriptions of their duties and responsibilities on the farm to reveal its daily operations and its cultural and political significance. This file

While many writers gained immediate authorization of their works, sometimes with only several days between the time of submission and authorization, several reasons contextualize their swift and positive response. First, authors such as Carmen de Icaza, Elizabeth Mulder, and Liberata Masoliver inherently supported the conservative ideology and published novels not only benign to the regime but sympathetic to its causes. Others selected narrative subgenres that were viewed as naturally non-threatening to the political climate, specifically the *novela rosa* or the *novela sentimental*. Authors such as Rosa María Cajal, under the pseudonyms María Martí, María Mogar, María Morgan, and Mónica Villar, as well as Susana March, under pseudonym Amanda Román, wrote many such novels primarily as a means to an economic end, considering that they could produce a great num-

---

was originally not made available to me in my initial request in 2014, with the explanation that it was not available, but, after requesting it again in 2017 I was permitted access. Before rendering the outcome of *denegado*, the 1968 report reads:

> Los autores han realizado un reportaje sobre distintos lugares de Cuba, especialmente entre las granjas socializadas y las comunas. Con magnetofón van recogiendo las respuestas de los encargados y responsables de estos centros, así como de algunos trabajadores.
>
> Naturalmente todas las respuestas son favorables a las tesis marxsistas [sic] y demuestran un espíritu de compenetración y adhesión al fidelismo. Entre todos los interrogados solo hay uno que dice no entender de política, por no alabar a Fidel Castro, inmediatamente es tachado de antiguo terrateneinte.
>
> Obra de una propaganda demasiado burda de los principios que inspiran la política castrista.
>
> NO ES ACONSEJABLE SU PUBLICACION. (File *Los nuevos cubanos*).

I leave for future inquiry the analysis of this essay for its classification as unpublishable during the dictatorship, as it falls outside the scope of this study on novels. Forest's husband was playwright Alfonso Sastre, whose work was systematically denied publication of her work and singled out by censors as subversive or as espousing values openly in defiance of the Franco regime.

ber of them in a short amount of time, with little if any censorial opposition, and to relative commercial success. The practice of featuring adolescents or young adults as adopted by Carmen Laforet and Ana María Matute suggests that the characters preclude any sense of ideological threat. For example, we have seen that the two censors' reports on *Nada* dismiss its literary worth and render it as facile, and therefore non-threatening. Further, the file for *Primera memoria* (1960) attests to the youth of the protagonist and recognizes the political innocuity: "La infancia de una niña sensible con sus reacciones al encuentro con la complicación y malicia del mundo de los mayores. Un repudio de lo artificial, lo hipócrita y lo violento, en nombre de la ternura y la sinceridad. Pasajes de cierto mordiente social y político, pero en nombre y en busca de lo humano" (File *Primera memoria*).[4] Other writers have practiced self-censorship to the degree that they purposefully produced writing that avoids censure, and it is contended that still others more subtly modified their literary output so that it aligned in its content, character portrayal, semantics, and themes with the values that would free them from censorial stricture.

As will be demonstrated, a taxonomy of reasons emerges from the files on novels censors denied publication. We return to the paradigm that what reaches readers' hands is not the censored textual material but the text the censors authorized for publication. Censored material, revised in such a way as to alter the intended message of the author or that is stricken from the original text, does not. By teasing out nuances in meaning to distinguish between texts that have undergone censorial-mandated revision or erasure, read for instance by Montejo Gurruchaga as textual mutilation, we begin to see that readers gain access only to read authorized material rather than the actual censored material.

This section builds on previous studies on censorship in women's writing during the 1950s and 1960s in terms of novels that censors denied publication and the reasons for this. For previous studies on

---

4   For Patricia O'Byrne these works gain censorial approval because the protagonists are orphans who have been deprived of solid moral foundation due to lack of role modeling (205).

novels that were not initially authorized but then underwent extensive revision in order to see publication, the following discussions on the processes and the ramifications on the text provide insightful contextualizations. In *Discurso de autora: género y censura en la narrative española de posguerra*, Montejo Gurruchaga examines, among others, the case of *Una mujer llega al pueblo* (1957) by Mercedes Salisachs, *Nosotros, los Rivero* (1953) by Dolores Medio. Nino Kebadze's "Censorship and Sense-Making in Elena Soriano's Trilogy *Mujer y hombre*" provides an overview of censorial practices and theories in addition to evaluating Soriano's experience with the censorship process. This chapter discusses novels initially denied by Rosa María Cajal, María Josefa Canellada, Dolores Medio, and Susana March.[5]

---

5   It is important to recognize that Ana María Matute's (1925-2014) *Luciérnagas* (1993) would optimally be included in this chapter. The novel was originally submitted for evaluation on 20 October 1953; however, efforts to locate the original censorship report have proven unfruitful (in the Archivo General de la Administración and in the Ana Maria Matute Collection of the Howard Gotlieb Archival Research Center, Boston University, and by contacting the publisher Planeta). The process by which *En esta tierra* would merit inclusion in this study would entail a word-by-word comparison with the original typescript, which is inaccessible. In the Archivo General de la Administración, the archive's database lists the novel, and a file does exist, but it is incomplete. The file contains the typed novel with red ink on first page that reads: "Se agradecerá devolver el otro ejemplar que es el corregido mecanograficamente." In the typescript, free from censor markings, Matute indicates that she wrote novel between 1950 and 1953 "con etapas en blanco" (File *Luciérnagas*). The report's cover page, lists the author's contact information, title, publisher (Planeta), number of copies to be published (3000) and the price (60 pesetas). The file also contains a blue index card on which is stamped "Suspendida el 30-11-53" (File *Luciérnagas*). Missing among the documents is the censor's evaluation, and there is no reference to what specific portions of the text were subject to revision or excision, which only allows for limited interpretation in the context of this study. These remarks are indicative of the difficulty with which Matute published the novel under a new title *En esta tierra* (1955), only after incorporating substantive changes, although these changes presumably are not specified in the censorship documentation. *Luciérnagas* is one of the few texts that has been recovered to be

ROSA MARÍA CAJAL: *UN PASO MÁS* (1956)

Rosa María Cajal (1920-1990?)[6] is an author and journalist whose writing has been understudied, although she has been the focus of recent critical analysis undertaken by Patricia O'Byrne that examines, through the portrayal of female protagonists in the context of their societies, the ways characters in Cajal's novels conform to or contest prescribed gender roles (*Post-war Spanish Women Novelists* 149-72). O'Byrne offers this study as a path toward the recuperation of historical memory that serves as testimony to daily living during Francoist Spain. Cajal was a prolific writer, and through her publishing she was able to earn a living. Spanning a period of over two decades, Cajal published four novels under her own name: *Juan Risco* (1948), *Primero, derecha* (1955), *Un paso más* (1956), and *El acecho* (1963). The first and third novels were finalists, respectively, for the Nadal Prize and the Ciudad de Barcelona Prize. Under the pseudonyms most often used of María Morgan and María Martí, Cajal also authored "over one hundred and fifty *novelas rosas*, mostly with the publishing house Bruguera, between 1955 and 1968" (O'Byrne 155). The turn to the romance novel was one of practicality as it afforded her the opportunity to support herself as a writer. Critics often overlook Cajal as a serious writer because of the high volume of love stories she published and because she shifted professional gears to work as journalist to supplement her income. While true that the trope of the young girl falling in love characterizes much of her writing, Cajal's stories capture social

---

published, in 1993, in its original form. Of her return to the novel to prepare it for press, the author remarked that "me ha hecho recuperar la mentalidad y los sentimientos de entonces, de una época marcada por la brutalidad de la guerra, porque el libro es de la guerra. [...] No es una novela política, sino que es humana" (Moret). I leave for future inquiry the comparison of *En esta tierra* with *Luciérnagas* as it will no doubt require an extensive analysis, one that moves beyond the scope of this present study.

6 There are conflicting dates of Cajal's passing. O'Byrne has traced her life to at least 1974 through her connection to Carmen Laforet, as gleaned from the latter's biography, *Carmen Laforet, una mujer en fuga* (Caballé and Rolón-Barada). The Real Academia de Historia website includes a biographical entry that lists the date as "12.XII.1990" (Hernández Cano).

nuances and exhibit literary creativity that position them as worthy of critical attention. In Cajal's own words, the themes she endeavors to develop point to "Todo aquél donde existe problema humano—lucha, decaimiento y superación" (Díaz 556).

Un paso más was a problematic text for the censors, who considered its original content "inmoral y destructivo" and therefore unpublishable (File *Un paso más*). To see publication, it would need to undergo extensive revision in both character and plot development. Manuel L. Abellán, offers a substantive explanation of the novel's reception within the censorship board that merits including it here in its entirety:

> La obra quedaba irremediablemente prohibida sin dejar de omitir que el motivo, 'confidencialmente hablando', se debía a la inmoralidad general que impregnaba la novela. Advertida la autora, ésta se ponía inmediatamente en contacto directo con los responsables de la censura. Se le leía el correspondiente informe en el que la novela se consideraba altamente inmoral. El jefe de censura procedía entonces a sugerir las enmiendas que habrían de limar muchas de las asperezas y prometía indulgencia en caso de demanda de revisión. [...] La escritora ante estos ardides no tenía más remedio que someterse a las exigencias censorias cambiando para ello si era necesario la psicología del personaje de tal manera que entre las razones que primitivamente habían motivado el arrepentimiento de algunos de sus actos, algunas de ellas coincidieran con lo que por contrición propósito de enmienda se entiende en la doctrina cristiana. (165)

O'Byrne identifies the protagonist's moral shifting between typescript and published novel to construct a paradigm of accountability outside of the teachings of Catholicism, "in which religious and sinful considerations are no longer the factors that determine the protagonist's behavior" because "fear of exposure represented a threatening force" (*Post-war Spanish Women Novelists* 167).

In contradiction to the numerous revisions censors required to Alejandra's words, actions, and character development, they make no such demands of the male characters, whether related to morality or politics. Óscar, the adulterer; Juan, the communist sympathizer; and Eugenio, the presumably Republican soldier, stay true to their portrayals in the original typescript.

The axis of the narrative action spans the 1930s when Alejandra leaves her provincial town and moves to Madrid where she first lives in a *pensión* and then moves into the home of Óscar and his wife Elvira, who is the daughter of her mentor and tutor. Óscar offers Alejandra work in his bookstore, and the two develop romantic interest in each other, leading to an extramarital affair. At the outbreak of the Spanish Civil War, Elvira and Óscar hurriedly leave the country heading for Argentina without explanation as to why, presumably to put distance between Óscar and Elvira, although the quick departure out of the country for a time period that roughly coincides with the war suggests the motive of ideological dissonance. At this moment in the narration, Alejandra realizes that her relationship with Óscar is over, and she is left to carry on during the wartime years as a single woman, feeling alone and abandoned.

Cajal's mention of the Civil War merits attention, as censors make no demands to revise these references for their seemingly tangential portrayal to the actions in the novel. Although Cajal avoids espousing ideological undertones, censors completely gloss over references to the war, including references to Eugenio as an injured combatant who convalesces in a hospital over the course of several chapters. Cajal incorporates carefully positioned ellipses and contrives plot ambiguity to negotiate the morally bankrupt issue of suicide by making the unrequitedly loved Eugenio fall to his death not intentionally but accidentally, when he slips through the window while hanging curtains. The censor references this plot point and identifies the character's pathology, but does not require textual modifications.

The first censor to evaluate the manuscript, dated as completed in 1949, does so on 8 March 1954. He summarizes the plot in the lengthy report's first paragraph and in the second explains the problematic portrayal of the unrepentant and amoral adulteress, before offering concluding remarks on the secondary characters and assessing the novel as unsuitable for publication:

Puede resumirse esta novela diciendo que es la biografía de un adulterio, iniciado en el primer cuarto de la obra y mantenido a lo largo del resto. La protagonista, Alejandra, es una joven que carece de principios morales, por lo que el adulterio no significa nada para ella. Debe su educación precisamente al suegro de su amante, pero, ni bien perdida la virtud accidentalmente, y enamorada del marido de otra mujer, no vacila en mantener sus pecaminosas relaciones sin tener en cuenta el sufrimiento de la esposa. Hay también una muerte, sospechosa de suicidio (páginas 257-261), cuyo antecedente psicológico se encuentra en la página 143. La situación entre ambos amantes llega a hacerse extremadamente difícil al verse sometidos a la vigilancia de la esposa engañada, quien, por su parte, no llega a la certeza del adulterio.

Dado el fondo de la novela, que puede clasificarse entre el surrealismo vigente, es un constante despliegue de inmoralidad y de cruel ingenuidad. Podría explicarse así el pecado, si se acepta la inconsciencia de Alejandra. Esta sólo se dedica a romper los lazos que la unen al adúltero, cuando comprende que la vida no le puede deparar satisfacciones. Pero en su acción no interviene el arrepentimiento ni el conocimiento del daño que causa. Se trata de una amoral, cuya conducta tampoco es lógica en lo psicológico, ya que ha recibido una educación suficiente para distinguir el bien y el mal.

Como buen complemento de este personaje central, los restantes que desfilan son también una buena colección de cínicos e impuros, que matiza fuertemente el desarrollo de la acción.

Creo, por tanto, que esta novela, literariamente buena, no debe autorizarse, pues su esencia inmoral y destructiva así lo exige. (File *Un paso más*)

Cajal responds in a hand-signed letter to her editor, Sr. Úbeda dated 10 April 1954 with the original typescript in which she incorporated the requisite "numerosas rectificaciones," as she explains:

Tal como acordamos tengo el gusto de enviarle el original de la obra "UN PASO MAS" con numerosas rectificaciones, pues ateniéndome al informe que tuvo Vd. la amabilidad de leerme, he cambiado la psicología de la protagonista y las razones de su arrepentimiento. He procurado limar todo lo que me ha parecido contrario a las normas que rigen esa censura de libros, y espero que me haga Vd. el favor de tomarlo con interés para que la lean de nuevo y me conceden la autorización para publicarla, pues como Vd. ya sabe esta obra obtuvo un premio y no puedo devolver lo que he cobrado por los derechos de edición.[7]

Espero que encontrará usted acertados los cortes y la modificación de conceptos.

Muchas gracias y en espera de sus noticias le saluda cordialmente Rosa María Cajal. (File *Un paso más*)

The most significant modification deals with the protagonist's psychological corrective to express remorse for committing adultery. Cajal indicates that her protagonist undergoes a shift in standpoint and proceeds to request a second evaluation to attain authorization to publish, considering as well the financial imperatives due to the prize and prizemoney she received. Her letter illustrates the author's role in advocating for the publication of her novel and reveals the steps she took to comply with censorship restrictions. Responses from the authors directly to the censors, while not commonplace, at times do appear as part of the censorship file documentation and demonstrate that some authors chose to petition a second evaluation as a way to potentially rescue their text. This was also the case with Susana March and Ricardo Fernández de la Reguera's *La boda de Alfonso XIII*, discussed below.

Upon its second evaluation, the censor then granted authorization to publish after acknowledging Cajal's revisions of the textual references under scrutiny and the protagonist's transformation:

---

7   *Un paso más* was the runner up to Carmen Conde's *Las oscuras raíces*, of the Premio Elisenda de Montcada in 1953, for which they garnered the sums of 15,000 and 25,000 pesetas respectively ("Entrega de los premios 'Elisenda de Montcada'" 38).

Se tachan unos detalles para completar las correcciones de la autora, al querer transformar la psicología de la protagonista, convirtiéndola en una mujer con creencias religiosas y sentido moral. En la primera versión eran calificados de 'prejuicios atávicos' los leves remordimientos que sentía por su adulterio y, su único dolor, la idea de no verse correspondida igualmente. Se señalan dos alusiones que parecen afirmar una como superación de trabas morales al alcanzar la edad madura (¿) y algún otro matiz. Ver pgs. 38, 121, 165, 189, 190, 201, 223, 265, 267, 268-69, 270 y 271. (File *Un paso más*)

The remainder of this section outlines the changes Cajal made to the original text in order to gain authorization to publish *Un paso más*. Upon her arrival in the capital city, Alejandra contemplates the vertiginous surroundings on the Paseo de la Castellana with the surreal perspective that reveals to her "huesos recubiertos de carne, vísceras, risas y lágrimas" (Ts. 38, Ms. 38), which appears in both the typescript and printed novel. However, the censor strikes Cajal's subsequent expression of existential anguish that teeters toward the agnostic, erasing the following rhetorical questions: "¿Qué era lo que encerraba un cuerpo a más del ritmo regular de sus palpitaciones? ¿Qué era aquel soplo incógnito que poseía y a dónde huía para morir?" (Ts. 38). This textual omission removes the suggestion that Alejandra's chaotic meandering throughout the city should be attributed to some unknown force.

In the next textual revision, when Alejandra imagines her tutor don Gabriel's response to learning of her affair, and invokes his encouraging words to overcome adversity, the original paragraph below appears here with brackets around the text the censors struck in red ink, which were removed from the printed novel due to their focus on the fulfillment she found in her affair: "¿Es que no das importancia a tu propio criterio? Sabes que no es noble ni limpio encorajinarse al perder, [y si fuiste feliz aquellos días y lo has sido también, por cuanto vivía en ti durante tres años ¿qué más puedes pedir?] Hay que seguir, Alejandra, hay que avanzar siempre un paso más" (Ts. 121, Ms. 107). The censor struck the passage to erase the sentiments of happiness Alejandra experienced in the relationship and required Cajal to leave the duration of the relationship unspecified, both excisions that minimize the significance the relationship held for Alejandra.

In the next marked section, the narrator recalls that the adulterous relationship existed but that it was less meaningful for Óscar than for Alejandra. The original typescript, with the censor strikethrough between brackets, refers to Alejandra's inner struggle to reconcile the relationship:

> En alguna ocasión se empeñaba en razonar apoyándose en los consejos de don Gabriel. "No soy, ni mucho menos, la primera mujer del mundo a quien sucede algo parecido. Yo me enamoré de él y Óscar no dio importancia a nada, porque estaba muy lejos de compartir mis sentimientos. [Supongamos que la última vez que rozó el tema demostrando que "no había olvidado," fue por obra del "champagne" o por el vértigo de un momento de intimidad. Eso no supone nada a mi favor. Entonces... si él ha olvidado, o más claramente, no da importancia alguna al recuerdo puesto que nada trascendente la significó, ¿por qué no procuro olvidar también? Han pasado años y tengo alguna experiencia. Puedo juzgar los hechos sin aturullarme. Nadie muere de un desengaño. El poso que la deje es cuestión aparte.] Lo razonable sería que procurase sin vivir sin constituir de este problema la base fundamental de mi existencia. "¿Por qué no puedo?" (Ts. 165)

In the printed novel, Cajal drastically altered the text:

> Entonces procuraba razonar apoyándose en los consejos de don Gabriel. Recurría a un análisis crudo sobre sí misma, y llegaba a la conclusión de que sería inútil esperar la paz y tranquilidad de su conciencia siguiendo los impulsos de su corazón. (Ms. 143)

Substantive and significant excisions alter the way Alejandra deals with the crisis of reconciling what society would call her sexual indiscretions. Her resolute determination in making sense of the failed relationship by relying on Gabriel's advice is reduced to a mere attempt to do so. In the original version, adultery appears as a societal woe, not softened to appear limited in scope to Alejandra's situation. Further,

her positioning as someone cast off or abandoned who should simply forget the experience just has Óscar seems to have done is replaced with the self-reproach that she would not achieve peace of mind were she to follow her heart.

Of note in the revision process is that Cajal abbreviated a paragraph on a page that does not appear on the censor's report, although parts of it were stricken in blue ink on the typescript. This nuance is concrete evidence of self-censorship, the act of refraining from including original text even though the censorship board does not require its removal. The original text refers to Alejandra's inner thoughts surrounding Óscar's absence and the possibility they will reunite in the future, with brackets around the text the censor marked in blue ink:

"Porque llevo demasiado hincado; porque sin él, todo pierde interés. [Entonces, ¿por qué no le hablo? ¿Por qué no procuro una explicación?] Y si todo llegara a aclararse [y favorablemente para mí,] ¿qué? No puedo ser su mujer. Tendría que conformarme con..." No se atrevía a pronunciar la palabra. [Tampoco es eso lo que quiero; creo que no podría resistirlo.] "Entonces, ¿qué?" Le repugnaba, y sufría con el solo pensamiento de ser capaz de llegar a ello. (Ts. 144)

Cajal revised this portion to:

"Porque llevo demasiado hincado; porque sin él, todo pierde interés. Pero si todo llegara a aclararse, ¿qué? No puedo ser su mujer. Tendría que conformarme con..." No se atrevía a pronunciar la palabra. Le repugnaba, y sufría con el solo pensamiento de ser capaz de llegar a ello. "Entonces, ¿qué?" (Ms. 144).

Alejandra's bravado in confronting Óscar is simply reduced to the "if" clause without the glimmer of hope for their future. With the removal of the last sentence, the possibility that she might have to accept the undesirable role of the concubine, or synonymous word, is implied by the mid-paragraph ellipsis.

The censor also strikes the words *atavismo* and *atávicos* to describe Alejandra's impulses, so that their removal in the printed novel portrays her as a more proper young woman by society's standards. Likewise, references to their age difference disappear from typescript to published manuscript. The first phrase in question that Cajal removes—bracketed to indicate censor strikethrough—presents Óscar's point of view regarding his affair with Alejandra as more socially prejudicial to her than to him:

> Óscar sufría al comprender sus vacilaciones, sus miedos... [Por él nada le importaba, puesto que ya tenía bastantes años y le sería más fácil acoger lo que fuere con filosofía, pero] se sentía culpable de haber desvirtuado la existencia se Alejandra. (Ts. 201)

In published form, this becomes:

> Óscar sufría al comprender sus remordimientos, sus miedos... Se sentía culpable de haber desvirtuado la existencia se Alejandra hacia derroteros que la privaban de toda tranquilidad. (Ms. 173)

A second instance of the erasure of the age difference originally appeared as Alejandra realizes that her separation from Óscar was imminent and asked him to leave. The bracketed text below, crossed off by the censor, was omitted from the printed version:

> — Sí, vete, [y quizá pasado algún tiempo... cuando tenga más años...
> — Entonces seré yo demasiado viejo, murmuró él.
> — Nadie puede decir lo que ocurrirá entonces. Yo comprendo que de este modo nuestra vida se haría imposible y además...pues, sí, mira, no puedo hacer sufrir a Elvira.] (Ts. 265, Ms. 228)

The printed version omits the references to the hypothetical obstacles their future together would hold. Although the censor strikes Alejandra's proposal that the passage of time may suffice for their relationship to resume, he allows Óscar's idea to remain, "Yo haré todo lo que quieras" (228), revealing a double standard in behavior norms. The protagonist's behavior and her opinions about her behavior are also at the center of the next excised section, in which Óscar benevolently expresses his willingness to proceed according to Alejandra's wishes. The narrator conveys her difficulty in articulating her thoughts: "continuaron faltándole palabras para expresar sus complejos sentimientos" (Ts. 223, Ms. 193). Although the preceding quote appears in the printed novel, censors required the removal of the following, as indicated by the strikethrough in pen:

> No, no obraba mal, todo su ser se volcaba en Óscar y sin embargo, existían sombras, sombras profusas empañando su conciencia. Juzgaba que nada irreprochable había en su cariño hacia él, pero entonces ¿por qué su constante descontento hacia sí misma? ¿Por qué aquellos esbozados reproches que apenas si se atrevía a admitir, contra su manera de vivir? Solo junto a él, sin temas que rozaran o despertaran el recuerdo de los demás, era feliz, mas una vez sola, ella tan amante en otros tiempos de la soledad, los acontecimientos tomaban proporciones gigantescas y amenazadoras. (Ts. 223)

Five of the 15 excisions affect the last chapter and significantly alter the intended conclusion. In the original, Alejandra grapples with ending the relationship with Óscar, even though she has exercised her agency to do so, with stricken text that would have appeared on page 231 of the printed novel: "Día tras día se le hacía más difícil aceptar lo establecido y se decidió rotundamente" (Ts. 267). The revision avoids addressing the transgressive nature of her inner conflict as difficult to accept. The vacillating also applies to don Gabriel, who is aware of the love triangle and the complications it has caused. The censor marked the following passage containing Gabriel's self-dialogue upon the impending departure from Spain of his daughter and son-in-law:

> Demonio, demonio, murmuraba. ¿Por qué se complicará todo de ese modo? Claro que... ¿Cómo solucionarlo? Las dos tienen derecho, a su manera, claro. Luego dicen que no existen los imposibles. ¡No, qué va! — Se encaró repentinamente con su yerno: Por eso te he tenido siempre tanta antipatía, por eso te temía. Eres como yo hubiera querido ser, tener tu temple, tu espíritu disciplinado que

sabe resignarse, amoldándose a las circunstancias, al menos aparentemente. (Ts. 268)

The deletion from the printed novel thwarted a double threat to morality: the original text would have established that both women were entitled to their relationship with Óscar and would have condoned Óscar's actions as conduct Gabriel wished he could emulate. In the original draft, Gabriel also holds both women accountable for the marital infidelity, but censors required the excision of "y las dos sintieron débilmente culpables" (Ts. 270), which would have appeared on page 233 in the novel.

Then, in anticipation of Óscar's departure, Alejandra questions her decision to ask him to leave, and again the censor requires striking this section that would have appeared on page 234:

¿No hubiera sido mejor desgarrarse, poder tenerle al lado? ¿No era preferible pasar por todo, a la angustia loca de no verle? Sí, había sido una locura. Era preciso detenerle, que no se fuera.... Correr a su encuentro, interponerse en su camino y abrazarse a él para toda la vida. (Ts. 271)

The censor moves Cajal away from portraying an emotionally fraught Alejandra as a way to mitigate the inner turmoil that arises from the conflict of engaging in an adulterous relationship.

A few lines below, the last textual revision appears. In reference to tenets contrary to religion rather than to questionable moral behavior, the censor aims to quell the existential anxiety Alejandra experiences amidst the cacophony of her surroundings upon Óscar's impending departure by striking the bracketed:

Más bullicio en la calle, ruido de puertas que se abrían, cierres metálicos que se levantaban... Eugenio. [¿Existiría Eugenio todavía en alguna parte?] ¿Le vería a ella y podría hacerse cargo de su dolor? (Ts. 271, Ms. 234).

Censors deemed *Un paso más* in its original form as threatening to morality and religion but authorized publication when Cajal granted her protagonist a sense of culpability for her adulterous relationship. The revision conveys Alejandra's knowledge that her affair broke with the gendered code of conduct in Francoist Spain, though Óscar's portrayal did not undergo any such transformation. The censors allow for the textual ambiguity surrounding the circumstances of Eugenio's death as accidental rather than intentional. Further, this novel illustrates an example of the author's direct intervention in the editorial process through her correspondence that advocated for a second evaluation by the censorship board.

MARÍA JOSEFA CANELLADA: *PENAL DE OCAÑA* (1965)
A prominent philologist of mid-twentieth century Spain who moved in prestigious cultural circles of her time, María Josefa Canellada (1912-1995) contributed to the advancement in Spanish linguistics of phonetics and dialectology, positioning her among the top in her field. She published only one work of fiction during the Franco dictatorship. Canellada was an educator, not only in Spain in the University of Salamanca, but also in universities worldwide including in the United States (Middlebury), Mexico, and Denmark.

Canellada's only work of fiction published during the dictatorship was *Penal de Ocaña*, a novel consisting of a wartime nurse's diary entries on her work life and on the deleterious effects of the war on her psyche. It was a finalist for the Café Gijón literary prize, the year that Carmen Martín Gaite earned this distinction for *El balneario*. The novel was adapted for the theatre in 2013 as a one-act monologue by Ana Zamora, Canellada's granddaughter, and was performed as recently as September 2019 in Miami.[8] The online playbill for a 2016 performance in Madrid calls the adaptation "el intenso testimonio de aquella estudiante, que se va haciendo a sí misma a través de las elecciones que toma en su periplo cotidiano descubriendo a través de su angustia, más que de la propia razón, lo que es la verdadera existencia" (*Penal de Ocaña*, Corral).

---

8 The play first opened in Segovia and was later performed in Madrid by Zamora's company Nao d'amores.

Textual similarities with the author's biography abound. Canellada was a university student at the outbreak of the Spanish Civil War. In the years she postponed her studies before obtaining her degree, she was a nurse, and the novel's text, according to her granddaughter, Ana Zamora, originates from the author's personal diary from that time. The first-person accounts of the disillusionment with the war and its destruction are at the crux of a quest for survival where wounded soldiers and narrator alike find themselves in constant danger with little recourse for protection. The uncertain fate of the diary writer (although she is presumed to have been killed as a consequence of war), however, breaks with the author's path, as Canellada resumed her studies after the war to finish her doctoral degree in 1940.[9] She swiftly garnered the critical attention of prominent writers of her time, including Pedro Salinas, Ramón Menéndez Pidal, Tomás Navarro Tomás, and the man who would become her husband, writer and dialectologist Alonso Zamora Vicente.

The diary trope reveals protagonist María Eloína Carrandena's experience as a twenty-year-old university student mobilized as a wartime nurse in a Republican hospital in Madrid that was subsequently dismantled and transferred to the repurposed titular location during the first year of the Spanish Civil War. The action around María Eloína's life transpires between 2 October 1936 and 30 November 1937, with an unnamed first-person narrator explaining in the epilogue that he or she found it and is revealing the contents in diary format as they originally appeared.

Fundamental to the discussion of Canellada's creation of the 1955 novel is the role of memory in constructing María Eloína's written narrative. Two factors play a role in mediating fact and fiction, first that Canellada kept a diary at the time in her life that coincides with the narrative action, and second that she must have reconstructed at least some the events based on recall. Frederic C. Bartlett's theories on ways of remembering are useful to navigate each of these circumstances:

---

9   Canellada's doctoral dissertation "El bable de Cabranes" examined a regional dialect in her native Asturias; it was written under Dámaso Alonso and published in 1944.

The most persistent problems of recall all concern the ways in which past experiences and past reactions are utilised when anything is remembered. From a general point of view it looks as if the simplest explanation available is to suppose that when any specific event occurs some trace, or some group of traces, is made and stored up in the organism or in the mind. Later, an immediate stimulus re-excites the trace, or group of traces, and, provided a further assumption is made to the effect that the trace somehow carries with it a temporal sign, the re-excitement appears to be equivalent to recall. (197)

Bartlett's paradigm fosters a reading of Canellada's novel as a collection of stored traces activated by a stimulus, whether this stimulus is her own diary or recollections she endeavors to put on paper. The robust details she includes in her descriptions of the patients' wounds and a tone that conveys a combination of bewilderment, ennui, and hopelessness, amidst the drive to work with utmost decorum, position María Eloína as a reliable narrator.

The narrative structure determined by the internal writer of a diary or letters proves an insightful tool to convey the protagonists' life stories, whether they are meant solely for the journal-keeper or for specific readers. The voice that narrates Canellada's *Penal de Ocaña* seems to have been keeping a personal journal with no other purpose than to document her experiences as a wartime nurse. The added purposing of her words as a commentary on war isolates her experiences from a denunciatory message and presents them as unfiltered thoughts. This writing captures the Bakhtinian notion of heteroglossia:

> another's speech in another's language, serving to express authorial intentions but in a refracted way. Such speech constitutes a special type of double-voiced discourse. It serves two speakers at the same time and expresses simultaneously two different intentions: the direct intention of the character who is speaking, and the refracted intention of the author. (324)

This is mediated through a double-voiced and internally dialogized text. Canellada copies the language of eye-witnessed war injuries and serves as her own interlocutor.

Canellada's poignant story is a testimonial novel fraught with existential imperatives that pepper the protagonist's thoughts as expressed in her journal entries: "Desde el punto de vista literario, quizá el contacto principal entre esta novela y la narrativa existencialista, radique en el reencuentro de la heroína consigo misma y con los otros, como resultado de un proceso de autorreflexión solitaria y libre que la lleva a clarificar su propia existencia" (Zuleta). The reader, then, becomes the mediator of the text, another of the protagonist's interlocutors, a role molded and influenced by María's ways of seeing through her female gaze, which then turns the reader into the spectator of war: "Hoy mi casa es el Hospital. Mis hermanos son una pena honda que se me ablanda en lágrimas. Mi vida, el andar medio ahogada, con la tragedia como el pan de cada día. El no ver claro. El querer resistir por encima de todo. Y el echar mano de todos los restos de mi serenidad" (55). The existential bent in the novel evokes the 1940s literature that at the time of publication would have been a vestige of Spain's literary past, which for Óscar Barrero Pérez touches upon the themes of "duda, incomunicación, pesimismo, vacío, tedio, culpa, dolor, la vida como perpetuo estado de lucha contra una realidad superior, y al final de ella, la muerte con su misterio definitivo" (59).

According to Raquel Conde Peñalosa *Penal de Ocaña* reads almost like a historical chronicle (244) rather than a literary artifact: "se publica fuera de su contexto, en un momento histórico y literario que no le correspondía, cuando los intereses narrativos ya se alejaban de la contienda y el realismo iba perdiendo vigor. Poca difusión y casi nulo reconocimiento en los estudios de la posguerra" (243).

This section discusses the novel's circuitous route to publication, initially rejected by censors when Canellada submitted it for review in 1955 and then published almost entirely in its original form after its second submission to the censorship board nine years later (1964), more than a generation's temporal remove from the incidents the narrator memorializes. Further, as seldom happens, the book was reprinted in 1985 in its original form, with a prologue by Zamora Vicente.

The circumstances surrounding the creation of a text relative to the timing of the events it narrates are problematized—scrutinized because of the nature of these events—when the text's publication takes place years or even decades after those events. In the case of *Penal de Ocaña*, the events narrated are twice removed from publication date given that *Penal de Ocaña* was submitted for censorial review in 1955, rejected, and then resubmitted in 1964, significant because with the passage of time the second censor interpreted the protagonist through the lens of gender, defined through patriarchy. The original typescript was rejected for publication without explanation in its report dated 17 May 1955 that simply reads: "Denegada" (File *Penal*). Absent the usual plot summary, the record stands out for the censor's complete silence save that one word. It is the only time in viewing over 200 reports that I came across such a sparse record. Canellada would likely have been known to censors for her marriage to Zamora Vicente (1946), and for their connection to the literary world, in particular the literary circles of the famed members of the Generation of 27. Censors would likely not associate this type of publication—a gruesome war story not of battle but of its immediate aftermath—with a woman of Canellada's prominence. Censors would have deemed the María Eloína's likely death in the end an unjust punishment for her benevolent actions toward healing the wounded fighters because typically the morally lax or otherwise deviant characters were punished by dying, suffering an accident or violence, or being relegated to a life of ostracization or solitude. Censors also would have considered the realistic portrayal of wartime injury too damning even though the injured and mortally wounded soldiers belonged to the Republican side. Highlighting the consequences of representing the ideology of the vanquished was often a deciding factor leading to authorize publication, such as Liberata Masoliver's *Barcelona en llamas* (1961) and Concha Alós's *El caballo rojo* (1966). Further, the action would have presumably taken place during their lifetime and the "fictional" events recounted in a first-person narrative would have been too temporally close to real time and appeared so vivid as to be authentic.

The graphic descriptions of the aggressed male body help the reader visualize torn limbs, concussed heads, triturated bones, displaced organs, and other gruesome combat injuries as well as imagine the smells of rotting flesh and coagulating or oozing blood. Even away from the battlefield, references to the fear of nightly bombings, scarcity of resources, and an overall sense of despair permeate the novel. It seems that the wounds were still too deep, less than a generation removed from the Civil War, for censors to consider authorizing publication. The unsuccessful first pass through the censorship process, however, gave Canellada the opportunity to rework the novel; many of the revisions had little to do with potentially suspect material, but rather were stylistic modifications and textual revisions the author considered would improve the content, adding, for example, one of Jorge Manrique's *coplas* in a poetic juxtaposition with the description of suffering, injury, and death.[10] An example of Canellada's reworking of the novel appears in the entry dated 21 December (1936) in which she discusses the presence of a group of French soldiers eating in a tavern at day's end. Through María Eloína's translation of their conversation, the readers learn that they were responsible for a bombing in the university zone earlier that day. When one of them boasts: "Y voló *toda la Universidad*" (Ts. 48, Ms. 52, emphasis original) the diary writer in the original 1955 typescript reflects: "Lo dicen vanagloriándose con un aire canalla y ruin. ¿A qué habrían venido aquí estos chiquillos de tabardo gris y cascos de acero? ¿En nombre de qué dios del odio vienen a matar hermanos nuestros?" (Ts. 48). Canellada omits the last last question, however, in the 1964 version and replaces it with "La Universitaria es mía y nuestra" (Ms. 52). The excision elides the conflation of religion with the concept of civil war as fratricide and instead offers a statement that reflects an ethos of solidarity.[11]

---

10   I am grateful to the personnel in the Archivo General de la Administración (AGA) for allowing me to view the two typescripts side by side, page by page, to detect textual differences. AGA protocols only allow for the viewing of materials in one box at a time, and to allow me to view these typescripts that are stored in two different boxes, I was granted permission to access the contents of both boxes in a separately monitored section.

11   Whether an oversight or intentional, the statement of solidarity rather than the rhetorical question also appears in the 1985 edition on page 70.

The second typescript, resubmitted in 1964, gained swift authorization, which required only one revision. With portions underlined in red ink by the censor, the report summarizes:

> Bajo la forma de un pretendido diario la protagonista refiere sus actuaciones e impresiones como enfermera en un Hospital de sangre en la zona roja, primero en Madrid y luego en Ocaña. Prescindiendo de valor que como relato más o menos histórico pueda tener la obra, en <u>ella no se hace más que reflejar los sentimientos caritativos y cristianos de la protagonista con respecto a los heridos de guerra</u>, en su labor de enfermera con estudios universitarios. (File *Penal*, underline original)

Reading the diary as a work of fiction about a woman performing the role of a nurse moves the contents away from the author's firsthand account of her own, real-life experiences. The novel's assessment not as historical, but "more or less" historical, also suggests that it is more of a fictional account than perhaps it likely was, especially considering that with the passage of time the ideological threat the novel initially constituted was assuaged. Further, by accentuating the traditional role of woman as nurse (and man as doctor), the novel's premise and characters are complicit with social norms of the time.

The report continues:

> <u>La obra es publicable</u>, si bien recomiendo eliminar la frase "de Alemania" en la pag. 34 y allí tachada en rojo, por referirse a las maravillas técnicas de esa nación con las que tenían que enfrentarse los rojos luchando con el texto a palos. Por lo tanto fuera de esto puede autorizarse la publicación. 18/mayo 1964. (File *Penal*, underline original)

The phrase in question appears in the context of weaponry. The narrator explains that Russian tanks have arrived to protect Madrid to avoid another clash ending with heavy casualties as occurred on 3 September 1936 during Battle of Talavera. Although the battle cost both sides many lives, it was especially detrimental to the Republican forces as the city represented one of the last lines of protection of Madrid from the Nationalist troops. Instead of the original "ya no puede pasar lo que en el desastre de Talavera aquel, que íbamos a matar como corderos, sin fusil siquiera, a pelear con palos contra las maravillas técnicas de Alemania" (Ts. 46), the last phrase in final version appears as "...a pelear con palos contra las maravillas de la técnica" (Ms. 50). This leaves the readers "protected" from knowing the provenance of the technical marvels and all that the country of origin implies in the context of World War II atrocities.

A second censor reports that:

> Es un diario de memorias escritas en zona roja durante nuestra guerra de Liberación por la joven enfermera, universitaria, María Eloína Carrandena, un alma angelical que derrochó los tesoros de su ternura sobre los soldados heridos que quedaban confiados a su cuidado, siendo principalmente el hospital militar de Ocaña donde desarrolló su humanitario apostolado. Autorizable. (File *Penal*)

According to the report, the story reads in 1964 not as a testimony of wartime cruelty but as the memoirs of a benevolent, Christian wartime nurse. Mary Nash explains the significant contribution women made during the war, especially in the first months, including the training and militarization of nurses who worked warfront and in war hospitals (*Defying* 146-52). They worked "long hours" under "dreadful conditions" to tend "to the escalating number of wounded soldiers" (Nash, *Defying* 151-52). The codified message of femininity as medical support staff debases the text's implicit or explicit politicized message and perpetuates a discourse of gender roles that portray the woman as caregiver. This view centers the debate on gender representation that positions the nurse on the dialectic of political vs. the sexual intimate in terms of the Power (with a capital P) structure, where we read politics as Kate Millet posits: "The term 'politics' shall refer to power-structured relationships, arrangements whereby one group of persons is controlled by another" and the relationship between the sexes on the binary is one "dominance and subordinance.... whereby males rule females. Through this system a most ingenious form of 'interior colonisation' has been achieved" (23), which is most readily perceived in the power hierarchy in the hospital marked by the language of military titles that María Eloína uses when addressing the doctors—*mi general*, for example—and when she acts to follow orders.

The male body suffers the egregious and unrelenting attacks in the midst of a country at war. The numerous gruesome combat injuries confront the reader with the harsh realities of the bloodshed and loss of life. While some men recover, others succumb, and the nurse who witnesses in real time the aftermath of the armed battles provides testimony to the devastating effects of war on the male body from a space of subtle emotional detachment that prevents her from transferring the distress to her own existence. Although sympathetic, she fulfills her duties at the *hospital de sangre* in Madrid and assists in its relocation to the Penal de Ocaña where her work resumes.[12] Her body appears to be numb from the hostilities that surround her as a way of coping with the trauma of war: the physical pain of her patients, the scarcity of food, the cold, the chilling sound of the repeated bombings, and the deficient medical supplies. She seeks solutions to lessen her patients' suffering and demonstrates tremendous resiliency.

While many soldiers succumb to their wounds, María Eloína vanishes amidst the horrors of war, presumably killed in a mortar attack, as her diary entries inexplicably abruptly end. Her journal was found and delivered to her brother, a member of the Republican 50th Mixed Brigade. Her presumed death reminds the readers that she was living in a war-torn society in which death is a very real and frequent occurrence.

The medical discourse María Eloína articulates to represent wartime life as she experiences it proves a valuable testimony to the ways she alleviated the suffering of the wounded soldiers. Her diary entries also reveal the inner turmoil of negotiating the daily perils to survival in a war-torn society. Beyond the text, Canellada's trajectory in publishing the novel reveals the importance of the passage of time between the novel's creation and its suitability for public consumption,

---

12   This penitentiary is located in Toledo and was converted into a hospital during the war out of necessity as its original location in Madrid became too vulnerable when the city was under siege. Miguel Hernández spent the latter part of 1940 and the beginning of 1941 in this jail before being moved to Alicante where he would die the following year.

a generation removed from the events María Eloína memorializes in her diary.

DOLORES MEDIO: *CELDA COMÚN* (1963/1996)
Asturian-born Dolores Medio (1911-1996), author and political activist, enjoyed a successful literary career over a four decade period. After winning the Nadal Prize for her 1952 novel *Nosotros, los Rivero*, Medio gained the reputation of a writer whose works represented the social mosaic of Francoist Spain's middle class, most notably demonstrating the daily lives of these individuals in the 1952 novel and also in others such as *Funcionario público* (1956) and *El pez sigue flotando* (1959). While the latter two were authorized for publication either with no modifications (File *Funcionario público*), or with the removal of one paragraph that critiqued chaotic social order by attributing the cause to "los curas" (File *El acuario*),[13] censors heavily scrutinized *Nosotros,*

---

13 The censorship report on *Funcionario público* reads: "Novela ambientada en Madrid, época actual donde se pretende reflejar la vida mediocre de un funcionario de Telecomunicación que tiene que luchar diariamente para atender a los gastos familiares, y dentro de ello se enlaza una breve suceso de interes [sic] femenino hacia una desconocida persona. PUEDE AUTORIZARSE" (File *Funcionario públic*o).

The censorship report on *El pez sigue flotando*, appears under its original title *El acuario*: "Es una novela en la que se describe la vida en una casa de inquilinos. Aparecen, en cuadros aislados, sin mucha relación entre sí, una escritora, un portero, una muchacha que trabaja, una bailarina, un matrimonio joven, etc. La autora presenta la vida de cada uno de estos personajes, intentando unirlos con el sútil [sic] hilo de la vida en general. PUEDE AUTORIZARSE LA PUBLICACION" (File *El acuario*).

However, following the final sentence, the handwritten words "quitándose el párrafo de la p. 14" appear. This paragraph consists of dialogue in which the clergy is painted in a negative light. Medio handled the revision of the text marked in parenthesis by removing it from the printed version:

(— La culpa de lo que sucede la tiene los curas.)
José Cilleiro no sabe exactamente por qué los curas tienen la culpa de que los pantanos no se llenen de agua y de los apagones del servicio de Electricidad. Pero insiste terco:

los Rivero, initially denying its publication on grounds that it constituted threats to "los Ministros," "la moral," and "el Régimen y sus instituciones" (File *Nosotros, los Rivero*). What is notable regarding this prizewinning novel is that Medio wrote a letter to the censorship board to petition for a second evaluation, explaining that her novel was the product of careful creation based on her academic background in psychology and that any irreverence was unintentional. She agreed to edit the sections censors had highlighted with the hope that her apology and willingness to adapt the text would conform to the demands of the censorship board; in the end she gained authorization to publish.[14] Montejo Gurruchaga documents this interaction in greater detail and sheds light on the precarious situation in which Medio found herself, particularly in light of Medio's desire to pursue a literary career ("Dolores Medio" 212-17).

Medio's *Celda común* captures disagreeable descriptions of a women's jail as observed by the protagonist Teresa Vega, incarcerated for her participation in a public manifestation in support of Asturian coalminers on strike to demand better working conditions. In April 1962, when the coalminers refused to descend the labyrinthine passageways underground to render a day's work in abysmal working conditions, for about 100 pesetas, they set the stage for the first of many labor strikes that would disrupt the image of social harmony the Franco regime aspired to cultivate. The protests resulted in harsh retaliation against the striking workers and their families until the *gobernador civil* of Asturias, Marcos Peña Royo, entered in discrete negotiations to restore a sense of normality in the region. The strikes in Asturias

---

(— Los curas. Y nadie más que los curas. Se van con los ricos. No hay moralidad. Y uno va en el tranvía o el Metro, y ¡zas!, corte de fluído. [sic] ¿Quién tiene la culpa?)
En el cerebro de José Cilleiro todo es confusión. La conclusión es siempre la misma:
(— ¿No decía yo? Los curas. La culpa de todo lo que sucede la tienen los curas. No hay moralidad.)
— Cuando llega a esta conclusión, José Cilleiro queda satisfecho. (Ts. 14).

14   *Nosotros, los Rivero* saw publication in 2017 in its original form, including previously censor-stricken passages.

were met with parallel demonstrations of protest across Spain as well as other countries including France and the United States. One such protest took place in Madrid's Puerta del Sol on 15 May 1962. Among those arrested was Dolores Medio.

Faced with the choice of paying an exorbitant fine of 25,000 pesetas or serving jail time upon her arrest, Medio "chose" the latter, likely not a choice at all due to financial realities of the time. Her one-month stay in prison, which began in a common, or holding, cell, served as inspiration for her manuscript *Celda común*. Although written in 1963, the novel only saw publication in 1996, due to the freeze and subsequent outcome of "rejected for publication" by censors, effectively derailing the possibility of its publication during the dictatorship. The entire corpus of its contents was deemed immoral, so much so that revising the manuscript was not an option. The novel recounts, through third-person narration focalized on Teresa, the moments of her initial detainment and processing as well as the first four days of her incarceration in the large holding cell until she would be assigned a place within the general population of Madrid's Ventas Prison.

The historical and political context of the subversive act of participating in the protest that gives rise to Medio's incarceration situates her writing as revolutionary as she clamors for humane treatment of the incarcerated women with whom she interacted: sex workers and criminals of varying degrees. Through her protagonist and in her own life, Medio staunchly advocated for women's education as a means to rise above discrimination and gender-based injustices. Foundational paradigms in the context that integrates Medio's self-history with Spain's national history mirror Kristine Byron's work on Dolores Ibárruri, La Pasionaria, famed opponent of Fascism who defiantly shouted "No pasarán" upon the Nationalist troop's arrival in Madrid in 1936. Byron's understanding of Marie Marmo Mullaney's concept of women's positioning on the spectrum of "the triple oppression of law, family, and workplace" (Qtd. in Byron 144) may be extended to this present study to emblematize Medio's interplay between Vega and the jailed women. Medio's voice in *Celda común*, silenced for decades through the delayed publication of her novel and thereby relegated to the nebulous region of the margins, is now unsilenced and as such casts light on the plight of women precluded from advocating for themselves.[15]

Medio mediates her plight as an incarcerated woman through her alter ego, Teresa Vega. Medio's own autobiographical accounts provided in various interviews reference a parallelism between her own experiences and those she narrates. Janet Winecoff Díaz confirms that Medio's work references "considerable autobiographical elements in setting, background and events, and [...] a strong social impetus. Her sympathy for the underdog [...] is not merely a political stance" (245), two predominant themes Linda Gould Levine identifies: economic and emotional deprivation (213), which are cornerstones in *Celda común*.

Because of the novel's late publication date, however, it may be argued that the author's message—to shed light on the deficiencies of the carceral state that women endured in Francoist Spain—has been diluted. Indeed, this holds true for the time contemporary to the novel's creation. Nonetheless, reaching readers' hands some 30 years after the manuscript was completed reveals telling details about how Medio viewed her civic responsibility to honor the women, the "underdogs," who shared the confined space with her by granting them the humanity of which society had stripped them for their inferior social status, specifically the case of the sex workers. This discussion avoids euphemistic terms for sex worker ("streetwalker," "lady of the evening," etc.) as well as the socially charged term "prostitute," terms that emphasize their marginality and vulnerability, and highlight their objectification. In a society that views prostitution as shameful and dishonorable, euphemistic phrasing accentuates a portrayal as an act of dramatic or entertaining performance. In their peppered and colorful language the sex workers explained the financial exigencies or family dysfunction that contributed to their plight. Where Medio and Vega first perceive these women as uncivilized, they quickly gain an appreciation for and nuanced understanding of their situation, immediately positioning

---

15 Medio's account of her incarceration vastly differs from the stark portrayals of physical and sexual violence Mercedes Núñez Targa narrates based on her incarceration in the same prison during the Spanish Civil War in *Carcel de Ventas*, published in Paris in 1967.

the narration under the rubric of testimony for *la recuperación de la memoria histórica*.

What can narrating a mere four days of incarceration reveal? Or from another angle, what about these days in jail was deemed so threatening to the regime or to morality that the censors denied authorizing the novel's publication? The answer moves beyond the reason that Medio or Vega were arrested for their political activism, resting as well upon the attitudes, actions, and ideas of the other jailed women, defined by an inadequate legal system and presented in a way that hints toward their victimization.

The censorship database does not contain an entry on *Celda común* despite Medio's affirmation that censors would not authorize publication without numerous textual revisions, revisions she chose not to incorporate; the reasons for this absence are not apparent. Readers today do, however, have access to Manuel L. Abellán's summary and interpretation of the report. To gain a better understanding of why the novel was relegated to obscurity until after the Franco regime, Abellán explains:

> Censura le sugirió supresiones y cambios de diversa importancia. El cambio más notorio, y exponente inconfundible de la pudibundez censoria, acaso sea el relativo [a] [...] una prostituta, que debía mutarse en delincuente encarcelado por falta incurrida contra la Ley de Tráfico. *Lex dura*, esa que arroja directamente a sus infractores en los calabozos de la Dirección General de Seguridad. ¿Se percató el censor de la insensatez y temeridad cometida a sugerir tan livianamente semejantes cambios? ¿Hubiese tolerado el ministro de Gobernación de la época la publicación de tal descabello? La congelación voluntaria del manuscrito evitó, sin duda, disgustos e innecesarios quebraderos de cabeza a esa respetable escritora, pese [...] a las mejoras propuestas por la administración censoria. (Abellán, *Censura y creación* 81)

Admittedly, the sex workers have broken the law, spew vulgarities, and lack decorum in their behavior. Yet this way of being does not define them. Many of them convey in practical terms an understanding of the commodification of the female body, including the relationship between maternity and the inability to work. They are skilled in creativity in their work to maximize their earnings. They realize that they are punished by a judicial system when their male customers are not, whereby unjust laws criminalize only the female's role in sex worker industry by positioning their profession as one they willingly and voluntarily enter. In what can be considered a literary diatribe against the violation of incarcerated women's rights, the irreverent characters in *Celda común* embody the fear of sexual repression.

Additional vulnerability relates to the women's lack of protection of a parental figure. One woman's mother transacted her daughter's entry to the sex worker industry whereas another's father lost sight of his daughter's actions that led to her perdition. Medio's portrayal of the families who failed their daughters is born of Francoist ideology of the family unit, to borrow from Mary Nash, as the salvation that will lead to Spain's future prosperity (*Pronatalism* 162). In other words, the institution of the family, whereby parents are entrusted with ensuring the well-being of their offspring, is under attack. The women's maternal role in particular is under attack on a double bind: motherhood negatively affects their ability to work, which leads them to the periphery as they engage in taboo practices of avoiding pregnancy or undergoing illegal abortions.

As the novel opens, Teresa is forcibly leaving her apartment under police escort after hurriedly packing the few essentials in her travel bag she believes will be permitted in jail but not considered standard issued: a small amount of clothing, a brush, a toothbrush, soap, and some notepads. Officers transport her to the Dirección General de Seguridad, police headquarters, for questioning upon her arrest. The third-person narrator identifies the reason she is arrested with less precision than would have actually been the case in the author's experience, as if to distance truth from fiction: "Le detuvieron por solidarizarse con los conflictos laborales de Asturias, según parece" (23). Then, the balancing of the narration with dialogue and thoughts brings Teresa's voice to the fore, with a gradual shift in the dialogued voice as the narration unfolds. While thinking of ways to combat the solitude of her first night under arrest, she hears others singing without reproach and decides to sing the hymn "Asturias, patria querida" from her cell, in hopes that someone will recognize the call to camaraderie: "se acerca a la puerta, pero apenas puede cantar. Dice sólo: Asturias... La voz le sale apenas de la garganta"; she recalls the images of her homeland and gains the courage to shout "¡Asturias!" (23).

Once transferred from the Dirección General de Seguridad to the Ventas Prison, Teresa realizes the gravity of her surroundings, as she lives in filth and squalor the narrator describes in detail. It is worth noting that the Ventas Prison website marks the site's significance in terms of historical memory. The facility, open from 1931 to 1969, "fue la prisión femenina más poblada de la historia de España. Concebida originariamente como 'Prisión Modelo' para mujeres por Victoria Kent—dentro del nuevo proyecto penalista de la Segunda República—en 1939 acabó convirtiéndose, con el triunfo franquista, en todo lo contrario: un gigantesco 'almacén de reclusas' en el que mujeres y niños se hacinaron en las peores condiciones imaginables" (Cárcel de Ventas). The majority of the novel's action takes place in and around the holding cell, and specifically in one of the *galerías* that houses between 30-40 women.

Despite the prison's abhorrent conditions, the necessity of correctional institutions reflects official discourse as summarized by one of the guards: "Figúrese usted qué ganado tenemos: ladronas, asesinas, prostitutas... Cada una de estas mujeres lleva a cuestas una historia de infamante. Si se las dejara actuar libremente, convertirían esto en un manicomio, en un prostíbulo... La cárcel tiene que ser para ellas un saludable castigo" (168). In parenthetical text, the guard reflects upon her differentiation of the types of criminals: "Estas cochinas políticas van a darnos más guerra que un millar de putas" (169). Teresa challenges the guard's erroneous interpretation that reflects the official political discourse of the criminalized sex workers, which holds that the women choose this employment to attain luxury, by positing instead that they work for survival, to cover the basic necessities of food and shelter.

Although Teresa realizes that she cannot remedy society's injustices that privilege the wealthy at the expense of the poor, whether in or out of the prison system, she capitalizes on the power of her written words to shine a light on the societal woes that lead women to commodify their bodies. Medio's writing reveals what she learns from the stories the sex workers tell, such as one mother who commodifies her four daughters, an act that even the guard describes as "es criminal" (170). Teresa believes this social ill is curable only by destroying the root cause, yet she realistically understands that she alone cannot solve the problem. What is in Teresa's purview, though, is to take action permissible within the structure of the correctional facility. Social hierarchies in Francoist Spain spill into the jail, with its pecking order determined not by force or violence but by the length of time spent in jail and also by the amount of money each prisoner could access from the outside. Teresa benefits from both circumstances as she moves up a notch or two when new prisoners arrive after her and when those around her quickly realize that she has a source of financial support from her family.

At the beginning of the novel, Teresa is the sole political prisoner in the facility. Despite the compassion she begins to feel for the "true criminals" around her, on day two of her stay she seeks out familiar faces among the new detainees, certain that other women involved in the protest will eventually join her. When three more *políticas* arrive, they team together to clean and then occupy a nonfunctioning shower room. Their collective role becomes one of alterity and then shifts to articulate a narrative not of similarity but of difference, setting them apart from the rest of inmates because their crimes are different—politically rather than morally driven—and they hail from a different walk of life.

This division underscores injustice: those with financial means bribe the guards to assign tasks to those unable to pay for a reprieve. The unpleasant or painful tasks include cleaning toilets without cleaning products and with minimal water or scrubbing grease off of the air vents of the kitchen equipment in the summer heat, with a brick-like tool and, again, no cleaning products. The division is voiced by one of the guards who seems inclined to give Teresa special treatment but is precluded from doing so because, as she repeatedly remarks, she is following the rules (113). Teresa belongs to the category of the "haves" whereas the sex workers constitute the "have-nots," in terms of their financial mobility and, even more precariously, their level of education.

Teresa's language of confinement mimics the language she employed before her incarceration, with which she articulates the idea that there is strength in numbers to combat social or political injustice. Within the jail walls, she clamors "Hay que organizarse y trabajar en equipo" (137), before the prospect of an uneven distribution of cleaning and maintenance tasks assigned to the inmates. The injustice is compounded when those who maneuver through the system with financial means can bribe the guards to assign tasks to those unable to pay in exchange for a reprieve. Teresa's call to organize prompts her political prisoner comrades to pool their resources in terms of their personal items as a way to join forces. The *políticas* break up the established order by refusing to pay the guards to assign their cleaning chores to others, despite having the money to do so. In solidarity, the women defiantly refuse to adhere to the "pay to rest model," and instead complete the work. "Nos van a estropear la cárcel si siguen aquí mucho tiempo" one guard bemoans in parenthetical thought (179). Teresa equates cleanliness with order and order with a sense of improvement in her surroundings, an analogy of the order she aspires to beyond the prison: for Teresa "es cuestión de conseguir un poco de orden," as she adapts to the group mentality dynamic and negotiates the realities of the scarcity of food, disgusting bathrooms and offensive odors, bed bugs, hard straw beds—pungent and stained with evaporated perspiration and dried menstrual blood—and eating meager rations with dirty tableware.

Another area of concern for Teresa is the inadequate medical care in the jail. Common in-house knowledge about the condition of the maternity ward and the treatment women receive there suggests that it is not a desirable place to be because of a stricter regimen, and also because it houses the young children born to their incarcerated mothers. Although the details surrounding the maternity ward do not explicitly reference when the women became impregnated, the reader is left to infer the level of sexual violence that took place in the jail in the context of this narrative silence. Since Teresa does not visit this area, she can only rely on limited descriptions she hears from others. She does, however, visit the infirmary because she fears infection due to her blistered then bloodied hands after completing her cleaning chores. The text reveals the doctor's biases against her as well as the inadequacies of medical treatment in the jail, as she enters the room. The doctor's authoritative voice downplays Teresa's wounds: blisters to be cleaned with soap and water. When Teresa retorts that her hands are infected and she needs penicillin, the doctor refuses, stating there is none. When Teresa protests and explains that she will pay for medicine from a pharmacy outside the jail, he insults her by attributing the wounds to soft hands of political prisoners: "acostumbradas a hacer nada... y la menor cosa..." (187). His course of treatment: he dispatches her with a bottle of rubbing alcohol. Summarily dismissed, she walks past two patients: one moaning in pain with a gangrenous leg she saw when she first entered who now desperately shouts "que me la corten... Ya he dicho que me la corten" (188) and the "revirgadora de Embajadores" (189). This inmate is in the infirmary due to facial injuries she sustained after having sulfuric acid thrown on her face in retaliation for trying to trick a man into believing his fiancée and then wife (actually a former sex worker) was a virgin after her "restorative treatment" by the celestinesque figure of the *revirgadora*. The vengeful act is justifiable according to official rhetoric, as the culprit remains free, because it restores the social order that punishes amoral behavior in the weak and downtrodden.

Social class disparity is also debilitating in terms of educational level. Teresa attempts a symbolic bridging of this gap by promoting literacy. Teresa's efforts harken back to Irene Gal, the protagonist of Medio's earlier novel, *Diario de una maestro* (1961), in her role as a teacher during the Second Republic who was charged with educating students in a rural Asturian town (Soliño 30-31). In *Celda común*, Teresa and her fellow jailed activists listen in stupor as the women share their origin stories, stories of moral corruption that began with one woman at the young age of seven years and also incuded another woman named Coral, repeatedly objectified by being passed from one man to another to the point that "se acostumbraba" (201). She recounts that "al principio no me gustaba, ¿sabes? Cuando me cosían [...] porque a ellos les gustaba romperme eso... Cuando venía algún amigo nuevo a comer con el amo, pues el amo me compraba un pañuelo o unas medias y me decía: 'Tú, Rocío, como si nada, como si es la primera vez, ¿comprendes? Chilla lo que quieras.' Pero yo gritaba porque me dolía. [...] Cada vez era más difícil y cada vez me hacía sufrir más. Pero ellos se divertían" (201). Teresa realizes that, through this shocking story, she has gained entry to a *submundo* whose existence was heretofore unknown to her, a watershed moment that springs her to action. To the reader's surprise, Teresa asks Coral to stop sharing her story, not to silence her, since she through Medio's writing the story will endure, but to help her cope with the trauma and begin to forget (or in today's verbiage "process") the atrocity; and to replace the traumatic past, Teresa forges a modest path of enlightenment, as well as dignity, for Coral, the first sex worker she teaches the rudimentary steps to read and write. For this teacher, "todas las armas son lícitas para ganar una pequeña batalla contra la ignorancia" (206). Reducing the incidence of future crime through increased literacy, indeed, is an enduring humanitarian endeavor that exists as an avenue to social and financial betterment and empowerment.

Although Teresa and her friends realize that correcting the injustices surrounding the sex worker industry is beyond their reach, they recognize that "hemos de resignarnos a poner siempre nuestro granito de arena" (235), as the narration winds down. Another political prisoner enters the holding cell, poised to adapt to her surroundings just as the other *políticas* had done in the days before. The novel draws to a close "in media res" amidst the daily obscenity-laced banter and verbal jabs among the prisoners, an indication of the repetetiveness associated with the passage of time in jail.

In *Celda común*, Dolores Medio captures a moment in time and place she experienced firsthand. She imbues in her protagonist Teresa Vega the qualities that she herself exhibits in yearning for justice for all, with eyes keenly trained on women who commodify themselves in order to survive. It remains clear that, although some of the women believe that they exercise their free will in choosing their profession, the judicial system creates and applies gender-infused laws. Compounded by social inequities, this paradigm perpetuates financial hardship, coupled with the lack of access to education, and overrides the women's exercising of agency.

Medio combines her self-history with national history, to draw attention to multiple levels of injustice affecting the jailed women. Medio's spotlight on the unjust legal system through the incarcerated sex workers' own words gives voice to these fighters from the margins as they begin to move out of the obscurity of the *submundo*. Medio suggests that one key factor in combating injustices rests in the role of literacy and takes the symbolic step of doing her part by beginning with "un granito de arena" with the character aptly named Coral.

Susana March y Ricardo Fernández de la Reguera: *La boda de Alfonso XIII* (1965)

Susana March (1915-1990) initially gained attention for her poetry, with her first collection, *Rutas*, published in 1938, followed by seven additional collections between 1946 and 1987. As a novelist, her writing includes *novelas rosas* and neorealist fiction, with the last one of those novels published during the dictatorship, *Algo muere cada día* (1956), in addition to *Cosas que pasan* (1983). In the gap between the last two novels appears her most substantive contribution to Spanish literature of her time, a series of 12 *Episodios Nacionales Contemporáneos* that follow the model of Benito Pérez Galdós's *Episodios Nacionales* she coauthored with her husband Ricardo Fernández de la Reguera (1912-2000), published by Planeta between 1963 and 1979.[16] Indeed, March is not the sole author of the novel studied here, *La boda de Alfonso XIII* (1965); however, her contributions are significant, and she takes an active role in the censorship process when the authorization to publish is in peril. According to Pilar Palomo, both authors collaborated on all volumes although they alternated primary authorship

---

16   The novels' central action takes place during and surrounding the events that begin with the Spanish American War in 1898 to the postwar period of the 1940s: *Héroes de Cuba, Héroes de Filipinas, El fin de una Regencia, La boda de Alfonso XIII, La Semana Trágica, España neutral: 1914-1918, El desastre de Annual, La Dictadura, La caída de un rey, La República, La guerra (1936-1939)*, and *La posguerra*.

from one title to the next.[17] March indicates in her interview with Laureano Bonet that the series is a joint project, adding that "Vamos tomando juntos los datos y después cada uno redacta su respectivo libro. No obstante las novelas van firmadas por los dos" ("Dos escritores" 13).

Palomo and Blanca Ripoll Sintes examine the literary nexus of the contemporary series with the Galdosian *Episodios*, but very little has been said in the way of critical inquiry on any one of the novels in Fernández de la Reguera and March's series that not only continues the tradition of one of the most influential writers of Spain's modern literary tradition but also significantly serves as a precursor to the historical fiction cultivated post-dictatorship. In considering these 12 novels as testimony to a politically constructed past, in the vein of social realist writing,

> history is rendered in a way that simultaneously affirms and negates time. That is to say, the confluence of fictional and historical narration for the social realists hinges upon 'historical' circumstances that are experiential rather than narratively reconfigured (time affirmed), and upon a historical past from which the social realists

---

17   Future inquiry may uncover, perhaps through corpus comparison of any of the coauthored novels with one written by March and one written by Fernández de la Reguera, the distribution of work in the coauthored writing of this series. Palomo states that Fernández de la Reguera and March "Al parecer, alternaban la realización de los episodios, pero los dos colaboraban en todos (631, n. 52). However, we are not to read "alternating" as "every other one" since she surmises attribution, of the first (*Héroes de Cuba*) to Fernández de la Reguera and the third to March (*El fin de una Regencia*). Palomo attributes the seventh (*El desastre de Annual*) to Fernández de la Reguera as well as, indirectly, the fifth (*La Semana Trágica*), by pointing out that character of Luis Gómez de la Riba in *La Semana Trágica* is of March's creation, according to Alfredo Fernández de la Reguera, the couple's son (631, n. 52). The likely attribution is the first two to Fernández de la Reguera for their thematic uniformity and then *Fin de una Regencia* and *La boda de Alfonso XIII* to March—for thematic transition and overlap with Barcelona—such that the remaining episodes could have alternated in primary authorship. This conjecture is also supported by March's direct correspondence with the censorship board.

are excluded by a political State that holds the past and its history as its own (time negated). (Herzberger, *Narrating the Past* 41).

As an example of historical fiction in the Galdosian sense, it emerges in a context that Mar Langa Pizarro sandwiches between "la actitud crítica del realismo social de los años cincuenta [que] se centró en mostrar la cotidianidad del momento; y la experimentalidad de los sesenta y los primeros setenta [que] se volcó más en el desarrollo formal que en la temática" (109).

Because comments that address March's writing in the series are usually limited to the likes of "A prolific writer, Susana March has collaborated with Fernández de la Reguera, her husband, on several historic novels set in the twentieth century" (Stycos 1009) or simply state that the historic novels are "set in the early twentieth century rather than the nineteenth" (Pérez, "March" 369), the analysis of the fourth installment of the series, *La boda de Alfonso XIII* fits with the parameters of this study in light of its multiple readings before the censorship board, the first of which rendered the decision to deny authorization to publish. Further, given the extensive length of both each novel and the series in sum, in conjunction with the relative absence of critical study—in particular for its historical focus—*La boda de Alfonso XIII* is worthy of inclusion here also because it is illustrative of the transactional relationship between the censorship board and author. *La boda* was heavily marked in its typescript form, and censors identified dozens of passages threatening to political dogma in response to the question on the censorship evaluation form, revealing that factually driven, historical fiction is not exempt of censorial stricture. Manuel L. Abellán explains that *La boda* was "suspendida íntegramente por la censura aunque, más tarde, tras ímprobas negociaciones y numerosos cortes fuera autorizada" (*Censura* 207), and it also needed the authorization of *censores militares* (207), for its focus on political ideologies dealing with anarchy and communism in the context of early twentieth century Spain.

The first three novels in the series attained swift authorization for publication. Of *Héroes de Cuba* (1963), the censor remarks "desfilan por este volumen los más destacados acontecimientos de la Historia y de la política española de 1898" (File *Héroes de Cuba*). The report for *Héroes de Filipinas* (1963) reads "Un trabajo de integración subjetiva, integrado por lo novelesco y creador, y la información racional copiosa y verídica, destacándose sobre todo la inmortal hazaña del General (entonces modesto oficial) Cerezo, a quien el censor que suscribe tuvo el honor de tratar en su juventud" (File *Héroes de Filipinas*). The historical reality of narrative location referencing a historical time beyond Spain's borders and in a political climate distanced from the dictatorship would also have contributed to their authorization. Further, the authors would have been perceived as sympathetic supporters of the regime considering that Fernández de la Reguera supported the Nationalist cause during the Spanish Civil War.[18] The censorship report on the third novel in the series, *Fin de una regencia* (1964), classifies it a story of "una sencilla acción familiar que acontece en la España de fines de siglo y comienzos del presente" (File *Fin de una regencia*) pertaining to a widower, Ignacio, and his three sons of differing political views. The censor concludes that "La acción está conducida con acierto y buena traza literaria" and devalues the historical content: "sobra historia—pues tampoco se trata de novela histórica" (File *Fin de una regencia*). The perceived lack of historical content relating to the transition of the monarchy from the Queen Regent María Cristina in 1902 to her son Alfonso XIII shifts the censor's interpretation of the novel to conclude that although "algunos episodios amatorios a cargo de Ignacio [son] un poco subidos de tono pueden excusarse en atención a la buena calidad del relato. Desde el punto de vista político tampoco hay nada rechazable" (File *Fin de una regencia*). With the temporal-spatial divide in the first two novels of the series, and the minimal lack of po-

---

18   Fernández de la Reguera's *Vagabundos provisionales* (1959) was heavily marked and could only be published after the author incorporated revisions on approximately 25 pages. The censor who evaluated the typescript signaled in his report threatening text in various categories: to morality for "por el lenguaje soez y de prostíbulo que emplean de continuo los tres personajes y el mismo autor cuando habla por su cuenta," to the government officials whom "Los tacha de ignorantes y groseros (202-04) y de codicia y mala educación," and to political institutions "con críticas simples y alusiones indirectas" (File *Vagabundos provisionales*).

litical undertones in the third, the closer proximity of events and their politicized nature that pit anarchist Mateo Morral against the king in *La boda de Alfonso XIII* resulted in a more scrutinized approach the censors took in evaluating the fourth installment, which narrated the events surrounding the domestic terrorist act intended to destroy the monarchy by assassinating the king.

A daily account in third-person narration, the novel's 14 sections correspond to each day the coauthors identify by day and date, beginning on Sunday, 20 May 1906, with Morral's departure by train from Barcelona to Madrid, and ending on Saturday, 2 June 1906, the day he commits suicide. With about 85% of the novel's 437 pages dedicated to the days leading up to the failed assassination attempt on Alfonso XIII during his wedding procession on 31 May, ample discussion and description of the political climate informs the plot.

The novel received three evaluations, 13 and 19 November 1964 and 14 December 1964, concluding that the novel was not publishable. Although the first report allows that it may be published with cuts on 15 pages, the second advises against publication before the third definitively classifies it "No autorizable," citing offensive text on over 30 pages and denying publication. The first censor writes a scathing report in which he questions the value and veracity of the novel's plot and characters:

> un *relato folletinesco y ramplón*, sin imaginación en el aspecto novelesco ni autenticidad en el histórico. *Mateo Morral es el desgraciado protagonista* y casi todos los personajes que le rodean imaginariamente son muñecos de trapo que ni siquiera llegan a la altura de comparsas. Una verdadera desdicha es esta absurda narración que aspira a contarnos un "episodio nacional contemporáneo." (File *La boda*, emphasis original)

This summation represents a vast difference from the perceived innocuous writing in the first three novels in the series that contained "información racional copiosa y verídica" conveyed through action "con acierto y buena traza literaria," which is perceived to have dramatically devolved into the absurd and inauthentic, notwithstanding the painstaking accuracy with which the authors weave the reported facts of the events into the narration.

The second censor notably discounts Susana March's co-authorship in his plot summary:

> La obra del Sr. Fernández de la Reguera es una reconstrucción novelesca del ambiente en que se incubara el atentado de Mateo Morral contra la vida de Alfonso XIII el día en que éste regresaba por la calle Mayor desde el templo de los Jerónimos, de contraer matrimonio con la princesa de Battenberg. (File *La boda*)

This second censor indicts Fernández de la Reguera for displaying a predilection for values

> <u>que idealizan al regicidio y exaltan el altruismo y honrada sinceridad de sus cómplices y correligionarios anarquistas, en contraste con el grosero avallasamiento del pueblo por parte de un clero corrompido y de un ejército usurpador</u>, encastillado en su arrogante Ley de Jurisdiciones [sic], tan grata al <u>militarista Alfonso XIII</u>. (File *La boda*, emphasis original)

Although he distinguishes the extremist ideals of certain characters as separate from those of the author, he surmises that the unfavorable and unflattering portrayal of conservativism, through character or ideological representation, does not bode well for the novel's publication. His final assessment establishes: "Por lo que el suscrito opina que la obra examina, en cuanto ensalza en el fondo la intrepidez y altruismo de los secuaces de la violencia política, constituye un peligro para la exaltación de romántica de los lectores jóvenes y NO SERÍA PRUDENTE AUTORIZARLA" (File *La boda*).

After briefly summarizing the plot, the third censor divides his remarks based on two readings of the novel, the first of which is the narrative: "transcripción casi literal de las noticias aparecidas en la prensa de aquellos días sobre el atentado (V. por ejemplo el "ABC" de entonces)" (File *La boda*). Notably, this assessment contradicts the erroneous claim of historical inaccuracy the first censor reported. In addition, in the 24 May 1906 edition of *El Imparcial*, the list of royal guests and dignitaries and the types of carriages that will transport them from the San Jerónimo church to the Royal Palace (2) is a close reflection of what appears in the novel. In fact, one of the characters is holding the newspaper clipping that describes the wedding cortege (369-71). The second reading yields content that consists of "*comentarios* que supone el autor en boca de Morral, sus amigos, conocidos ocasionales y demás personajes" (File *La boda*, emphasis original). Unlike the first reading that references the historical record already in circulation that contains no objectionable material, the obstacles to publication appear in the second reading in which "el elevado n° [de revisiones] que se ha tenido que hacer—por motivos especialmente de índole política— obliga a proponer la denegación" (File *La boda*). His additional comments on Morral offer further insight to the questionable portrayal of the bomber as "*un hombre distinguido, culto, amante de las flores y de la buena literatura y que quiere regenerar la sociedad*" (File *La boda*, emphasis original). The irony is not to be lost on the method of delivering the Orsini bomb—hidden in a bouquet of flowers Morral lobbed over the balcony—and on the references to Morral's interactions with notable Generation of 1898 writers of the of time that included Pío and Ricardo Baroja, Miguel de Unamuno and Ramón del Valle-Inclán.

As the novel journeyed through the censorship process, both authors receive a letter dated 28 January 1965, about six weeks after the third report, which conveys that authorization to publish has been denied. Normally, correspondence of this nature does not form part of the censorship file on any given novel. However, the transactional nature of the censorship process surfaces through this communication just as it did in the case of Rosa Cajal's *Un paso más*.

After learning of the outcome on the censorship report, March responds with a letter dated 2 February 1965 in which she asks for a rereading of the novel with certain revisions incorporated, followed by another letter dated 3 March 1965 in which she explains that the book took about a year to compose and is part of a series; it is the fruit of exhaustive archival research that requires such a portrayal of the happenings in order to present an accurate, fictionalized account. She then identifies other assassinations, or attempts, to highlight their grounding in historical reality, and she also explains that the reconstruction of events requires that they (the co-authors) give voice to the anarchist, who must say disparaging things to lend credibility to his characterization. She agrees to edit the novel to incorporate the minimally necessary suggested revisions and submit for subsequent review, in a negotiation of terms of publication that seldom surfaces in the censorship reports. The novel's publication was authorized after the revisions indicated on about 40 pages, rather than approximately 100, were incorporated. The fact that March wrote the letter to advocate for authorization to publish the co-authored novel prompts the questions as to why it was she rather than her husband, whether or not the censors would have perceived her role as secretarial or secondary in the creative process, or whether a letter written by Fernández de la Reguera rather than March may have seemed more confrontational. The correspondence reveals that the censorial outcome, in this case, was subject to negotiation.

I highlight here seven representative examples of questionable text that censors demanded be removed or revised, each dealing with political references that ultimately the authors incorporated in the novel's final version. To begin, on his train ride from Barcelona to Madrid, Morral's conversation with a fellow traveler enters the realm of politics with a discussion of the recently passed Ley de Jurisdicciones (24 April 1906). The law authorized martial law under the leadership of Alfonso XIII and was met with fierce protest in Barcelona, whose citizens considered the law a threat to their local rule. As Brian J. Dendle explains, "In 1906 [Segismundo] Moret obtained passage of the Ley de Jurisdicciones, which reserved to military courts the trial of any offenses against the army, police, or nation. The army now formed a state within the state. For Fernández Almagro, approval of the Ley de Jurisdicciones revealed not only the militaristic nature of the monarchy but also the total impotence of Spanish liberalism" (82).

In the novel, Morral describes the scene in the Plaça de Catalunya, with 200,000 protesters, led by prominent Republican political figures of the time that advocated for Catalunya's sovereign rule, listed (mostly) by surname: Nicolás Salmerón, Gumersindo de Azcárate, Morote, Francisco Pi y Arsuaga, Rodrigo Soriano, Junoy, Ventosa,

Giner de los Ríos, Pi y Suñer, Raimundo de Abadal Calderó, Alberto Rusiñol.

The original typescript begins with Morral's remarks, with the censor's strikethrough in pen:

— [...] Los militares han conseguido que se aprobara la ley de Jurisdicciones. ~~Pero en Barcelona se les ha dado una lección que no podrán olvidarla.~~
— Usted es muy optimista. ~~No cree que los militares acepten lecciones de nadie. Son una casa muy cerril y de vanidad tan grotesca que se creen los depositarios exclusivos del honor y del sentimiento de patria.~~
— Lo peor no es eso. Lo peor es que están engañando al Rey.
— Un engaño a sabiendas, porque don Alfonso sigue muy complacido el juego ~~militarista~~.
— No estoy conforme...cuidado, ~~porque los cepadones [sic] le arrastrarán a su perdición.~~ (Ts. 11)

The revised text appears in the novel as:

— Los militares han conseguido que se aprobara la ley de Jurisdicciones, que dará mucho que hablar. Lo peor no es eso. Lo peor es que están engañando al Rey.
— Un engaño a sabiendas, porque don Alfonso sigue muy complacido el juego.
— No estoy conforme. Le engañan y le han hecho dar un paso muy peligroso en el vacío. Debe tener cuidado. (Ms. 17)

The excisions and rephrasing soften the projected humiliation and criticism of the central government and eliminate the foreboding of the king's demise at the hands of the *capadones*, a term the censor also marked in need of revision four pages later and which the authors replaced with "oficiales levantiscos" (Ts. 15, Ms. 21). The revisions temper the tone by removing the qualifier from the phrase *juego militarista* in referring to the passage of the law. Further, the veiled threat to the king's downfall (*perdición*) now appears as Morral's vague conjecture and only indirectly references the monarch. Censors disapprove of identifying Alfonso's reign as militaristic, so that the original description of the passage of the *Ley de Jurisdicciones*—"aprobada, ~~corroborando, ya de un modo irrevocable, la tendencia militarista del reinado de Alfonso XIII~~" (Ts. 16, censor strikethrough)—is simply identified as "aprobada" in the published version (Ms. 22).

When Morral arrives in Madrid and begins to reacquaint himself with the city where he had briefly lived several years earlier, he marvels at his surroundings in the Plaza de Cibeles. As he turns his gaze to the Banco de España, he reminisces about the city's grandiosity and waxes poetic at the great amount of loss he perceives: loss of aristocracy, discontinued masquerade balls at the Fernán Núñez Palace, languishing literary discussion circles, the death of Nuñez de Arce, and disregard for current writers. The atmosphere Morral navegates in the capital city he no longer recognizes forebodes its impending destruction: "Se iba ciegamente hacia el más cruel de los materialismos, hacia la explotación implacable, el egoísmo brutal, la insolencia y el poder aniquilados, aplastante, el dinero" (Ts. 39, Ms. 49-50). The censor considered the next lines too threatening for public consumption and required their excision: Madrid "[s]e iba hacia la muerte. ¿Qué culpa tenía él? La sociedad había armado su mano. La armó la injusticia. Le estaban pidiendo todos, a gritos, exigiéndolo—pobres y poderosos—que descargara el golpe mortal. No; no podía acusarle. Ellos, todos, lo habían querido" (Ts. 39). Exculpating Morral by attributing the rationale for his impending attempt at regicide to the injustices he is experiencing shifts the blame away from Morral himself, an interpretation the censor would wish to quell so that in the end Morral alone is held accountable for actions he undertook.

The censorship report also addresses depictions of Spain's history. Fernández de la Reguera and March were aware of many intricacies of the Spanish-American War from the research they conducted for the first two novels in the *Eposidios* series and attempted to extrapolate some of its statistics for inclusion in *La boda de Alfonso XIII*. However, because the numbers relating to the loss of lives painted Spain in an unfavorable light, the authors were not permitted to include the death toll nor reference the daily reality of thousands of deaths of women and children in Spain. In a conversation between a journalist named

Pedro Acosta—whom Morral approached to arrange for a falsified press pass for the day of the royal wedding—and four domino players in a local café, the discussion turns toward the political, in which Acosta extols the virtues of anarchy and destruction as a path to rebirth and renewal. He challenges one of the players who decries violence as an end to justify the means approach to enacting political change.

The original typescript reads:

— Sus escrúpulos son muy curiosos — replicó Acosta — ~~Pero ¿no le repugna que murieran 200.000 infelices soldados españoles en la última guerra y más de 200.000 inocentes reconcentrados cubanos, tan sólo durante la sublevación de Baire? No le repugnan los miles y miles de mujeres y niños que fallecen cada día en España,~~ en el mundo entero. (Ts. 111, censor strikethrough)[19]

This is revised to:

— Sus escrúpulos son muy curiosos — replicó Acosta —. Le repugna que en un atentado parezca hombres, mujeres y niños inocentes. ¡También a mí! Pero, ¿no le repugnan los miles y miles de hombres, mujeres y niños que fallecen cada día en el mundo entero, de hambre, de frío, de enfermedad? (Ms. 128)

---

19   The 200,000 figure refers to the approximate number of Spanish soldiers who fought in the war, though the death toll hovers around 20,000 Spaniards who lost their lives during the war or during the aftermath, due in large part to disease. Further, the *Grito de Baire* (1895) was the call to arms that launched the third and final Cuban War of Independence. Although Fernández de Reguera and March conflate this event with reconcentration, the latter, begun in 1897 and in effect until the end of the war under the leadership of Valeriano Weyler, consisted of relocating rural populations who were likely to join the rebel cause to concentration camps where they were subjected to inhumane treatment, enduring famine, filth, and disease. The death toll due to reconcentration is impossible to ascertain. Figures range from about 60,000 by some accounts and up to 400,000 by others, but historian John L. Tone has arrived at a range of 150,000 to 170,000 lives lost by comparing census reports against statistical documentation from the various camps (209-23).

The complete textual extraction of the circumstances and loss of lives in the war, Spaniards and Cubans alike, satisfies censorial exigencies because it downplays Spain's defeat and doubly shields readers from the perception of both the *infelices soldados españoles* and the projection of the *reconcentrados* as innocent, when they were perceived by Spanish troops as a threat to Spanish sovereignty for the likelihood that Cubans living in rural populations would take up arms against colonial rule. The censor would have viewed as favorable the absence of marking Spain as a site with a daily death toll, which in the revised text is extrapolated to be a global malady caused by hunger, cold, and disease.

Another example of malleablizing Spain's stance on wartime loss of life appears in a dialogue between a former soldier in the Philippines, José Miguel Asensio Berzunces, as he describes his body scarred by both knife and bullet. When questioned about his financial situation, his response in the original typescript reveals:

> — No prosperé por la guerra propiamente. ¡No te digo lo que hay! Prosperé por un casual. En la guerra no le agradecen a uno nada. La guerra es una basura. ~~Así reviente todos los que mandan a los hombres a matarse.~~ ¿Ustedes han oído hablar de Baler? (Ts. 293, Ms. 341)[20]

The sentence the censor struck is removed in the printed novel, to erase the military's accountability for sending soldiers to their likely death during the war, in an effort to spare readers from the suggestion that a cavalier government devalues human life.

Textual erasure of threats to conservative ideology is another way censors addressed the following section of the typescript, in which the censor evaluating this novel called for striking a reference to a failed attempted in 1893 on the life of Antonio Cánovas del Castillo. An ac-

---

20 The Siege of Baler (1 July 1898 to 2 June 1899) took place in the Philippines during the Philippine Revolution, which in part coincided with the Spanish American War. Spanish soldiers unaware the war had ended refused to surrender and continued holding ground in the church where they had taken cover.

count of the bombing appears in the 21 June issue of *El Imparcial* and is somewhat mirrored in the typescript. The reported details of the crime allude to the bomber's miscalculation of the timing of the fuse, whereas the text in the typescript would suggest the bomber's remorse at the potential to kill an innocent woman and children. This detail, however, contradicts reporting en *La Época* on 22 June 1893 stating that the bombing happened "cuando ya no pasaba gente y el día declinaba" (2):

> Hacía años un anarquista intentó colocar una bomba en La Huerta, la lujosa mansión de Cánovas del Castillo en la Castellana. Al ir a retirarse, después de dar fuego a la mecha, vio llegar a unos niños acompañados de una criada. El anarquista se precipitó a retirar la bomba. Le estalló entre las manos, arrancándole un brazo y causándole la muerte. (Ts. 299)

The censor strikes this passage to avoid spotlighting the vulnerability of Cánovas's conservative leadership while likewise mitigating the idea that an ideology aligned with anarchy has existed for decades, suggesting that anarchy be cast as a contemporary ill. Readers in the 1960s perhaps would not immediately recall Cánovas's eventual death at the hands of anarchist bomber Michele Angiolillo in 1897.

The passage above continues to elevate the profile of anarchists as defenders of Humanity and to criticize Alfonso's aunt, the *infanta Isabel*, for her role in indoctrinating her nephew's authoritarianism. The original typescript describes the following, in the context of Morral's eavesdropping on a conversation between two women and a man in a café on the eve of the bombing: "hablaban con afecto y admiración de la infanta Isabel" (Ms. 349). In the typescript, Morral rhetorically wonders about the fellow patrons and then elaborates his position:

> ¿Comprenderán esto? ¿Comprenderán que los anarquistas aman a la Humanidad? Kropotkine, su doctrina de amor, un Cristo moderno, un Cristo ácrata. Él, Morral, [...] ama a una mujer, ¿ama a sus semejantes? Probablemente, pero odia a la sociedad. ¡Todo es mentira, una apariencia, trágica farsa! Doña Isabel se acerca al pue-

blo y, sin embargo, nadie ignora su orgullo, la intransigencia radical en sus prerrogativas. No, no han sido culpables del autoritarismo de Alfonso XIII, ni su madre, ni su preceptor, el jesuita Padre Montaña; lo es, sobre todo la infanta Isabel. Ella ha contribuido, como nadie, a ensordecer a su sobrino, a configurar los fantasmas de la dictadura, del absolutismo que cada día se concretan más. Si el déspota no es derribado, ¿qué va a ser de España? (Ts. 299)

The suggestion that Morral is acting to snuff Alfonso's absolutism would in parallel suggest that this absolute authority exists in the first place. The censorship board would have been opposed to this inferred smear on Alfonso's leadership, justifying the entire removal of this passage and placing the weight of Alfonso's authoritarian rule on the *infanta* Isabel's wishes more than a *de facto* reality. As a result, the previous lines were replaced by the following sentence, again, with the ideas originating with the three café patrons: "Aseguran que el profundo afecto que la Infanta Isabel siente por su sobrino está estropeando a don Alfonso y contribuyendo a afirmar su carácter autoritario" (Ms. 350).

The circumstances under which Fernández de la Reguera and March published *La boda de Alfonso XIII* affords the opportunity to examine the threats to ideology even through a narration set in the beginning of the twentieth century. Preserving a carefully cultivated historical image of a glorious Spain was paramount to reflect the strength of the dominant discourse during the dictatorship. That March corresponded with the censorship board to successfully advocate for the revision of less than half of the combined revisions censors marked on 35 pages, some of them representing paragraph-length passages, reveals that the power of negotiation in the censorship process.

Observations

Each of the texts in this chapter has a distinct reason for the denial of publication when first appearing before the censorship board. Threats to the tenets of censorship legislation were too egregious to allow these texts to reach readers hands. The primary infraction in Cajal's novel was the protagonist's blatant disregard for moral precepts dictated by the Catholic Church. The first censor to evaluate the text repeatedly referenced Alejandra's amorality and sinfulness—questioning her psychological soundness for her lack of regret for and awareness of her transgressions—and called the novel's contents immoral. An emboldened and undeterred Cajal petitioned for the second evaluation of her revised novel that would ultimately grant her authorization to publish. Requisite revisions included altering Alejandra's originally unrepentant standpoint and erasing references to the age differences between Alejandra and Óscar as well as Óscar's placing of blame on both Alejandra and his wife for his transgressions. Of note, Óscar is consistently unrepentant of his adulterous actions in both the original and the published versions.

In the case of Canellada's novel, it can be surmised that the passage of time assuages censorial concerns about the publication of material that graphically described wartime injuries in the context of the *hospital de sangre* where protagonist María Eloína worked as a nurse. The decade between the first and second requests to publish that the censorship board initially denied without explanation allowed for a greater temporal distancing to situate the war wounds in the locus of the gradually maturing awareness of historical memory. The vivid images of injuries the soldiers sustained in battle marked their mangled bodies and served as an indictment against the war that was punctuated by the protagonist's implied death at novel's end. That there were no substantive changes to between the two versions attests to the shift as perceived by the censor in protagonism, away from the titular Penal de Ocaña, to María Eloína as the benevolent nurse who displays "sentimientos caritativos y cristianos" in a gender-prescribed role. Institutional representation is also at the center of Medio's novel, yet it is too inflammatory to gain authorization for the sympathetic portrayal of the downtrodden female detainees, many of whom are sex workers, as well as the women whose participation in a protest was deemed to have contributed to civil unrest. Medio describes the grotesque standard of living of the incarcerated women, obviating any physical or sexual violence they likely endured while in prison. The protagonist lends her ear so that through her narration, the voices of the marginalized women are not only heard but memorialized.

Subversive political motivations in *La boda de Alfonso XIII* led censors to deny publication until co-author Susana March interceded to negotiate the terms for authorization. Even though the narrated events transpired half a century earlier, censors deemed the novel a threat to political stability for its protagonist's anarchist ideology, as if the assassination attempt on the monarch would inspire similar activity in present day. By advocating for the would-be assassin's ability to propagate his ideals on anarchy through his own fictional voice, March breathes life into the fictional representation of the historical figure Mateo Morral to render his (fictionally) authentic yet unsympathetic portrayal before her readers.

Women writers who negotiate discursive spaces in Francoist Spain produce a robust corpus of narrative works that put on display a cross-section of plots, themes, and characters. When normative representations fall within the edges of moral, religious, institutional, and political propriety, that is, they are non-threatening to preservation of the values associated with the official discourse, their works gain authorization to publish. This holds true for non-normative representations of the same provided that sufficient context debases these representations in ways that include a moral or spiritual conversion, textual retribution—such as the suffering or death of transgressive characters—or characters' marginal positioning in their respective societies. Further, publisher and author intervention directly with the censorship board debunks the myth that censorship practices were simply accepted at face value. The process at times prompted unambiguous negotiation to rescue texts from obscurity, a recovery effort that endures as critics shift their focus outside the canon and begin to examine the wealth of literary accomplishments mid-century women writers have achieved.

Works Cited

Abellán, Manuel L. "Fenómeno censorio y represión literaria." *Censura y literatura peninsulares*, edited by Manuel L. Abellán, Rodopi, 1987, pp. 5-25.

———. *Censura y creación literaria en España (1939-1976)*. Península, 1980.

Aguilar Fernández, Paloma. *Memoria y olvido de la Guerra Civil española*. Alianza, 2007.

Alás-Brun, Monsterrat. "The Shattered Mirror: Colonial Discourse and Counterdiscourse about Spanish Guinea." *Arizona Journal of Hispanic Cultural Studies*, vol. 8, 2004, pp. 163-76.

Alborg, Concha. "Formica, Mercedes." *The Feminist Encyclopedia of Spanish Literature*, vol. 1, edited by Janet Pérez and Maureen Ihrie, Greenwood, 2002, pp. 242-43.

———. *Cinco figuras en torno a la novela de la posguerra: Galvarriato, Soriano, Formica, Boixadós y Aldecoa*. Libertarias, 1993.

Alós, Concha. *El caballo rojo*. Planeta, 1966.

Álvarez, Carlos Luis. "*Vispera del odio*. Concha Castroviejo." *Punta Europa*, vol. 47, 1959, pp. 134-35.

Álvarez, María and Cristina Somolinos Molina. "Censura y narrativa social escrita por mujer: *La madama* (1969), Concha Alós." *Represura*, vol. 4, 2019, pp. 172-222.

Amills, Rosa. "Liberata Masoliver Novel·lista." *Roser Amills, escritora mallorquina*, 19 Jan. 2008, https://roseramills.com/2008/01/19/liberata-masoliver-novel%c2%b7lista/.html, accessed 5 Mar. 2020.

Arias Careaga, Raquel. *Escritoras españolas 1939-1975*. Laberinto, 2005.

"El atentado anarquista." *La Época*, vol. 45, no. 16444, 22 Jun. 1893, p. 2.

Aznar Soler, Manuel, ed. *El exilio literario español de 1939*. Universitat Autònoma de Barcelona. Grupo de Estudios del Exilio Literario, 1998.

Bakhtin, Mikhail M. "Discourse in the Novel." *The Dialogic Imagination: Four Essays by Bakhtin*, edited by Michael Holquist, translated by Caryl Emerson and Michael Holquist, U of Texas P, 2016, pp. 259-422.

Barrero Pérez, Óscar. *La novela existencial española de posguerra*. Gredos, 1987.

Bartlett, Frederic C. *Remembering: A Study in Experimental and Social Psychology*. Cambridge UP, 2010.

Behiels, Lieve. "La recepción de Sartre en España: el caso de *La nausée*." *Espéculo*, vol. 32, 2006.

Belda, Ismael. "Elisa Brufal, el huerto dorado." *El Mundo*, 22 Jan. 2018, p. 21.

Beneyto, Antonio. *Censura y política*. Plaza & Janés, 1977.

Berlant, Lauren. "The Female Complaint." *Social Text*, vol. 19/20, 1988, pp. 237-59.

———. *The Female Complaint: The Unfinished Business of Sentimentality in American Culture*. Duke UP, 2008.

Bonet, Laureano. "Hacia la construcción literaria de Barcelona: dos textos olvidados de J. R. Masoliver y Mario Lacruz." *Quaderns de Vallençana*, no. 4, 2011, pp. 54-61.

———. "Dos escritores españoles tratan de llevar a la novela nuestra historia contemporánea." *Solidaridad Nacional*. 12 Mar. 1963. p. 13.

Bourdieu, Pierre. "Censorship and the Imposition of Form." *Language and Symbolic Power*. Harvard UP, 1991, pp. 137-59.

Brown, Joan Lipman. "One Autobiography, Twice Told: Martín Gaite's *Entre visillos* and *El cuarto de atrás*." *Hispanic Journal*, vol. 7, no. 2, 1986, pp. 37-47.

Brown, Joan and Crista Johnson. *Confronting Our Canons: Spanish and Latin American Studies in the 21st Century*. Bucknell UP: 2010.

Brufal, Elisa. *Siete puertas*. Suc. de Such, Serra, 1964.

Burns, Kate. *Censorship*. Greenhaven, 2004.

Butler, Judith. "Ruled Out: Vocabularies of the Censor." *Censorship and Silencing: Practices of Cultural Regulation*, edited by Robert Post, Getty Research Institute for the History of Art and the Humanities, 1998, pp. 247-59.

Caballé, Ana and Israel Rolón-Barada. *Carmen Laforet: Una mujer en fuga*. RBA, 2010.

Cajal, Rosa María. *Un paso más*. Garbo, 1956.

Calvo de Aguilar, Isabel. *La danzarina inmóvil*. Rumbos, 1954.

Camino, Mercedes. "'*Volvemos a empezar*': Return Journeys of the Spanish Maquis." *Journal of Iberian and Latin American Research*, vol. 17, no. 1, 2011, pp. 27-39.

Campo, Antonio. "*El rebelde* de Liberata Masoliver." *San Cugat. Semanario de Información Local*, no. 64, 24 May 1960, p. 8.

Canellada, María Josefa. *Penal de Ocaña*. Bullón, 1965.

———. *Penal de Ocaña*, edited by Alonso Zamora Vicente, Austral, 1985.

"Cárcel de Ventas." https://carceldeventas.madrid.es/ Accessed 6 Nov. 2018.

Carrasco González, Antonio. "Novelas de plantación en la Guinea Española: *Efún* y *La mujer del colonial* de Liberata Masoliver." 29 Apr. 2015. Accessed 25 Jul. 2019.

Castroviejo, Concha. *Víspera del odio*. Garbo, 1959.

"Catálogo de escritoras en lengua castellana." *Catálogo de escritoras españolas*. http://www.mujerpalabra.net/bibliotecademujeres/pages/catalogos_bibliografias/escr_esp.htm.

Cisquella, Georgina, José Luis Erviti Jimeno, and José Antonio Sorolla. *La represión cultural en el franquismo. Diez años de censura de libros durante la Ley de Prensa (1966-1976)*. Anagrama, 1977.

Colmeiro, José F. *Memoria histórica e identidad cultural: de la postguerra a la postmodernidad*. Anthropos, 2005.

"Concesión del Andersen 1966." *ABC*, 29 Sep. 1966, p. 43.

Conde Peñalosa, Raquel. *Mujeres novelistas y novelas de mujeres en la posguerra española (1940-1965): catálogo bio-bibliográfico*. Fundación Universitaria Española, 2004.

Conde, Carmen. *Cobre: Destino hallado* y *Solamente un viaje*. Estades Artes Gráficas, 1954.

———. *En manos del silencio*. José Janés, 1950.

———. *Las oscuras raíces*. Garbo, 1954.

Corujo Martín, Inés. "El árbol-narrador en *La sangre* de Elena Quiroga: lugar femenino de memoria y trauma en la posguerra española." *Lucero. A Journal of Iberian and Latin American Studies*, vol. 24, 2015, pp. 20-28.

———. "La voz femenina en los márgenes de la posguerra española: matricidio y transexualidad narrativa en *La careta* de Elena Quiroga." *Cuadernos de Aleph*, vol. 8, 2016, pp. 13-33.

Crespo Vázquez, Miguel, et al. "Análisis constructivo de la capilla de La Cadellada (1926-1944), Oviedo." *ReCoPaR. Red de conservación del patrimonio arquitectónico*, vol. 10, 2013, pp. 25-40.

Davies, Catherine. *Spanish Women's Writing, 1849-1996*. Athlone, 2000.

Del Arco. "Mano a mano: Mercedes Rubio." *La Vanguardia*, 9 Dec. 1956, p. 27.

Del Mastro, Mark P. "Deception through Narrative Structure and Female Adolescent Development in Laforet's *Nada* and *La isla y los* demonios." *Confluencia*, vol. 20, no. 1, 2004, pp. 45-53.

Dendle, Brian J. *Galdós: The Mature Thought*. UP Kentucky, 1980.

Díaz, Janet. "Rosa María Cajal." *Hispania*, vol. 58, no. 3, 1975, pp. 555-56.

Díaz, Janet Winecoff. "Three New Works of Dolores Medio." *Romance Notes*, vol. 11, no. 2, 1969, pp. 244-50.

DiFrancesco, Maria. "Censorship and Literature in Spain." *World Literature in Spanish: An Encyclopedia*, vol. 1, edited by Maureen Ihrie and Salvador Oropesa, ABC-CLIO, 2011, pp. 168-72.

Entrambasaguas, Joaquín de. "Las novelistas actuales." *El Libro Español*, vol. 2. 17 May 1959, pp. 286-97.

———. "Las novelistas actuales." *El libro español: revista mensual del Instituto Nacional del Libro Español*, no. 17, 1959, pp. 286-94.

"Entrega de los premios 'Elisenda de Montcada.'" *ABC*, 18 Dec. 1953, p. 38.

Escobar Sobrino, Hipólito. "Spain." *Encyclopedia of Library History*, edited by Wayne A. Wiegand and Donald G. Davis Jr., Routledge, 1994, pp. 593-95.

"Una explosión de dinamita en el palacio de Cánovas." *El Imparcial*, 21 Jun. 1893, pp. 2-3.

"Exposición infantil de dibujo intuitivo." *ABC*, 28 Mar. 1957, p. 36.

Fernández, Celia. "Entrevista con Carmen Martín Gaite." *Anales de la Narrativa Española Contemporánea*, vol. 4, 1979, pp. 165-72.

Fernández Almagro, Melchor. "*La careta* por Elena Quiroga." *ABC*, 15 Jan. 1956, p. 67.

———. "*Víspera del odio* por Concha Castroviejo." *ABC*, 1 Sep. 1959, p. 6.

———. "*La danzarina inmóvil*." *ABC*, 5 Sep. 1954, p. 39.

Fernández de la Reguera, Ricardo and Susana March. *La boda de Alfonso XIII*. Planeta, 1965.

Fernández Gutiérrez, José María. *La novela del sábado (1953-1955): catálogo y contexto literario*. Consejo Superior de Investigaciones Científicas, 2004.

Fernández Luna, Concepción. "Elizabeth Mulder: Retrato de madurez." *ABC*, 10 Jun. 1956, p. 33.

———. *Martín Nadie*. Novela del Sábado, 1954.

Fernández Luna, Concha. "Nuestro amigo Olaf y otras aventuras." *ABC*, 15 Apr. 1960, p. 58.

"Fichas de novelas presentadas a la censura. Primera serie: 1937-1962." *Represura*, 8 Feb. 2013. http://www.represura.es/represura_8_febrero_2013_sumario.html

File of *A punta de lanza*. 1 Aug. 1962. Archivo General de la Administración, Alcalá de Henares.

File of *A ras de las sombras*. 10 Apr. 1968. Archivo General de la Administración, Alcalá de Henares.

File of *A tientas y a ciegas*. 24 Dec. 1966. Archivo General de la Administración, Alcalá de Henares.

File of *El acuario* [*El pez sigue flotando*]. 22 Nov. 1958. Archivo General de la Administración, Alcalá de Henares.

File of *Agua estancada*. 25 Nov. 1963. Archivo General de la Administración, Alcalá de Henares.

File of *Al lado del hombre*. 22 Oct. 1959. Archivo General de la Administración, Alcalá de Henares.

File of *Algo pasa en la calle*. 19 Jul. 1954. Archivo General de la Administración, Alcalá de Henares.

File of *Barcelona en llamas*. 18 Jan. 1961. Archivo General de la Administración, Alcalá de Henares.

File of *Carta a Cadaqués*. 23 Feb. 1961. Archivo General de la Administración, Alcalá de Henares.

File of *Cobre: Destino hallado y Solamente un viaje*. 15 Jul. 1953. Archivo General de la Administración, Alcalá de Henares.

File of *Detrás de la piedra*. 7 May 1958. Archivo General de la Administración, Alcalá de Henares.

File of *Efún*. 11 Apr. 1955. Archivo General de la Administración, Alcalá de Henares.

File of *El caballo rojo*. 30 May 1966. Archivo General de la Administración, Alcalá de Henares.

File of *El mundo pequeño y fingido*. 18 Aug. 1953. Archivo General de la Administración, Alcalá de Henares.

File of *El pantano*. 27 Feb. 1954. Archivo General de la Administración, Alcalá de Henares.

File of *El secreto*. 19 Nov. 1953. Archivo General de la Administración, Alcalá de Henares.

File of *El último camino*. 14 Apr. 1961. Archivo General de la Administración, Alcalá de Henares.

File of *En manos del silencio*. 8 Feb. 1947. Archivo General de la Administración, Alcalá de Henares.

File of *Entre visillos*. 22 Jan. 1958. Archivo General de la Administración, Alcalá de Henares.

File of *Eran cuatro*. 21 Aug. 1954. Archivo General de la Administración, Alcalá de Henares.

File of *Fin de una regencia*. 22 Oct. 1964. Archivo General de la Administración, Alcalá de Henares.

File of *Funcionario público*. 2 Oct. 1956. Archivo General de la Administración, Alcalá de Henares.

File of *Héroes de Cuba*. 10 Dec. 1962. Archivo General de la Administración, Alcalá de Henares.

File of *Héroes de Filipinas*. 26 Aug. 1963. Archivo General de la Administración, Alcalá de Henares.

File of *Historia de un viaje*. 26 Jul. 1955. Archivo General de la Administración, Alcalá de Henares.

File of *La boda de Alfonso XIII*. 13 Nov. 1964. Archivo General de la Administración, Alcalá de Henares.

File of *La careta*. 30 Dec. 1955. Archivo General de la Administración, Alcalá de Henares.

File of *La ciudad perdida*. 24 Feb. 1951. Archivo General de la Administración, Alcalá de Henares.

File of *La danzarina inmóvil*. 21 May 1954. Archivo General de la Administración, Alcalá de Henares.

File of *La enferma*. 17 Mar. 1955. Archivo General de la Administración, Alcalá de Henares.

File of *La familia de Pascual Duarte*. 16 Jun. 1944. Archivo General de la Administración, Alcalá de Henares.

File of *La isla y los demonios*. 31 Dec. 1951. Archivo General de la Administración, Alcalá de Henares.

File of *La mujer del colonial*. 1 Feb. 1962. Archivo General de la Administración, Alcalá de Henares.

File of *La otra guerra de la postguerra*. 29 Dec. 1966. Archivo General de la Administración, Alcalá de Henares.

File of *La Retirada*. 23 Mar. 1967. Archivo General de la Administración, Alcalá de Henares.

File of *La sangre inútil*. 25 Apr. 1966. Archivo General de la Administración, Alcalá de Henares.

File of *La sangre*. 3 Aug. 1952. Archivo General de la Administración, Alcalá de Henares.

File of *La soledad* sonora. 26 Apr. 1949. Archivo General de la Administración, Alcalá de Henares.
File of *Las esquinas del alba*. 25 Nov. 1960. Archivo General de la Administración, Alcalá de Henares.
File of *Las hogueras*. 5 Nov. 1964. Archivo General de la Administración, Alcalá de Henares.
File of *Las medias palabras*. 11 Mar. 1960. Archivo General de la Administración, Alcalá de Henares.
File of *Las oscuras raíces*. 11 Jan. 1954. Archivo General de la Administración, Alcalá de Henares.
File of *Las siete muchachas del liceo*. 6 Apr. 1957. Archivo General de la Administración, Alcalá de Henares.
File of *Las últimas banderas*. 21 Oct. 1967. Archivo General de la Administración, Alcalá de Henares.
File of *Lola, espejo oscuro*. 29 May 1950. Archivo General de la Administración, Alcalá de Henares.
File of *Los Galiano*. 29 Jul. 1957. Archivo General de la Administración, Alcalá de Henares.
File of *Los nuevos cubanos: La vida en una granja del pueblo*. 18 Nov. 1968. Archivo General de la Administración, Alcalá de Henares.
File of *Luciérnagas*. 20 Oct. 1953. Archivo General de la Administración, Alcalá de Henares.
File of *Martín Nadie*. 26 Jul. 1953. Archivo General de la Administración, Alcalá de Henares.
File of *Me llamo Clara*. 31 May 1968. Archivo General de la Administración, Alcalá de Henares.
File of *Mi hermano y yo por esos mundos*. 31 Aug. 1962. Archivo General de la Administración, Alcalá de Henares.
File of *Mi vida en el manicomio*. 15 Jan. 1953. Archivo General de la Administración, Alcalá de Henares.
File of *Monte de Sancha*. 8 Sep. 1950. Archivo General de la Administración, Alcalá de Henares.
File of *Nada*. 20 Apr. 1945. Archivo General de la Administración, Alcalá de Henares.
File of *Nosotros, los Rivero*. 25 Feb. 1952. Archivo General de la Administración, Alcalá de Henares.
File of *Penal de Ocaña*. 17 May 1955. Archivo General de la Administración, Alcalá de Henares.

File of *Perdimos la primavera*. 6 Mar. 1948. Archivo General de la Administración, Alcalá de Henares.
File of *Pista de baile*. 3 Jun. 1955. Archivo General de la Administración, Alcalá de Henares.
File of *Plácida la joven*. 4 Feb. 1957. Archivo General de la Administración, Alcalá de Henares.
File of *Primero, derecha*. 20 Mar. 1953. Archivo General de la Administración, Alcalá de Henares.
File of *Primera memoria*. 15 Feb. 1960. Archivo General de la Administración, Alcalá de Henares.
File of *Puente sobre el deseo*. 21 Mar. 1966. Archivo General de la Administración, Alcalá de Henares.
File of *Segundos planos*. 30 Jan. 1953. Archivo General de la Administración, Alcalá de Henares.
File of *Selva negra*. 20 Mar. 1959. Archivo General de la Administración, Alcalá de Henares.
File of *Siete puertas*. 1 Nov. 1961. Archivo General de la Administración, Alcalá de Henares.
File of *Talia*. 14 Dec. 1951. Archivo General de la Administración, Alcalá de Henares.
File of *Telón*. 26 Jun. 1969. Archivo General de la Administración, Alcalá de Henares.
File of *Un camino llega a la cumbre*. 10 Dec. 1965. Archivo General de la Administración, Alcalá de Henares.
File of *Un hombre de paz*. 25 Nov. 1969. Archivo General de la Administración, Alcalá de Henares.
File of *Un paso más*. 8 Mar. 1954. Archivo General de la Administración, Alcalá de Henares.
File of *Una mañana cualquiera*. 8 Jun. 1965. Archivo General de la Administración, Alcalá de Henares.
File of *Vagabundos provisionales*. 28 Jan. 1959. Archivo General de la Administración, Alcalá de Henares.
File of *Vidas contra su espejo*. 29 Apr. 1944. Archivo General de la Administración, Alcalá de Henares.
File of *Viento del norte*. 22 Jan. 1951. Archivo General de la Administración, Alcalá de Henares.
File of *Víspera del odio*. 17 Jan. 1959. Archivo General de la Administración, Alcalá de Henares.
Formica, Mercedes. "El domicilio conyugal." *ABC*, 7 Nov. 1953, p. 5.

———. *Espejo roto. Y espejuelos*. Huerga y Fierro, 2004.
———. *La ciudad perdida*. Luis de Caralt, 1951.
Foucault Michel. "Intellectuals and Power." *Language, Counter-Memory, Practice*, edited by Donald F. Bouchard, translated by Donald F. Bouchard and Sherry Simon, Cornell UP, 1977, pp. 205-17.
García Blay, María Gloria and Tomás Ernesto Micó Escrivá. "La censura moral e ideológica durante el franquismo (1945-1975): ejemplos en la obra narrativa de Carmen Laforet." *Tonos digital*, no. 36, 2019, pp. 1-14.
García López, Silvia. *El cuerpo y la voz de Margarita Alexandre*. Universidad Carlos III de Madrid, 2016.
García López, Sonia. "*La ciudad perdida*. Spaces of Reconciliation and Dissidence in 1950s Spanish Literature and Cinema." *L'Atalante*, vol. 20, 2015, pp. 46-53.
García Viñó, Manuel. *Novela española actual*. Prensa Española, 1975.
Gardiner, Harold C. *Catholic Viewpoint on Censorship*. Hanover House, 1958.
Gil Casado, Pablo. *La novela social española (1942-1968)*. Seix Barral, 1968.
Godayol, Pilar. "Censorship and the Catalan Translations of Jean-Paul Sartre." *Perspectives*, vol. 24, no. 1, 2016, pp. 59-75.
Godsland, Shelley. *Killing Carmens: Women's Crime Fiction from Spain*. U of Wales P, 2007.
Godsland, Shelley and Anne M. White. "Popular Genre and the Politics of the Periphery: Catalan Crime Fiction by Women." *Crime Scenes: Detective Narratives in European Culture Since 1945*, edited by Anne Mullen and Emer O'Beirne, Brill, 2000, pp. 219-27.
González Ruiz, Nicolás *Antología de piezas cortas de teatro*, vol. 2. Labor, 1965.
Gordenstein, Roberta. "Kurtz, Carmen." *The Feminist Encyclopedia of Spanish Literature*, vol. 1, edited by Janet Pérez and Maureen Ihrie, Greenwood, 2002, pp. 326-27.
Gould Levine, Linda et al. *Spanish Women Writers: A Bio-Bibliographical Source Book*. Greenwood Press, 1993.
Guardiola, María Luisa. "La Salamanca censurada de la novela *Entre visillos*." *Hispania*, vol. 102, no. 1, 2019, pp. 26-28.
Gubern, Román. *La censura: función política y ordenamiento jurídico bajo el franquismo (1936-1975)*. Península, 1981.
Guillermo, Edenia and Juana Amelia Hernández. *Novelística española de los sesenta*. E. Torres, 1971.
Halsey, Martha T. "Antonio Buero Vallejo." *Censorship: A World Encyclopedia*, edited by Derek Jones, Routledge, 2001, pp. 368-69.

Heilbrun, Carolyn. *Writing a Woman's Life*. Norton, 2008.
Hermida, Xosé. "La escritora Elena Quiroga muere a los 74 años." *El País*, 3 Oct. 1995.
Hernández Cano, Eduardo, "Rosa María Cajal Garrigós." Real Academia de la Historia. Accessed 12 Jan. 2020.
Herzberger, David K. "Narrating the Past: History and the Novel of Memory in Postwar Spain." *PMLA*, vol. 106, 1991, pp. 34-45.
———. *Narrating the Past: Fiction and Historiography in Postwar Spain*. Duke UP, 1995.
Iglesias Laguna, Antonio. *Treinta años de novela española*. Prensa Española, 1969.
Ilie, Paul. *Literatura y exilio interior: escritores y sociedad en la España franquista*. Fundamentos, 1981.
"Índice de seudónimos." *Catálogo de escritoras españolas*. http://www.mujerpalabra.net/bibliotecademujeres/pages/catalogos_bibliografias/escr_esp.htm. Accessed 17 Jun. 2017.
J. V. P. "Carmen Martín Gaite: *Entre Visillos*." *Archivum*, vol. 367-70, 1958, p. 369.
Janés, José. Letter 032-008 to Carmen Conde. 13 Sep. 1945. Patronato Carmen Conde-Antonio Oliver. Cartagena, Spain.
———. Letter 049-098 to Carmen Conde. 29 Jul. 1948. Patronato Carmen Conde-Antonio Oliver. Cartagena, Spain.
Jansen, Sue Curry. *Censorship: The Knot That Binds Power and Knowledge*. Oxford UP, 2010.
Johnson, Roberta. "Personal and Public History in Laforet's Long Novels." *Feminine Concerns in Contemporary Spanish Fiction by Women*, edited by Roberto C. Manteiga, Carolyn Galerstein, and Kathleen McNerney, Scripta Humanistica, 1988, pp. 43-53.
Johnson, Roberta and Israel Rolón-Barada. "Carmen Laforet's *Nada*: From Letter to Novel." *Bulletin of Spanish Studies*, vol. 93, no. 9, 2016, pp. 1571-89.
Kebadze, Nino. "Censorship and Sense-Making in Elena Soriano's Trilogy *Mujer y hombre*." *Bulletin of Spanish Studies*, vol. 92, no. 1, 2015, pp. 65-89.
Kegan Gardiner, Judith. "On Female Identity and Writing by Women." *Critical Inquiry*, vol. 8, no. 2, 1981, pp. 347-61.
Kurtz, Carmen. *Al lado del hombre*. Planeta, 1961.
Labanyi, Jo. *Myth and History in the Contemporary Novel*. Cambridge UP, 2011.

Labrador Ben, Julia María. "*Una mujer fea* de Ángeles Villarta, Premio Fémina 1953." *Arbor Ciencia, Pensamiento y Cultura*, vol. 82, no. 720, 2006, pp. 489-503.

Laforet, Carmen. *La isla y los demonios*. Destino, 1952.

———. *Nada*. Destino, 1945.

Langa Pizarro, Mar. "La novela histórica española en la transición y en la democracia." *Anales de Literatura Española*, vol. 17, 2004, pp. 107-20.

Larraz, Fernando. "Gender, Translation and Censorship in Seix Barral's 'Biblioteca Breve' and 'Biblioteca Formentor' (1955-1975)." *Foreign Women Authors under Fascism and Francoism: Gender, Translation and Censorship*, edited by Pilar Godayol and Annarita Taronna, Cambridge Scholars, 2018, pp. 126-45.

———. "La 'operación retorno' de la narrativa en el exilio en la prensa diaria del Franquismo (1966-1975). Los casos de *ABC*, Informaciones y Pueblo" *Dicenda. Cuadernos de Filología Hispánica*, vol. 29, 2011, pp. 171-95.

Larraz, Fernando and Cristina Suárez Toledano. "Realismo social y censura en la novela española (1954-1962)." *Creneida*, vol. 5, 2017, pp. 66-95.

Laskaris, Paola. "La última tentación de la libertad: vida y andanzas de la obra de Nikos Kazantzakis en tiempos de censura." *Creneida*, vol. 5, 2017, pp. 198-238.

Lavail, Christine. "De la creación de la Sección Femenina (1934) a la campaña electoral de 1936: Modalidades de intervención de las mujeres falangistas en la esfera pública." *ARENAL*, vol. 15, no. 2, 2008, pp. 345-70.

Leggott, Sarah. "Negotiating Censorship in the Postwar Spanish Novel: Divorce and Civil Marriage in Elena Quiroga's *Algo pasa en la calle* (1954)." *UNED, REI*, vol. 2, 2014, pp. 121-43.

Lera, Ángel María de. *Las últimas banderas*. Espa Ebook, 2013.

Lima Grecco, Gabriela de and Sara Martín Gutiérrez. "Mujeres de pluma: escritoras y censoras durante el franquismo" *Represura*, vol. 4, 2019, pp. 76-104.

López, Francisca. *Mito y discurso en la novela femenina de posguerra en España*. Pliegos, 1995.

Mannheim, Karl. "The Problem of Generations." *Karl Mannheim Essays*, edited by Paul Kecskemeti, Routledge, 1952, pp. 276-322.

Martín Gaite, Carmen. *Entre visillos*. Destino, 1958.

———. "La chica rara." *Antología del pensamiento feminista español*, edited by Maite Zubiaurre and Roberta L. Johnson, Cátedra, 2012, pp. 381-95.

———. *Desde la ventana*. Austral, 1987.

———. *Usos amorosos de la postguerra española*. Anagrama, 1987.

Martín, Juan Carlos. "Civil War Literature in Spain." *World Literature in Spanish: An Encyclopedia*, vol. 1, edited by Maureen Ihrie and Salvador Oropesa, ABC-CLIO, 2011, pp. 206-09.

Martínez Cachero, José María. *La novela española entre 1936 y 1975*. Castalia, 1973.

Martínez, Josebe. *Exiliadas: escritoras, guerra civil y memoria*. Montesinos, 2007.

Maslow, Abraham H. *Motivation and Personality*. 3rd ed., Harper and Row, 1987.

Masoliver, Liberata. *Barcelona en llamas*. Barna, 1961.

———. *Efún*. Garbo, 1955.

Matute, Ana María. *En esta tierra*. Éxito, 1955.

———. *Luciérnagas*. Destino, 1993.

Mayock, Ellen C. *The "Strange Girl" in Twentieth Century Spanish Novels Written by Women*. University Press of the South, 2004.

Medio, Dolores. *Celda común*. Nobel, 1996.

Millet, Kate. *Sexual Politics*. Simon & Schuster, 1990.

Montaner, Joaquín. "Concesión del cuarto premio 'Elisenda de Moncada.'" *ABC*, 9 Dec. 1956, p. 79.

Montejo Gurruchaga, Lucía. "Algunas novelas de Darío Fernández-Flórez: de *Zarabanda* (1944) a *Alta costura* (1954): Temas escabrosos en tiempos de restricciones moralistas." *Revista de Literatura*, vol. 70, no. 139, 2008, pp. 165-85.

———. *Discurso de autora: género y censura en la narrativa española de posguerra*. UNED, 2010.

———. "Dolores Medio en la novela española del medio siglo: El discurso de su narrativa social." *EPOS*, vol. 16, 2000, pp. 211-25.

———. "Las mujeres escritoras de los años cincuenta: al margen de las tendencias dominantes. *Las mujeres escritoras en la historia de la literatura española*, edited by Lucía Montejo Gurruchaga y Nieves Baranda Leturio, Estudios de la UNED, 2002, pp. 153-66.

———. "La narrativa de Carmen Kurtz: compromiso y denuncia de la condición social de la mujer española de posguerra." *ARBOR Ciencia, Pensamiento y Cultura*, vol. 83, no. 719, 2006, pp. 407-15.

———. "La narrativa realista de Concha Alós." *Anuario de estudios filológicos*, vol. 27, 2004, pp. 175-90.

———. "Realismo, testimonio y censura en la obra de Carmen Kurtz." *Cuadernos del Marqués de San Adrián: Revista de humanidades*, vol. 3, 2005, pp. 207-29.

Moreno-Nuño, Carmen. "Criminalizing *Maquis*: Configurations of Anti-Francoist Guerrilla Fighters as *Bandoleros* and Bandits in Cultural Discourse." *Armed Resistance: Cultural Representations of the Anti-Francoist Guerrilla*, edited by Antonio Gómez López-Quiñones and Carmen Moreno-Nuño, vol. 10, 2012, pp. 79-99.

Moret, Xavier. "Matute recupera *Luciérnagas*, una novela de niños marcados por la guerra." *El País*, 26 Oct. 1993.

Morris, Pam. *Literature and Feminism: An Introduction*. Blackwell, 2000.

Müller, Beate. "Censorship and Cultural Regulation: Mapping the Territory." *Censorship & Cultural Regulation in the Modern Age*, edited by Beate Müller, Rodopi, 2004, pp. 1-31.

Muñoz García, María José. *Limitaciones a la capacidad de obrar de la mujer casada, 1505-1975*. Servicio de Publicaciones, 1991.

"Música y teatro." *La Vanguardia*, 24 May 1932, p. 27.

Nalbone, Lisa. "Moving through Time and Space in Mercedes Rubio's *Las siete muchachas del liceo* (1957) via Wagner's *Parsifal* in Barcelona, Spain (1914)." *Studies in Medievalism*, vol. 25, 2016, pp. 37-44.

Nash, Mary. *Defying Male Civilization: Women in the Spanish Civil War*. Arden, 1995.

———. "Pronatalism and Motherhood in Franco's Spain." *Maternity and Gender Policies: Women and the Rise of the European Welfare States, 1880s-1950s*, edited by Gisela Bock and Pat Thane, Routledge, 1991, pp. 160-77.

Núñez Targa, Mercedes. *Cárcel de Ventas*. Editions de la Librairie du Globe, 1967.

O'Byrne, Patricia. "El uso de técnicas narrativas para sortear la censura en la España de Franco: Un estudio del autor implícito en *La vieja ley* (1956) de Carmen Kurtz." *Creación y proyección de los discursos narrativos*, edited by Daniel Altamiranda and Esther Smith, Dunken, 2008, pp. 437-43.

———. *Post-war Spanish Women Novelists and the Recuperation of Historical Memory*. Tamesis, 2014.

———. "Spanish Women Novelists and the Censor (1945-1965)." *Letras Femeninas*, vol. 25, no. 1-2, 1999, pp. 199-221.

O'Connor, Thomas F. "The National Organization for Decent Literature: A Phase in American Catholic Censorship." *The Library Quarterly*, vol. 65, no. 4, 1955, pp. 386-414.

O'Leary, Catherine. *The Theatre of Antonio Buero Vallejo: Ideology, Politics and Censorship*. Boydell & Brewer, 2005.

Osborne, Raquel. "Good Girls versus Bad Girls in Early Francoist Prisons: Sexuality as a Great Divide." *Sexualities*, vol. 14, no. 5, 2011, pp. 509-25.

Palmer, R. Barton. *Shot on Location: Postwar American Cinema and the Exploration of Real Place*. Rutgers UP, 2016.

Palomares, Cristina. *The Quest for Survival after Franco: Moderate Francoism and the Slow Journey to the Polls, 1964-1977*. Brighton, 2004.

Palomo Vázquez, Pilar. "De *Episodios Contemporáneos*." *Galdós y la escritura de la modernidad*, edited by Yolanda Arencibia et al., Cabildo de las Palmas de Gran Canaria, 2013, pp. 602-32.

Penal de Ocaña. "Corral de Comedias." www.corraldealcala.com. Accessed 4 August 2020.

Pérez, Genaro J. *La narrativa de Concha Alós: texto, pretexto y contexto*. Támesis, 1993.

Pérez, Janet. *Contemporary Women Writers: Carmen Kurtz*. Twayne, 1988.

———. "March Alcalá, Susana." *The Feminist Encyclopedia of Spanish Literature*, vol. 1, edited by Janet Pérez and Maureen Ihrie, Greenwood, 2002, pp. 369-71.

———. "Portraits of the *Femme Seule* by Laforet, Matute, Soriano, Martín Gaite, Galvarriato, Quiroga, and Medio." *Feminine Concerns in Contemporary Spanish Fiction by Women*, edited by Roberto C. Manteiga, Carloyn Galerstein and Kathleen McNerney, Scripta Humanistica, 1988, pp. 54-77.

Perriam, Chris, et al. *A New History of Spanish Writing, 1939 to the 1990s*. Oxford UP, 2000.

Pilcher, Jane. "Mannheim's Sociology of Generations: An Undervalued Legacy." *British Journal of Sociology*, vol. 45, no. 3, 1994, pp. 484-95.

Powell, Robert. "Taking Pieces of Rand with Them: Ayn Rand's Literary Influence." *Journal of Ayn Rand Studies*, vol. 12, no. 2, 2012, pp. 207-35.

Preston, Paul. *The Spanish Civil War. Reaction, Revolutions and Revenge*. Harper, 2006.

Quiroga, Elena. *Viento del norte*. Destino, 1951.

Richmond, Kathleen J. *The Yoke of Isabella: The Women's Section of the Falange 1934-1959*. 1999. University of Southampton, PhD dissertation.

Ripoll Sintes, Blanca. "El modelo galdosiano en los *Episodios Nacionales Contemporáneos* de Susana March y Ricardo Fernández de la Reguera (1963-1988)." *Monteagudo*, vol. 25, 2020, pp. 133-45.

Rodríguez Puértolas, Julio. *Historia de la literatura fascista española*, vol. 2. Akal, 2008.

Rojas Claros, Francisco. "Mujer, censura y disidencia editorial en el segundo franquismo. Una aproximación." *Represura*, vol. 4, 2019, pp. 105-32.

———. *Dirigismo cultural y disidencia editorial en España (1962-1973)*. PU Alicante, 2016.

Rolón-Barada, Israel. "Carmen Laforet's Inspiration for *Nada* (1945)." *Spanish Women Writers and Spain's Civil War*, edited by Maryellen Bieder and Roberta Johnson, Routledge, 2017, pp. 116-28.

Rubio, Mercedes. *Las siete muchachas del liceo*. Garbo, 1957.

Ruiz Batista, Eduardo. "La censura en los años azules." *Tiempo de censura: La represión editorial durante el franquismo*, edited by Eduardo Ruiz Batista, Trea, 2008, pp. 45-75.

———. "La larga noche del franquismo (1945-1966)." *Tiempo de censura: la represión editorial durante el franquismo*, edited by Eduardo Ruiz Bautista, Trea, 2008, pp. 77-102.

Sáenz, Pilar. "Calvo de Aguilar, Isabel." *The Feminist Encyclopedia of Spanish Literature*, vol. 1, edited by Janet Pérez and Maureen Ihrie, Greenwood, 2002, pp. 87-88.

———. "Serrano y Balañá, Eugenia." *The Feminist Encyclopedia of Spanish Literature*, vol. 2, edited by Janet Pérez and Maureen Ihrie, Greenwood, 2002, pp. 555-56.

Sampedro Vizcaya, Benita. "Rethinking the Archive and the Colonial Library: Equatorial Guinea." *Journal of Spanish Cultural Studies*, vol. 3, 2008, pp. 341-63.

Santos, Nanina. "Concha Castroviejo, Unha muller na frontera." *Grial*, vol. 48, no. 188, 2010, pp. 132-39.

Secades Fernández, Patricia. "Los conjuntos arquitectónicos y su importante valor patrimonial: La parcela de la Cadellada como elemento dinamizador del entramado urbano." *Liño: Revista anual de historia del arte*, vol. 15, 2009, pp. 127-37.

Serrano, Eugenia. "En contra y en pro de las novelistas." *El Español*, 15 Apr. 1944, p. 4.

Serrano y Balañá, Eugenia. *Perdimos la primavera*. José Janés, 1952.

———. "Hacia un renacimiento de la novela española: Rafael Sánchez Mazas, Ledesma Miranda y Sánchez Ferlosio." *Correo Literario*, no. 23, 1 May 1951, p. 5.

Soldevila Durante, Ignacio. *La novela desde 1936*. Alhambra, 1980.

Soler Gallo, Miguel. "Hurgando en el 'Desván de los malditos': unas notas sobre Mercedes Formica." *Perífrasis*, vol. 2, no. 2011, pp. 40-55.

Soliño, María Elena. "Tales of peaceful warriors: Dolores Medio's *Diario de una maestra* and Josefina R. Aldecoa's *Historia de una maestra*." *Letras Peninsulares*, vol. 8, no. 1, 1995, pp. 27-38.

Soria, Mar. *Geographies of Urban Female Labor and Nationhood in Spanish Culture, 1880-1975*. U Nebraska P, 2020.

Spariosu, Mihai I. *The Wreath of Wild Olive: Play, Liminality, and the Study of Literature*. SUNY P, 1997.

Stasio, Marilyn. "Crime/Mystery: Murder Least Foul: The Cozy, Soft-Boiled Mystery." *New York Times*, 18 Oct. 1992, pp. 1-3.

Stehrenberger, Cécile Stephanie. "Manifestaciones (a)típicas del discurso colonial franquista en las novelas de aventura africana de Liberata Masoliver." *Iberoromania*, vol. 73-74, no. 1, 2012, pp. 61-75.

Stycos, María. "Susana March." *Dictionary of the Literature of the Iberian Peninsula*, vol. 2, edited by Germán Bleiberg, Maureen Ihrie, Janet Pérez, Greenwood, 1993, pp. 1008-09.

Tabori, Paul. *Anatomy of Exile: A Semantic and Historic Study*. Harrap, 1972.

Tone, John L. *War and Genocide in Cuba, 1895-1898*. UNC UP, 2008.

Torre, Guillermo de. Letter 22821/28 to Concha Castroviejo. 27 Jan. 1964. Biblioteca Nacional de España, Madrid.

Torres Nebrera, Gregorio. "La narrativa de Concha Castroviejo." *Anuario de Estudios Filológicos*, vol. 35, 2012, pp. 215-33.

Valabrega, Jean-Paul. "Fondement psycho-politique de la censure." *Communications*, vol. 9, 1967, pp. 114-21.

Valdivieso, L. Teresa. "El drama de lo tangencial en *Víspera del odio*." *Letras Femeninas*, vol. 12, no. 1/2, 1986, pp. 24-33.

Valiente, Guillermo. "La idea de reconciliación nacional durante la Guerra Civil española: los discursos de Yagüe y Azaña de julio del 38." *Aportes. Revista de Historia Contemporánea*, vol. 80, no. 3, 2012, pp. 73-96.

Verdegal Cerezo, Joan Manuel. *El premio Fray Luis de León de traducción. Historia, sociología y crítica*. Universitat Jaume I, 2013.

Villarta, Ángeles. *Mi vida en el manicomio*. Excelicer, 1953.

Vincent, Mary. *Spain 1883-2002: People and State*. Oxford UP, 2008.

Vivanco, Felip. "Era el 21 y me salvé." *La Vanguardia, Vivir en Girona*, 15 Mar. 2003, p. 6.

Wilcox, John C. *Women Poets of Spain, 1860-1990: Toward a Gynocentric Vision*. U of Illinois P, 1997.

Wilson, Katharina M. *An Encyclopedia of Continental Women Writers*. Garland, 1991.

Ynduraín, Domingo. *Historia y crítica de la literatura española, VIII Época contemporánea: 1939-1980*. Crítica, 1980.

Zatlin, Phyllis. "Writing Against the Current: The Novels of Elena Quiroga." *Women Writers of Contemporary Spain: Exiles in the Homeland*, edited by Joan L. Brown, U of Delaware P, 1991, pp. 42-58.

Zuleta, Emilia de. "Biografía de María Josefa Canellada." Archivo y Biblioteca, Diputación de Cáceres. http://ab.dip-caceres.org/. Accessed 14 Oct. 2018.

Index

A

Abellán, Manuel L., 34-36, 40, 41, 44, 173, 196, 205, 219

abortion, 42, 71, 95, 96

adaptation, 11, 117, 183

adultery, 42, 176, 178

agency, 22, 38, 39, 132, 145, 152, 162, 181, 203

aggression, 75

Albéniz, 62, 63

Alfonso XIII, 206-208, 210, 212, 216

Alonso, Dámaso, 184

Alós, Concha, 8, 12, 37, 88, 130, 152, 153, 155-58, 162-64, 187

anarchy/anarchist/anarchism, 42, 205, 207, 210, 213, 215, 218

ángel del hogar, 55, 108

Archivo General de la Administración, 45, 167, 171, 188, 223

Arias-Salgado, Gabriel, 32

Asturian coalminers' strike, 193, 197

autobiography/autobiographical, 21, 38, 41, 62, 85, 113, 153, 159, 195

B

Badajoz (Battle of/Massacre of), 160

Bakhtin, Mikhail, 185

Baroja, Pío and Ricardo, 209

Battenberg, Victoria Eugenie of, 208

Berlant, Lauren, 68

black market, 55, 126

estraperlo, 84

bomb, bombing, bombardment, 56, 81, 188, 209, 215

Bonet, Laureano, 84, 204

Bourdieu, Pierre, 25, 26

Brown, Joan L., 17, 18, 65

Brufal, Elisa, 130, 131, 134, 136, 163, 164

Butler, Judith, 38, 77

C

Caballé, Ana, 51, 172

Cajal, Rosa María, 8, 73, 89, 140, 169, 171-80, 182, 209, 216, 217

Calvo de Aguilar, Isabel, 130, 139, 140, 141, 143, 163, 164

Canary Islands, Las Palmas, 53

Canellada, María Josefa, 171, 183-88, 191, 217

canon/canonical, 13, 17-18, 29, 64, 147, 218

Cánovas del Castillo, Antonio, 214-15

Castroviejo, Concha, 13, 47, 69, 70-71, 75, 76

Cela, Camilo José, 92

censorship
transactional nature, 22, 127, 209

censorship legislation, 27-35, 117, 136, 155, 216

Chacel, Rosa, 13, 39, 69

chica rara, 51, 52

Cisquella, Georgina, 34, 36, 42

Colmeiro, José, 21

colonial, 79, 80, 82, 214

combat, 118, 174, 188, 191

concentration camp, 56, 213

Conde Peñalosa, Raquel, 12, 13, 60, 69, 72, 78, 84, 141, 186

Conde, Carmen, 12, 47, 89, 93, 94, 96, 99, 100, 127, 140, 176

confess/confession, 70, 73, 74, 117, 130

confinement, 51, 53, 58, 59, 145, 200

Congreso Femenino Hispano-americano Filipino, 113

Corujo Martín, Inés, 101

costumbrista, 60, 61, 131

crime novel, 141, 143

crusade/*Cruzada*, 74, 110, 149-51, 153, 157, 163

D

daily life (under dictatorship), 11, 14, 19, 20, 22, 28, 49, 50, 53, 60, 73, 79, 84, 87, 105, 122, 132, 168, 172, 191, 192, 202, 207, 212, 214

Davies, Catherine, 12

Dendle, Brian J., 210

detective (fiction, novel, story, writer), 140-41, 143-45

deviant, 187

Dirección General de Seguridad, 196-98
divorce, 42, 43, 71-73, 75, 76, 101, 112, 147
domestic/domesticity, 19, 61, 63, 75, 99, 108, 141, 147, 151, 152, 155, 163
  domestic violence, 73, 112

E
ecclesiastical censor, 135, 136
education, 12, 13, 41, 54, 65, 68, 109, 111, 121, 155, 163, 194, 200, 201, 203
ellipsis, 38, 144, 174, 179
ennui, 64, 185
Equatorial Guinea, 79
exile, 12, 13, 15, 69, 70, 100, 118
existential, 15, 50, 73, 76, 177, 182, 186

F
Falange/Falangist, 16, 28, 29, 31, 70, 108, 112, 113, 162
family, 21, 52, 64, 96, 151, 152, 154, 157, 197, 199
  displacement, 154, 158, 159
  dysfunction, 50, 94, 195
  impact of war, 156
  loss of, 132

female complaint, 68
feminine subjectivity, 19, 51, 77, 108, 111
Fernández Luna, Concha, 93, 120, 121, 124, 125, 127, 128
Fernández de la Reguera, Ricardo, 69, 176, 203-06, 208, 210, 212, 216
film noir, 114
Fisher King, 61
Forest, Eva, 168, 169
Formica, Mercedes, 69, 112, 113, 115-18, 123, 140
Foucault, Michel, 26
Fraga Iribarne, Manuel, 33
Franco, Francisco, 11
fratricide, 147, 151, 188

H
Herzberger, David K., 11, 20, 85
historical fiction, 204, 205
historical memory, 21, 56, 71, 87, 162, 198, 217
  Recuperation of, 16, 196
homosexuality, 42, 139
human rights, 112
hunger, 84, 155, 214
  food shortage, 43, 200

I
Ibárruri, Dolores (*La Pasionaria*), 194
incarceration/incarcerated, 71, 75, 86, 193-97, 200, 203, 217
Infanta Isabel, 215, 216
infidelity, 95-98, 121, 182
Instituto Femenino de Enseñanza (Salamanca), 66
interlocutor, 57, 186
irony, 11, 38, 122, 209

J
Janés, José, 94
Johnson, Roberta, 49, 53
JONS, 31

K
Kent, Victoria, 198
kidnapping, 86, 118, 119
Kurtz, Carmen, 37, 69, 89, 92, 130, 146-48, 150, 152, 167

L
La Cadellada Psychiatric Hospital, 55
La ciudad perdida (film), 117
Labanyi, Jo, 15, 73
Laforet, Carmen, 12, 15, 20, 29, 47-54, 73, 140, 170, 172
Larraz, Fernando, 16, 70, 135
lector (censor), 30, 32, 39, 40, 41, 80
Leggott, Sarah, 101
Ley de Jurisdicciones, 210, 212
Ley de Prensa, 28, 33
Ley de Tráfico, 196
Lima Grecco, Gabriela de, 50
literacy, 202
literary prize, 12, 18, 168
   Café Gijón, 64, 183
   Elisenda de Montcada, 59, 70, 79, 176
   Fémina, 54
   Hans Christian Andersen, 120
   María Fernández Luna, 120
   Nadal, 49, 64, 67, 91, 101, 172, 192
   Planeta, 90, 131, 146, 153, 158
literary trope, 61, 70, 79, 87, 88, 95, 99, 114, 145, 172, 184
London Blitz/air raid, 94, 99
Lost Generation, 20

M
Manrique, Jorge, 188

maqui/maquis, 115, 116, 118

March, Susana, 69, 169, 171, 176, 203-05, 208, 209, 210, 212, 213, 216, 218

Marco, Sixto, 131

marriage/matrimony, 12, 19, 58, 61, 67, 72, 73, 94, 95, 99, 109, 133, 142, 144, 145, 147, 150, 156, 164, 187

Martín Gaite, Carmen, 12, 20, 39, 47, 51, 64-68, 140, 183

Masoliver, Liberata, 47, 56, 77-79, 81, 82, 83, 85-87, 89, 165, 169, 187

maternal/maternity, 51, 99, 145, 197

   maternal loss, 53

   maternity ward, 200

matrimony, 99

Matute, Ana María, 11, 12, 20, 43, 69, 140, 170, 171

Mayock, Ellen, 51

medical world, 55, 56, 57, 58, 118, 190, 191, 200, 201

Medio, Dolores, 12, 37, 41, 69, 103, 140, 171, 192-97, 199, 202, 203, 217

memoir, 38

memory, 20, 81, 140

Menéndez Pidal, Ramón, 184

mental illness, 57, 123

Ministerio de Educación, 28, 31, 110

Ministerio de Información y Turismo, 16, 28, 32

Ministerio del Interior, 28, 29

Misiones Pedagógicas, 109, 111, 127

Montejo Gurruchaga, Lucía, 9, 27, 36, 41, 67, 74, 103, 146, 147, 149, 153, 170, 171, 193

Morral, Mateo, 207-210, 212, 213, 215, 216, 218

motherhood, 61, 63, 76, 111, 128

Mulder, Elizabeth, 89, 120, 140, 169

Müller, Beate, 14

murder, 32, 42, 121, 125

N

Nao d'amores (theatre company), 183

narrative strategy, 49, 88, 143, 164

Nash, Mary, 190, 197

National Organization for Decent Literature, 30

National Reading Service/Servicio Nacional de la Lectura, 120

Navarro Tomás, Tomás, 184

neorealist, 65, 84, 203

Novela del Sábado, 100, 121
novela rosa, 64, 86, 144, 146, 147, 159, 168, 169
nurse/nursing, 96, 155, 183, 184, 185, 189, 190, 191, 217

O

O'Byrne, Patricia, 16, 36, 40, 41, 54, 55, 170, 172, 173
Ocaña (military hospital, penitentiary), 189, 190, 191
Ofensiva de Levante, 158
Oliver Belmás, Antonio, 100
O'Niell, Carolota, 13

P

Palencia, Isabel, 13
Pardo Bazán, Emilia, 100, 101, 107
Parsifal, 60-62
patriarchal/patriarchy, 21, 61, 63, 64, 66, 68, 73, 76, 77, 82, 109, 147, 151, 156 187
Peña Royo, Marcos, 193
Pérez Galdós, Benito, 76, 203, 204, 205
performance, 123
picaresque, 44, 52, 92, 121, 122, 127, 128
political censor, 135

political prisoner, 199-201
post-traumatic stress disorder, 163
pregnancy, 109, 145, 164, 197
Primo de Rivera, Miguel, 93, 110
psychiatric hospital, 55, 123
publishers
  Bruguera, 172
  Garbo, 59
  Planeta, 149, 171, 203
  Rumbos (Júpiter y Danae), 141

Q

Queipo de Llano, Gonzalo, 158, 160-62
Quiroga, Elena, 12, 20, 93, 100-03, 107, 108, 127

R

racial/racialized, 30, 79, 82, 83, 86
Rand, Ayn, 116
rape. *See* sexual violence
ration card, 84
Real Academia Española, 93, 100
reconcentration, 213, 214
right of passage, 132
Rodoreda, Mercé, 12, 39

Rojas Claros, Francisco, 33, 35, 39, 40

Rolón-Barada, Israel, 49, 51, 52

Rubio, Mercedes, 47, 59-63

S

Salisachs, Mercedes, 12, 37, 171

Sastre, Alfonso, 169

Sección Femenina, 54, 55, 112

Second Republic, 43, 63, 71, 72, 75, 80, 109-11, 127, 198, 201

self-censorship, 26, 38, 54, 79, 162, 170, 179

Serrano y Balañá, Eugenia, 90, 93, 108, 109, 110

sex worker, 194-203, 217

sexual violence, 124, 125, 195, 200, 217

Siege of Baler, 214

social realist, 11, 14-16, 65, 68, 152, 153, 204

Soriano, Elena, 12, 69, 140, 171

Stockholm syndrome, 117

suicide, 42, 49, 117, 128, 174, 207

T

Talavera (Battle of/desastre de), 189, 190

temas malditas, 36, 42

testimonial, 50, 65, 78, 81, 163, 186

torture, 43, 84, 119

totalitarian, 15, 28, 61, 65, 74, 96, 99, 127

Trastienda (tertulia), 131

trauma, 191, 202, 221

tremendista, 15, 50, 76, 92, 121, 127, 128

U

Unamuno, Miguel de, 209

Ursuline Order, 121

V

Valle-Inclán, Ramón del, 209

vanquished, 15, 56, 74, 75, 88, 115, 153, 187

Ventas Prison/Cárcel de ventas, 194, 198

victors, 56, 75, 78, 88, 162

Villarta, Ángeles, 54-59, 77, 123, 140

W

Wagner, Richard, 60, 61, 62

war crime, 56

Werbo, Nadia, 120

widow/widower, 113, 126

World War II, 49, 94, 99, 118, 158, 190

Y
Yagüe, Juan, 160-162

Z
Zamora Vicente, Alonso, 184, 186, 187
Zamora, Ana, 183, 184

www.ingramcontent.com/pod-product-compliance
Lightning Source LLC
Chambersburg PA
CBHW021352300426
44114CB00012B/1194